New Defence Policy of India
–A Perspective

New Defence Policy of India

A Perspective

Col. (Retd.) S.C. Narang

Prashant Publishing House
DELHI - 110094 (INDIA)

PRASHANT PUBLISHING HOUSE
C-34, 28 Foota Road, Gali No. 3
West Karawal Nagar, Delhi-110094
Phone : 9810396373, 22963970

New Defence Policy of India : A Perspective

First Published : 2010

ISBN : 978-93-80565-00-2

PRINTED IN INDIA

Published by Mr. R. K. Jha M/s. Prashant Publishing House, Delhi and Printed at H.S. Offset Press, Delhi.

Preface

India's policies on defense-related acquisitions from abroad and production within India are believed to have been directed not only at ensuring India's security interests but also at promoting self-reliance and indigenous capability in this vital sector often involving advanced technologies. Whatever one's opinions about intentions, questions have often been raised, as to whether these goals have actually been achieved. Again, while the point may be debated, clearly there are major problems going by the evidence in the past two decades. India has been buying ever larger quantities of increasingly sophisticated military hardware from foreign suppliers, while its defense forces have not been able to acquire necessary comparable equipment from Indian state-sector manufacturers due to inadequate performance, inordinate time delays and massive cost overruns.

Despite this past experience, and in spite of some success in pressurizing vendors into more meaningful collaboration through the policy of direct offsets under DPP-2005/6, the defense ministry is in the process of modifying the DPP particularly is respect of offsets. It is no coincidence that this process has been initiated at a time when major Western military hardware vendors are salivating at the $30 billion Indian acquisition budget, and especially the massive $10 billion deal for multi-role combat aircraft, in the tender for which India has specified a 50 per cent offset condition, much to the open displeasure of US aviation majors Lockheed Martin and Boeing.

Democracy influences both the process and the content of defence policy. Thus, in a democratic set-up, defence policy is based on a consultative process. Its goals and objectives, as well as many finer details, are often debated in Parliament, the media, by think-tanks and during election campaigns. This process ensures a more participative, inclusive and transparent defence policy. This indeed is the case in India and other democracies. An important outcome of this process is that democratic governments cannot concentrate on militarisation alone.

National security implies not only safeguarding territorial boundaries but also that the nation is able to build a cohesive, egalitarian, technologically efficient and progressive society with a good quality of life. Compared with national security, defence policy is more focused, concerned with the protection of the state and its citizens from direct and indirect military threats and actions of other states. In defence planning, the emphasis shifts to national security concerns that are mainly military in nature. There are two concepts at this level: deterrence and defence.

Defence Research & Development Organisation (DRDO) works under Department of Defence Research and Development of Ministry of Defence. DRDO dedicatedly working towards enhancing self-reliance in Defence Systems and undertakes design & development leading to production of world class weapon systems and equipment in accordance with the expressed needs and the qualitative requirements laid down by the three services.

The Indian Navy of 2010-20 is already being built – the Air Defence Ship at Kochi, the Vikramaditya (Ex Gorshkov) in Russia, along with its complement of MiG 29K, the Naval LCA at Bangalore, the Scorpene submarines at MDL, and at last count about 22 Destroyers, Frigates, corvettes, LSTs, OPVs, and FACs at various shipyards around the country. We must, therefore, look at what is needed, and what is possible, for the time frame of 2020-2030, and what else is needed to fill the voids prior to 2020. In arriving at the final figures we must take into account the probable security challenges and maritime threats that we will need to counter and the maritime interests that we will need to protect, preserve and indeed promote; India's stature and position in the comity of nations; our economic potential; and finally our design, industrial and ship-building capability.

—Author

Contents

Preface

1. History of Indian Defence Forces 1
2. Defence Planning in India 43
3. Indian Defence Projects 76
4. India Defence Industry 110
5. DRDO: Providing the Technological Edge to the Indian Defence 121
6. India: New Policy on Defence Contracts Offsets 141
7. Democracy and Defence Policy 148
8. India's Defence Purchase Policy Attracts Global Attention 163
9. New Defence Modernisation Challenges and Strategies 165
10. Indian Army's Modern Plans 177
11. The Indian Navy in 2020 190
12. The Defence Scene and the Budget 203
13. India's Defence Industry in the 21st Century 213
14. India-US Defence Pact-II: Commitments may Fetter Judgment 254
15. Indian Defence Industry: Domestic Production and Imports—the Future Balance 259
16. The Indian Experience in the Use of Military Helicopters 292
17. Indian Foreign Policy 299
18. India's Defence Minister: Improve Quality, or Else 302

Bibliography 319

Index 320

1 History of Indian Defence Forces

THE INDIAN DEFENCE FORCES : ARMY

Historical Overview

In 1902, when Lord Kitchner took over as Commander-in-Chief of the Army, it was further reorganised as a regular force. By 1914, at the time of the outbreak of the First World War, the strength of the Indian Army had reached approximately 150,000. By the time the Second World War started in 1939, the strength of the Indian Army had risen to 189,000. In 1947, with the partition of the country, two-thirds of the strength remained with India and one-third went away to Pakistan. On the eve of our independence the strength of the undivided Army was nearly two and a half million. Indian soldiers served all over the world during the British regime.

They fought from China in the East to France and Africa in the West. They fought bravely during 1914-18 and 1939-45, during the First and Second World Wars. The tales of their valour spread from China in the East to Iraq, Africa, Italy and France in the West. The secret of success of the Indian Army has been its unflinching sense of duty, discipline and traditions of valour. On 15th January 1948 Lieutenant General K. M. Cariappa became the first Indian Commander-in-Chief (C-IN-C). 15th January is now celebrated every year as Army Day. On this occasion the Chief of the Army Staff (COAS) takes the salute at the Army Day Parade in the Delhi Cantonment. This is a grand parade held just before the Republic Day Parade. The rulers of some princely states were reluctant to join the new Indian dominion and many had to be coaxed by threat of force.

The Army was yet to reorganise its partition when the call of duty came from Junagadh and Hyderabad. The Indian Army bravely and without bloodshed consolidated out position in these states, which then became parts of Indian dominion.

The war raged in Jammu & Kashmir from October 1947 to January 1948. It ended in a proud victory for our Army and Pakistan failed to capture Jammu or Srinager. However a premature cease-fire was accepted by our Government which enabled Pakistan to hold large parts of Jammu & Kashmir state. These areas under Pakistan's occupation are called Pak-occupied Kashmir (PoK) and Northern Areas. From 1948 to 1962 Indian Army contingents did a number of peacekeeping assignments outside the country, in Korea, Gaza (Egypt) and Congo (Central Africa) on behalf of United Nations and earned great honour for the country.

In 1962 when China attacked India the Indian Army was rushed to fight them on the icy heights of the Himalayas for which they were ill-equipped and ill-prepared. A sort of 'code of honour' has come down to us from our great commanders and soldiers of the past eras. It is a matter of great pride that whenever India has been attacked the Indian Army stood by this code of valour, fidelity and honour. The tradition never to surrender has remained ingrained in our fighting men and our Army has resolute soldiers who are ever ready to do their duty unto death without hesitation. The main characteristics of Indian soldiers are:

Valour. Fearlessness in combat, in the face of the enemy even when fighting at a great disadvantage or facing sure death.

Spirit of selfless sacrifice. The tradition never to question but to do or die.

Fairness and honesty. Even towards the enemy, prisoners or wounded.

Discipline and integrity. Patriotism, honesty and courage under all circumstances.

Dogged determination. Even in defeat or adverse situations.

Non-discrimination. On account of caste, creed or religion. Total impartiality in performance of duty.

Comradeship and brotherhood of the brave. Within the armed forces regardless of caste, creed or religion.

Fidelity, honour and courage. Stand out as an example to others.

THE INDIAN DEFENCE FORCES : AIR FORCE

Historical Overview

The Indian Air Force is a young service. Its birth in 1932 and its growth to date can be conveniently divided into four 15-year periods: 1932-1947-1962-1977-1992. By a coincidence these dates correspond to the major changes in the structure, composition and the capability of the Air Force. The origin of the IAF can be traced to the recommendation of the Skeen Committee set up by the British in 1925. This committee looked into the local demand of Indians for a greater say in matters of defence. The committee, chaired by Sir Andrew Skeen (then Chief of General Staff) was formally constituted as the Indian Sandhurst Committee in 1925. It recommended, among other things, the induction of the Indians into the RAF College at Cramwell and the formation of an Indian Air Arm manned fully by Indians. As a follow-up of this report, 6 Indians were sent to the RAF college for the first time in 1930. When 5 out of the 6 successfully became pilots, the Indian Air Force came into being on 8 October 1932. The first unit of the IAF, No. 1 Squadron, was formed on 1 April 1933 at Drigh Road Airfield, Karachi.

The Beginning, 1932-46

It was a slow start. No. 1 Squadron was formed with only one light 4 aircraft, 5 pilots and 9 technicians. The rate of training was only two pilots per year. Pilots had to go to the RAF College for training as there was no facility in India. Three years went before the second flight was added. With only one more aircraft another flight was formed in June 1938, initially with no aircraft at all. The squadron so far had no real existence as a unit. The flights were being moved about as appendages to various RAF units. Then at long last, the three flights came together in Ambala in July 1938. A committee in 1938 recommended the formation of an IAF Volunteer Reserve (IAFVR) and 5 Coastal Defence Flights (CDF) manned by this. An act authorising the formation of the IAFVR was passed, but nothing much else happened. Even though the war cloud had by then started gathering over Europe, the colonial government did not seem interested in letting the Indian Air Force grow.

In the twenties and the thirties, the RAF was engaged in experiments to find out the best way to utilise air power. One of the expensive operations of the British Imperial Forces in those days was to mount punitive expeditions against rebellious tribes on the fringes of the empire, mainly in Iraq and Afghanistan. The RAF postulated that punitive expeditions could be replaced or at least largely supplemented by aerial strafing and bombing of the rebel strong-holds as a more economical alternative. This proposal was accepted.

RAF set up a number of airfields and secured a presence for itself in India. In 1920, it had 8 squadrons in India. This force was reduced to 6 squadrons in the thirties and again went back to 8 squadrons by the end of the decade. When the formation of the Indian Air Force became inevitable, the RAF wanted to use this token force as its appendage in the rebel-suppression role. 'A' flight of No. 1 Squadron was tried out for six weeks in this role in 1937. The 'C' flight was deployed for a couple of months in 1938. Technically the Indian units performed at par with the RAF units both in air and on the ground. No. 1 Squadron was then re-equipped with a slightly better aircraft, the Hart, and one of its flights was introduce to a new task of maritime air patrol while the other two flights went back to its air suppression role in the NWFP.

After Britain entered the war, it stopped training Indian pilots at Cramwell for the IAF. However, it took in a large batch of Indians for training. These pilots were commissioned into the IAFVR and were utilised by the RAF. Those pilots who survived their operational tour in Europe came back to the IAF in 1942.

In 1940 the proposed IAFVR coastal defence flights came into being. Pilots were recruited from British and Indian civilians in the five metropolitan cities of Karachi, Bombay, Madras, Cochin and Calcutta. Available aircrafts of the local flying clubs and some small airlines were pressed into service. The RAF squadrons in India were not in full strength. A decision was taken to fill the existing vacancies in these squadrons by training Indians. An RAF squadron at Risalpur was converted to training role. The initial recruits for IAFVR were trained in this squadron and sent to the coastal defence flights to RAF squadrons in India.

By 1941, it had become clear that the total requirements of air force for the defence of India could not be made available from the RAF. The assessed need was for 21 squadrons and 5 coastal defence flights, whereas the RAF could at the most supply 11 squadrons. Therefore the IAF had to be expanded to a 10-squadron force. Large scale induction into the IAFVR began. To cope with the increase training needs, two Elementary Flying Schools and one Service Flying School were set up at Begumpet, Jodhpur and Ambala. To train technicians and other supporting tradesmen, one airmen's training school was set up at Ambala. This proved to be inadequate. Soon airmen's training was spread over 20 schools all over the country.

Two squadrons were formed in 1941. No. 2 in April, and No. 3 in October. In July 1941, No. 1 Squadron changed over from Ha- to Lysanders and No. 2 Squadron discarded their Wapitis for Harts handed over by No. 1 Squadron. No. 3 Squadron didn't get their full share of aircraft for some time. In December 1941, Japan entered the Second World War. No. 1 Squadron was sent to Burma in February 1942, but came back in March of the same year when Rangoon fell to the Japanese. After returning from Burma, No. I Squadron converted to Hurricanes.

Four more squadrons were formed in 1942: No. 4 in February and Nos. 6, 7 and 8 in December. Throughout 1941 and 1942, IAF squadrons remained on training role in addition to air suppression duties in the NWFP. During the same period, the IAFVR coastal flights were closed down. It was not cost-effective to run these units with unsuitable aircraft and untrained crew. The task was taken over by better equipped and trained RAF units.

No. 9 Squadron was formed in 1943, but was able to start training only in February 1944. No. 10 Squadron was formed in February 1944. Between 1943 and 1945, some of the units took part in air operations against the Japanese. No. 1 Squadron operated from Kohima from January 1944 to April 1945. No. 2 Squadron from October 19 to May 1945 in Cox's Bazar and various airfields in Burma. No. 3 Squadron from January to April 1945 in Burma, No. 4 Squadron from Feni between April 1944 to April 1945, and then in Japan with the Allied Occupation Forces in 1946. No. 6 Squadron from November 1943 to June 1944 from Cox's Bazar, No. 7 Squadron from March to June 1944 from Uderbund near Kumbhigram in support of the Chindits Operation, and again between March and May from various airfields in Burma. No. 8 Squadron operated from Double Moorings near Chittagong between December 1943 and 1944, and again from July 1945 till the end of the war from Mingladon. No. 9 Squadron operated from April 1944 to April 1945 from Kulaura, and again from November 1945 to January 1946 from Hmawbi. For this second operational tour, No. 9 Squadron was accompanied by No. 10 Squadron. In recognition of the work done by the IAF units in the Arakaan the IAF was given a 'Royal' prefix to its name. From then on till the country became a republic in 1950, the Air Force was known as the Royal Indian Air Force or the RIAF.

By 1946, all units had come back to India, and by now the process of "Indianization" had also proceeded quite far. By 1943, the charge of Kohat airfield had been handed over to the Indian Air Force from then on, till August 1947, all Station Commanders were from the RIAF. Those RAF or Commonwealth personnel who had operated with the Indian units during the war went away by 1946.

New Branches

The equipment branch had received its first Indian Officer in 1932. A new branch called Administrative and Special Duties Branch was formed in 1940. Pilots who were unfit for flying duties were transferred to this branch. Fairly large-scale direct recruitment was also made into this branch. Apart from routine administration, this branch took over the duties of air traffic control and codes and cipher duties. The Meteorological Branch took its officers and men from the India Met Department. There was direct recruitment for the Accounts and Education branches. The Medical branch drew its doctors from the Army Medical Corps.

Up to the early forties, the aircrafts being flown by the Air Force were simple. The units didn't need an Engineering graduate as an Engineer Officer. Therefore, there was no direct recruitment for the technical branches. By 1942-43, when a need was felt for an engineer in the officer grade due to the increasing complexity of the aircraft and reduced time of the aircrew under the pressures of war to devote to matters technical, a steady stream of senior technicians were commissioned into these branches from the ranks. This solution was adequate for the needs of the unit, but it prevented the growth of a technical staff who would be able to take a broad view of the technical needs at higher staff levels notwithstanding the presence of a few very eminent personalities who thus rose through the ranks. The weakness was rectified after independence, but the later entrants have often had to struggle to get out of the grooves made by the pioneers.

Organisation in the Early Days

The Air Force was a tiny force for the first 10 years of its existence. No separate Headquarters existed for it. It was controlled as a part of the British Air Forces in India under the AOC India, who in turn was controlled by the Commander-in-Chief in India and the GHQ. The HQ of the AOC India was called AHQ(I) and it consisted of a single branch with a Senior Air Staff Officer (SASO) as its head, and about 20 officers. The AOC held the rank of Air Marshal. With the expansion of air activity in India, this organisation expanded and a second branch, Administration, was added under a Senior Officer Administration or SOA.

By 1942, the rank of the AOC India had risen to that of an Air Chief Marshal and his designation had become AOC-in-C India. Up to 1943, there was no room for IAF officers in the AHQ(I). But as the organisation grew further, certain number of RIAF officers were inducted into it at an Assistant Director level. By 1945, certain RLKF officers had reached the level of Deputy Directors. In 1946, an RIAF officer took over the directorate of training, and he was the first RIAF officer to enter the Air HQ at that level. It might be interesting to note however, that in 1943, AHQ(I) was divested of most of its functions including that of recruitment and training. With the formation of the office of the Supreme Allied Commander South East Asia (SACSEA), two new air headquarters were formed. Air Command South East Asia (ACSEA) controlled all the operations against Japan, while Base Air Forces South East Asia (BAFSEA) did the house-keeping chores for all the Air Forces operating in India including the RIAF. The AHQ(I) was left to perform only the 'Watch and Ward' duties in the NWFP which were carried out mainly by (and at times only by) the RIAF. This situation continued until the wartime headquarters were dissolved.

The Air Force upto 1945 was purely a tactical air force. It had no transport capability until No. 12 Squadron was formed in 1946. It had no long-range bombers. Apart from the few months of 1938 when a flight of No. 1 Squadron carried out Coastal Patrol duties, and the interregnum of the coastal defence flights between 1940 and 1942, it had not developed any maritime expertise. However, during the War, its equipment was progressively upgraded. Whereas in 1939 it had only one understaffed and under-equipped unit operating obsolete aircraft, in 1946 it had nine fighter and one transport squadron using equipment that were current if not state-of-the-art, and a reasonably balanced infrastructure. In retrospect, it is quite interesting to observe this metamorphosis.

The IAF was not meant to grow quickly. Both pilot and technician training schemes were of small intakes and long durations. There was no attempt to induct Indians into non-flying branches of the commissioned rank, notwithstanding the commissioning of one officer in the equipment branch from the first batch of pilot trainees. Selection of pilots was from the metropolitan cities with previous flying experience. This automatically restricted the choice to the westernised and affluent.

By 1940, immediately after the rate of recruitment was expanded, the then traditional source proved to be inadequate. Rich city boys were not really interested in joining the shooting war. In the initial days of the war, no one really knew how long it would last and how it would end. The Air Force, therefore, attracted the venturesome from the public schools who had no previous flying experience. This lot was also from a reasonably affluent background. But even this source was not large enough to fill the needs.

Recruitment was then expanded to include the young ones from the middle classes. Here, the recruitment drive came face to face with lack of air mindedness then prevalent. This problem was battled by formation of display flights which toured the country to fire the imagination of the youth from the smaller towns and induce them to join the Air Force. A sustained effort was also launched to induct university students through an Air Training Corps. Despite all these efforts, however, it was not possible to fill all the vacancies in the nine existing squadrons with Indian pilots. Right up to 1946, the units had some RAF and other Commonwealth pilots on their strength, albeit in a progressively reduced number.

The response to recruitment in the non-flying cadre was more prompt. Indeed, it became necessary to restrict the entries into the non-flying branches to only those who were medically or otherwise not found fit to become air crew. To increase the number of volunteers for air crew duties, army officers were permitted to join the Air Force temporarily. Some of them liked the Air Force enough to stay back permanently while some others returned to their parent cadre and still others went back to civilian life at the end of the war.

Not all air crew recruited were to become pilots. In the earlier types of aircraft, there was room for an additional air crew called the OBSERVER. In the first decade of the existence of the IM, two pilots used to crew each other in the Wapiti. However, under the pressures of war, when training institutions were formed, training of a separate Observer's stream within the general duties branch commenced. After a few courses, direct recruitment of this stream was discontinued, the vacancies being filled by pilot rejects. At that stage, some of the earlier Observers opted to re-train as pilots and did so successfully. With the phasing out of the two-seat fighters from the service, some of the Observers were transferred to the newly formed A&SD Branch while some others were employed in various ground duties retaining their General Duty status. Later, with the induction of the Dakota, the Observers were utilised in the Navigator's role. For the first decade, No. 1 Squadron did not move about much. From April 1933 to April 1936, 'A' Flight of No. I Squadron stayed put at Karachi. With the formation of the 'B' Flight, it moved to Peshawar, Multan, and Sialkot for training exercises. After the 'B' Flight had stabilised, it moved to Bangalore for exercises and then moved into Ambala as its permanent base. In 1938, the 'C' Flight joined the 'B' Flight at Ambala. From then on, the three flights took turns to operate from Miranshah and Fort Sandaman, two of the most used forward airfields, in the air suppression role; and did short army-air cooperation exercises all over the country while maintaining Ambala as the home base.

When the rush of formation of new squadrons came, the RAF spread its wings to many new bases in the country. The IAF units moved at random to these stations. The most frequently used were Kanpur, Allahabad, Calcutta, Ranchi, Begumpet and Amarda Road. With the formation of SACSEA, the peninsular airfields become active. The IAF used Trichinopally, Tambaram, Sulur, Yellahanka, Kolar and Arakonam. More airfields became active in the North and East. Delhi, Bhopal, Chharra, Pune, Vizag, Kumbhigram, Chittagong, Cox's Bazar, Kohima, Feni and a whole host of small and big airfields in Burma and Thailand were used.

The Air Force got to know India from one corner to the other. This habit of treating the whole country as one unit, along with its recruitment base being devoid of any caste, creed, region or faith, gave the Air Force a stamp of secularity that has withstood the test of time.

Changes in Equipment

Like its change in size, the change of equipment came to the IAF in an explosive jolt. From 1933 to 1938, the IAF flew the Wapiti which was obsolete even in 1933. No wonder that the aircraft acquired the nickname of What-a-Pity! This was followed in 1938 by the Audax and the Hart which were by no means modern. These were the products of the transitional period where propellers were made of wood and had a fixed pitch, unable to match the engine speed with variable airspeed. The designers were not sure of making aircraft fully out of metals. Wood and fabric were still considered as major construction material for aircraft. The Audax and Hart were followed by the Vengeance and Lysander which were both slow limbering army cooperation aircraft with poor armament capability. The IAF had to fight a war with these planes where its task was often in the offensive role. The IAF displayed a great deal of innovation in usage and maintenance of these aircraft. Two famous examples were the fitment of a bomb rack on the Lysander and the fitment of a wooden tail wheel on the Vengeance when regulation metal ones were out of stock!

Aircraft design in the UK was revolutionised with the arrival of the Hawker Hurricane and Supermarine Spitfire. Both these aircraft entered the RAF just before the war, but reached the RIAF only by 1943-45. Anyway, they were still modern when they came. By the time the War ended, all Air Force units were equipped with various marks of these aircraft in the Western world. The aircraft factories were still producing modem aircraft that were no more required by the RAF. India had a very healthy balance-of-payment situation with the British Government. Independence was also on the horizon. The Air Force therefore found itself discarding its semi new Hurricanes and Spitfire Mark VH aircraft for Spitfire MV which again gave way to Tempest IIa and Spitfire XVIII within the short span of 1946-47. There was no British transport aircraft in the market at that moment. The new Transport Squadron was therefore formed with war-surplus Douglas DC3 Dakota aircraft. The Indian Army had formed a parachute brigade. A Paratroop Training School was therefore established at Walton with the Dakota as its mount.

For training purpose, no specific aircraft was initially provided for. After basic and advanced training with the RAF, the pilots flew the aircraft allotted to their units. The Wapiti, Audax and Hart had the second cockpit fitted with flying controls. The Squadron Commander or the Flight Commander could therefore use the operational aircraft to test or train the unit's aircrew. When the Flying Training Schools came about they used the DH Tigermoth and the North American Harvard. These two aircraft proved to be very hardy, and continued in their respective roles even beyond 1947. With the re-equipment of the fighter unit with single seat aircraft, a couple of Harvards were added to the unit establishment for dual checks and instrument flying practice. The IAFVR flew a large variety of aircraft during its short life span. The more exotic varieties like the Atlanta and the Blenhim did not find a place in the regular units when the coastal defence flight were closed down.

When the EFTSs and the SFTS were formed, they were manned fully by RAF personnel. As the war progressed, a sprinkling of India flying instructors, trained at the RAF's Central Flying School Little Risington, took their place in these units. By 1946, Indians formed the majority of instructors, though the units were still commanded by RAF personnel. A number of fighter pilots were also trained in UK as Pilot Attack Instructors. Indian pilots, by and large performed very well at these courses.

By 1946, the Air Force had digested its explosive growth in size and technology fairly well and had become a fairly stable Service. It was also unfortunately realised by then that the impending independence would bring with itself a partition of the country and a partition of the Air Force. For an organisation that was cosmopolitan and secular by design and upbringing, a partition on religious lines was not an easy concept to digest. Many non-Muslim men and officers hailed from areas that were to constitute Pakistan, just as there were many Muslim men and officers who had their roots in what to continue as India. Each and every such person had to decide for himself which side of the fence he wished to be on. Many such decisions were invariably influenced by the communal holocaust had engulfed the country or by the uncertainties that prevailed about the future of the two new nations. When the dust settled, however we found that although almost all non-Muslim men and officers had opted to stay back in India irrespective of their place of birth a large segment of Muslim personnel with their roots in India had done the same and remained with the country of their birth.

The nitty-gritty of division of assets was amicably sorted in four months preceding 15 August 1947. The assets of 1, 6 and 9 Squadrons were handed over to Pakistan and these units were number-plated. Similarly the depots and other assets were partitioned and relocated. Personnel were suitably relocated and moved safely with close mutual protection. On 15 August 1947, the first phase of the Air Force came to an end and a new phase began.

THE INDIAN DEFENCE FORCES : NAVY

Our Maritime Heritage

India's maritime heritage goes well beyond the past than some of us might comprehend. With the Himalayas in the north, Indians for centuries have depended on sea routes for trade and communication with rest of the world. Vital sea links therefore emerged over a period of time for the exchange of trade, commerce and culture. Historians and scholars have traced our associations with the sea way back to the Harappan culture, around 3000 BC.

Excavations at Mohenjo-Daro and Harappa reveal personal ornaments of shell and pearls, picked up possibly from the Indian or Persian Gulf coasts. It is believed that Harappans came from, what is presently Jamnagar, to the Gulf of Cambay. A naval dock unearthed at Loothal in Ahmedabad district further confirms presence of large ships capable of being used at sea. Besides, there is overwhelming evidence that commercial contact existed between the inhabitants of the Indus Valley and the people of Egypt, Central Asia and Persia.

Appearance of Warships in the Indian Ocean

Towards the middle of the fifteenth century the Ottoman Turks had emerged as a major power in West Asia and Eastern Europe, and continued their thrust into Central Europe. Western trade routes were therefore cut off over land with the East, with the fall of Constantinople (now Istanbul) into the Turkish hands. Western Europe had therefore to find an alternative route for their trade and import of spices from Asia. The Portuguese were the first to take the initiative and in 1497 Vasco da Gama sailed on a long voyage around the African continent to explore the East.

His San Gabriel was a warship and was accompanied by two others. Portuguese efforts bore fruit when they landed at Calicut 10 months later. While the Indians had used the sea for military transportation earlier, San Gabriel was the first ship of war, fitted with 20 guns, to touch the Indian shores. Vasco da Gama was granted trading permission and the Indians seemed quite content as long as their requirements from abroad were met and their own trade was promoted.

The Portuguese initiative would have given them very long-term benefits had they not made the mistake of selling Indian spices at very high prices to rest of the West European community. Their second mistake was in not being able to maintain cordial relations with the Indian community from the beginning. Their mistakes drew the other European navies into the Indian Ocean. In due course rivalries and hostilities grew within them, and finally the British emerged powerful and diplomatic enough to remain a pro dominant power in the area.

Portugal-Calicut relations worsened with Vasco da Gama refusing to pay the usual customs levy to Indians, Vasco da Gama and his soldiers indulged in acts of barbarism unparalleled in Indian maritime history. The situation further worsened due to Portuguese interference with Arab trading interests at Calicut; the latter having had long and friendly trade with the Indian coast. The Portuguese had, therefore, to seek other avenues.

They sought Cannanore and Cochin. Besides capturing trade, their primary aim was to gain supremacy over the India Ocean and trade routes. They remained persistent in sending more and more ships to the Malabar coast and went to the extent of pronouncing that no Indian or Arab ship could ply without their permission.

It is important to review the political conditions of India during this period. India was weak and divided into several small states and kingdoms. There was a Hindu-Muslim divide and even states belonging to the same religion had serious differences and rivalries. India's maritime importance had ebbed giving way to rob traders. Armed traders of the West, therefore, took advantages and established their bases with full assent of the weaker rulers. On the west coast Portuguese ships started raiding Indian and Arab merchant ships which ventured without their permission. Following differences with Calicut, the port was subjected to a blockade and therefore commercial starvation. Portuguese intervention at Cochin further aggravated the traditional feud between the rulers of Cochin and Calicut while these states raised their own armed flotillas, their individual seas power was no match for the Portuguese men of war on high seas and Lisbon continued to consolidate its influence in the Indian Ocean and made other settlements along the west coast of India and Ceylon.

The Dutch followed the Portuguese initiative and ventured east. Their first settlements were in Java and Sumtra which seemed to be their primary interests. In India, after making their initial base at Masulipatnam on the East coast, they spread southwards on the Coromandal coast. The arrival of the Dutch fleet was taken as a positive infringement by the Portuguese on what they by now considered as their area of influence. The two forces clashed at Pulict, Nagapatnam, Quilon, Cochin and Goa frequently. Having penetrated Portuguese naval influence and established a base at Patna.

Having broken the Portuguese monopoly of Indian trade in Europe the Dutch also demanded exorbitant prices for pepper and other Indian goods. This motivated the British to establish their presence in the Indian Ocean. The East India Company was formed in England in 1599. Four ships sailed and these were operated by privateers at Sumantra for the first two voyages. On their voyage in 1609 an attempt was made to trade with India but was met with Portuguese protests.

The East India Company, realizing the obstructional policy of the Portuguese, fitted their ships with armed merchant men and dispatched a squadron which reached Surat in 1612. The two forces had a encounter off the port during which British ships, being better constructed and better armed, emerged victorious. The British remained persistent and in 1615 formal trading rights were granted to the British by the Mughal court. The British established trading centres at Surat, Ahmedabad and Cambay.

From Indian Marine to Indian Navy

The Indian Marine was formed in 1613 in England for the protection of the East India Company's ships and trade. The company established its first trading centre at Surat and expanded further. For the British it was not an easy task to overcome the Dutch and Portuguese resistance in the Indian Ocean. Many battles were fought, and later with the French, to gain supremacy in the region. Besides, there was also the Maratha threat to counter. Besides the rivalry for the Indian coastal region, they struggled for the neighbouring areas also. Their navies clashed for obtaining bases in the Persian Gulf, Aden, Mauritius, Java etc. It seems that of all, the East India Company remained pragmatic and persistent for the cause. The Indian Marine therefore continued to grow with an increasing number of ships.

In 1661, Portugal ceded Bombay to the British Crown as a part of the dowry of their Infant Catherine when she married King Charles II. Seven years later the Crown leased Bombay to the East India Company at a rent of 10 pounds a year. Bombay, therefore, came rather easily to the British which they used greatly to their advantage. Its strategic location and ship-building infrastructure proved to be an asset. By 1735 a full-fledged ship-building dockyard was established and named Bombay Dockyard. With continued encounters with the Maratha Fleet the British found it more convenient to shift major forces and trading establishment from Surat to Bombay in 1688. The Indian Marine thereafter acquired the name Bombay Marine.

By 1782, the British had firmly established their control over the Indian Ocean area and the hinterland. The force was augmented and it underwent some transformation, and very early in the twentieth century was renamed "The Royal Indian Marine". Its main role was trooping and hydrographic surveys of ports and coastline. All officers and key sailors were British while the other staff were recruited from India, predominatly from the Konkan Coast.

The Royal Indian Marine (RIM) participated in the First World War and expanded considerably. But the end of the war brought severe retrenchment and the RIM was reduced to a very small force capable of only defence duties of a few ports. A large number of Indians therefore lost their jobs. The maritime defence of India was entrusted to the British Navy depriving Indians of valuable seafing experience.

On the insistence of some prominent citizens, the British relented to introduce a small fighting force in the name of 'Royal Indian Navy'. Bombay became the Headquarters of the RIN and it was agreed that in due course it will predominantly be manned by Indians.

Recruitment of officers into the Royal Indian Navy started in the early thirties. With the commencement of the Second World War in 1939, RIN expanded rapidly and some merchant ships were also converted into men-of-war. More and more Indians were inducted into the service and they gave a very good account in maritime combat. Quite a few were given gallantry awards.

In 1950, when India became a Republic, the word 'Royal' was dropped and the nomenclature was changed to 'INDIAN NAVY'.

The Indian Navy has very wisely followed the path of indigenisation and the day is not very far when the Navy of India will be truly Indian. In the earlier days we took what came, but today we endeavour to make what we want. We are now in a position to write our own agenda-our own staff requirements. From a Buyer's Navy, we are fast becoming a Builder's Navy. Indian Navy's ship requirements can be met indigenously, provided we place orders on our shipyards in time and with conviction, and also make the money-flow available. Some specialist equipment may of course have to be imported.

Rationale

At the outset, it needs to be made clear that India does not need a Navy designed to project power. A power projection Navy is for nations which have defence commitments outside their shores. What India needs is a medium sized blue water Navy which will deter aggression and safeguard our maritime interests in our region, and since we do not belong to any alliance, whatever we wish to defend has to be done all alone and by ourselves, This naturally calls for a different kind of preparedness where costs necessarily escalate. The shape and size of our country and the location of our island territories compels us to deploy our naval units in two or three distinct groups/tasks forces but there is no doubt that for sometime to come North Arabian Sea will continue to be the area of focus for us.

This does not mean that vast areas of the sea in the rest of the Arabian Sea, Bay of Bengal, Indian Ocean Region (IOR) and the Andaman Sea are any less important and can be neglected.

They are very much our responsibility and adequate forces will have to be assigned to safeguard our interests therein. We next come to the element of reach-this has been defined as the distance from home port at which operations will need to be carried out. This presupposes that for any naval force, the reach for some operations may be different from that of others.

For convenience, we can broadly divide this into two zones. An outer zone extending to 1000 nautical miles from base, where the main threat will be from submarines, missile fitted surface combatants and shore-based multipurpose aircraft and an inner zone extending to 200 nautical miles (within EEZ) from our shores where the operation will be of a different nature which will include clandestine activity, mining, submarine operations and attack by shore-based a.rcraft. In our case sea conditions on both seaboards are far from comfortable for much of the year and, therefore units operating in the outer zone will have to have the capability to operate in all weather conditions and for sufficiently long periods. With this background, let us now look at our requirements and how best we can meet them.

Surface Heat

We next look at the surface combatant element of the fleet. These are the main workhorses of the Navy called the Frigate/ Destroyers. They have to have all-purpose capability and excellent sea-keeping qualities and should have weapons and sensors to be able to perform anti-ship, anti-submarine and anti-aircraft role. They must also carry their own integral air in the form of a helicopter. Bearing in mind the sea conditions around us a frigate or a destroyer of 3000 tons plus is the smallest platform capable of fitting into this role. They form the primary units of the carrier task force. A minimum of 5 for each task force/fleet is absolutely necessary. With allowance for refit and maintenance, a force of 15 Frigate/Destroyers with afloat support would be required to maintain ten on station.

Though not so versatile, a smaller version of Frigate/Destroyer called the Corvette is built for specific roles and naturally costs much less. They complement the Frigate/Destroyer in their specific role as components of the carrier task force. They also help in the protection of offshore resource platforms and, if required, in escorting merchant ships. A force of 20 would be required to maintain 14 on station. Realistic tasking levels would indicate that 15 of the 35 (20+1 5) combatants should be Destroyers or Frigates.

Bearing in mind the geographic location of our island territories, in particular the Andaman & Nicobar islands which are almost 800 nautical miles away from the mainland, the requirement of sealift capability would become obvious. These ships are required to quickly move a Brigade group with all its paraphemalia-armour, vehicles and guns, at feast for the first assault which may have to be launched in the face of opposition. For them to be of worthwhile use, they should be able to carry a complement of commando helicopters and smaller LCUs and other assault vessels. Any shortfalls can be made up by requisitioning vessels from trade for subsequent build up. We also need fleet auxiliaries to support the fleet at sea-these could be Tankers, Depot & Repair ships and submarine rescue vessels.

We next come to smaller category of ships like the Missile Boats, Patrol vessels and Minesweepers. Missile Boats carry a lot of punch for their size though their sea-keeping qualities are limited, so also the range. They are therefore, most suitable in a defensive role and mainly operate in the inner zone or for swift raids on targets not too far away and for effecting a quick getaway. We also need relatively cheap patrol vessels with long endurance to maintain vigil over our large EEZ. Minesweepers are a must to keep our strategic ports open and safe for ship movements, In each of these categories, one can never have enough numbers. One would be lucky if one could have 1 5-20 of each.

Submarines

To complete the three dimensional picture let us look at the deadliest of the class-the submarine. They are vessels of stealth, and visibility or presence is not their hallmark. They play a very crucial role in denying the use of the sea to the enemy. Submarines now run deeper, are more silent, faster and have considerably enhanced endurance. They can take swift evasive action in both horizontal and vertical planes. Their ability to fire precision guided high speed torpedoes and anti-ship missiles make them extremely potent strike platforms. If one can go nuclear, the submarine can become a strategic asset with an ability to remain continuously submerged and move at high speed underwater. Conventional submarines can be deployed on patrol independently and far away from our shores in all kinds of weather or off enemy ports. Looking at areas around us a fleet of 12-15 conventional submarines would be the minimum needed to fulfil these tasks, considering that only 66% of these would be available on task, rest being under refit/maintenance.

Indigenous Capability

As stated earlier, shipbuilding capacity in the country has grown over the years and while some specialised equipment may have to be imported, in-house ship designing and construction ability exists. MDL at Bombay and GRSE at Calcutta can build Frigates/ Destroyers, Corvettes and Missile Boats. Goa Shipyard can take on the construction of minesweepers and other smaller vessels. The Air Defence Ship has so far not been built in the country but the one being contemplated can quite easily be built at Cochin Shipyard. Cochin Shipyard can also take on the task of building tankers and other support vessels. Submarines have been built at MDL and it is unfortunate that this line had to come to a grinding halt because of political sensitivities-HDW connection. This has to be restarted, the sooner the better-otherwise we will fall miles behind in our Submarine replacement programme.

Our shipyards are capable of producing a Frigate/ Destroyer and submarines ever 2 years and one each of Corvette, Patrol vessel/Minesweeper and Missile Boat every year. Amphibious ships of about 5000 tons can be built every 4-5 years and ADS one every 10 years. I am confident that this production rate can be improved upon if firm orders are placed, money supply guaranteed and the work culture in shipyards improved.

Conclusion

A time has come for the political leadership to evolve a mechanism which will stipulate realistic and firm force levels for the three Services avoiding ad hoc decisions which sometimes get taken.

In the foreseeable future, therefore, the Navy that would meet India's national interests will have to have adequate forces to deploy in sea areas around us and in all weather conditions. Our shipyards and associated industries will have to be geared up to produce the ships/submarines and hardware that is needed. Infrastructure support too will have to be provided. This is only possible if clear direction is given and adequate resources made available to ensure a smooth and realistic naval growth.

MILITARY INTELLIGENCE IN INDIA : AN ANALYSIS

Sources of Military Intelligence

The first section examines the components of MI and its main sources. Any intelligence, strategic or tactical, that is of interest to the defence capabilities of a country, which influences, in peace or war the military security of a nation, may be termed MI. It is possible that this intelligence may arise from a variety of sources. Wherever this intelligence is of relevance to an Air Force, Army or Navy it can be categorised as MI. For example, if India were to find out from photographic aerial reconnaissance that Pakistan has moved two divisions close to our borders, it should alert the defence planners to this move. Of curse, like in any other intelligence organisation there has to be collection, analysis and dissemination of information in MI, but the point is that certain specific categories of intelligence are of greater interest to MI than others. There are seven sources of intelligence.

Human intelligence (HUMINT) is perhaps the oldest of them all. From the covert agent, POW, defector, to the overt military 'reconnoitre', it has been the human being who has been the most prolific source of intelligence before the advent of writing and the invention of the pictograph. In course of time man learnt to transmit messages by writing them down. The interception of such communication became Communication Intelligence (COMINT). HUMINT & COMINT remained for hundreds of years the main source of information to civilian and military organisations. With the invention of printing in Europe a new source of information became available. Books, magazines and journals began to appear over the next few centuries on specialised subjects relating to military science and studies, which provided a wealth of information on foreign armies, their organisation, strategy and tactics. The introduction of wireless, radio and other methods of transmitting messages in the ether provided a new source of intelligence.

The ability to intercept such messages gave man Signal Intelligence or SIGINT. By the 1840s, the arrival of the telegraph and Morse code gave COMINT a new dimension, the ability to tap enemy communication lines. COMINT was particularly important for Britain in the First World War. The invention of photography and man's ascent to air, opened up two new sources of MI. One was Imagery Intelligence (IMINT) and the other was Photographic Reconnaissance (PR). A spy could now support his case with photographs of classified documents. And as technology progressed, small and higher resolution cameras eased the task of espionage. As the aircrafts took to the air, they in part took over the role of the spy, collecting images far beyond the reach of HUMINT and giving MI valuable insights into the enemy's order of battle, and logistic capabilities.

For instance, a PR Spitfire had spotted an additional Panzer corps in the Ardennes forest before Op *Market Garden* in 1944, but unfortunately the report was not believed. PR became important to MI during the Second World War. It was in the realm of SIGINT that Britain had considerable success during World War II with the recording and decoding of the signals traffic of the Luftwaffe and Wehrmacht which provided in many cases a decisive edge. SIGINT is usually a more profitable source at the strategic level as the time taken to defeat security at the tactical level reduces its importance on the ground.

The development of RADAR just before World War II provided a new method of acquiring tactical intelligence on the battlefield. With rapid improvements in electronics technology, a new and important source of MI became available i.e. Electronic Intelligence (ELINT). ELINT covers a field far beyond battlefield surveillance, it encompasses electronic eavesdropping upon electromagnetic emissions of a wide variety of devices. In recent times imagery from space satellites, ELINT from monitoring of nuclear explosions, and radars provides MI with a whole new range of information.

The collection and analysis of much of this raw data is done by computers today. In fact in all spheres of intelligence activity computers are playing an important role and help in the speedy dissemination of real-time intelligence of technical importance. They are also used to code and decode transmissions at a strategic and tactical level. In the past few decades, the information explosion has resulted in the availability of a number of published sources that provide a wealth of military information.

These specialised magazines, journals and papers, though not quite on the scale of their covert sources, provide a great deal of information if collated and analysed properly. For instance, there is enough available in both India and foreign publications on India's defence situation and yet the government does nothing to amend the Official Secrets Act. If any intelligence organisation were to broaden its net and collect information from radio broadcasts, science journals, books and TV programmes and use it in conjunction with classified information, very comprehensive intelligence tool will become available.

As a matter of fact one of the tasks of a Military Attaché (MA) is to collect information from the above mentioned sources and send it to his own country. Basically the Military Attaché acts as an observer in the foreign country and uses his eyes and ears to pick up stray bits of information which may later lead to a bigger picture. The defector is an other valuable source of MI, particularly if the defector is of rank and has served in sensitive departments of a foreign army. Equally important can be low grade clerks and operators who work in SIGINT and COMINT establishments. Lt Igor Gouzensko, who defected to Canada in 1945 was a cipher clerk to the MA in the Soviet Residency at Ottawa. He became one of the most useful sources of information for western intelligence agencies for over two decades. And finally, if an intelligence organisation has friendly links with another country's agency, valuable information can be obtained.

MI Organisations of Some Nations: In this section, it would be appropriate to examine some worldwide organisations specifically charged with the collection of MI. In America, under the National Security Act of 1947, the CIA was created, but the Department of Defence and the Armed Forces continued to have their own organisations. In 1961, the Defence Intelligence Agency (DIA) was created by the Secretary of Defence to have a central coordinating body for military intelligence. The Joint Chiefs of Staff thus had one place to look for MI, instead of arguing over the estimates of each armed force. Essentially each armed force now maintains an intelligence division for technical intelligence, apart from counter intelligence activities.

The US Army has an assistant chief of staff for intelligence (referred to as G-2) under whom Army intelligence is organised. This unit looks after the works of military attaches in other countries. The Naval intelligence is similarly organised with a Naval Intelligence Command (NIC) headed by an Assistant Chief of Naval Operations (intelligence). The US Air Force is in charge of PR and ensures against surprise attack. Thus each American Armed Force has its own agency charged with carrying out various intelligence activities, including counter-intelligence.

In the erstwhile Soviet Union and Russia today there, is Central Intelligence Office or GRU-the Chief Intelligence Directorate of the Army General Staff. The GRU deals primarily with military intelligence. A full General commands this post. The agent networks are controlled by the first four directorates, each headed by a Lt General.

In the United Kingdom, each armed force has its own intelligence unit. Like the American DIA, they have a Defence Intelligence staff that combines the talents of all three services to provide inputs to the JCS. For COMINT and SIGINT they have GCHQ at Cheltenham, which is responsible for electronic surveillance and cryptology. This is like the American National Security Agency. The National Defence Staff's Second Division in France is in charge of MI. While in Israel the AMAN-the Intelligence Corps of the IDF looks after MI. Its chief is the advisor to the Defence Minister.

MI in India: In India today, all three armed forces have their own Intelligence units and all are headed by a Director of MI under whom is a directorate which collects intelligence and prepares it for dissemination. The root of India's MI organisation can be traced to 1885 when Maj. Gen. Sir Charles Mac Gregor was appointed head of the Intelligence Department of the Indian Army.

The new department had its HQ in Simla and was principally concerned with gathering and evaluating information about Russian troop dispositions in Central Asia.

It was during the Second World War, after the retreat from Burma, that the British Army set up a group, staffed by Intelligence officers to collect intelligence about Japanese designs and to tackle counter-intelligence. GCHQ had a separate section looking after cryptology in the Far East with HQ at Delhi.

In 1942, the Intelligence Corps was created with HQ at Karachi for undivided India to train JCOs and NC0s. For most part of the war the intelligence work was done by British officers, and when they left the Intelligence Corps in 1947, nothing remained to go on as they destroyed most of the records. The fortunes of MI at the time of independence were at a low ebb. Not only did the British officers leave, but they took a host of records which left the organisation in India with a scanty database. The other problem was that MI was not given proper authority and was staffed and headed by officers with little intelligence experience and virtually nil resources.

In 1951, the Himmatsinhji Committee (also known as the North and North-East Border Committee) made a survey of the frontier situation. With regards to intelligence collection on the border, the committee recommended that this work be entrusted to the Intelligence Bureau (IB). The committee may have felt that MI organisation was not upto the job. Whatever the facts, it is a reflection of the prevailing malaise affecting MI of both mind set and organisation, as it did not argue that this job, which in pre-1947 days had been a military job, was rightly theirs.

The importance given to intelligence in the military hierarchy in those days is well reflected by the fact that both MI and military operations were headed by an officer of the rank of Lt Col. Officers and Jawans who were inducted into the Intelligence Corps in these early days were not trained for the job and the main function assigned to such people was field security. With little resources, cryptology also suffered. That, left the armed forces in a poor condition as far as intelligence was concerned. In the fifties, two suggestions came up to improve this situation, but nothing came out of it. One came from Lt Gen. Thorat, who suggested that officers from the armed forces be sent abroad on undercover assignments with the aim of building up a network of defence intelligence officers. Then in 1954, the Government decided to set up a Defence Intelligence organisation to serve as a clearing house for intelligence from all services and to advise the Chiefs of Staff. Plans were drawn up to induct around 30 officers from the three services. The idea was for the organisation to work in liaison with the external cell of IB. But due to the financial constraints and a shortage of suitable officers, it did not take off. The Army in the meantime went ahead with organising or rather reorganising its MI set up.

What actually happened in the sixties was that MI was nurtured as a field security service rather than as an external intelligence agency, This resulted in MI policing the army rather than carrying out intelligence activity. Worse than that, it was given the job of checking corruption and misuse of facilities/ equipment amongst army personnel; this animosity exists to a considerable degree even today.

The very organisation and functioning of MI meant that it was not prepared to handle the various facets of Military Intelligence, both external and internal. This is clearly what made the '62 debacle and subsequent 'failures' to provide either strategic or tactical intelligence. The other fact in this regard is that IB was given the task of external intelligence right from 1951, which did not give MI the chance to recover from its state of organisation since independence.

In the various conflicts India has been involved in since 1947 and in the numerous internal security operations involving the armed forces, MI has been largely involved in providing tactical intelligence. The scale of operations and levels of success achieved so far in both conventional and unconventional conflicts leave little room for complacency. What has become clear in the recent past, is the fact that with the increasing use of the army in aid of civil authority, MI has had to adapt quickly to the needs of counter-insurgency situations. In terms of equipment, adequate systems are available to provide tactical intelligence. Much of the present equipment is of Russian origin, including specialised direction finding and monitoring equipment.

In India there is provision for organisations within the MI which deal with SIGINT (both COMINT and ELINT. There is an inter-services Joint Cipher Bureau which is in-charge of cryptology and SIGINT. There are other organisations within the MOD which have similar mission profiles. The problems in this realm really exist due to the multiplicity of organisations performing similar roles. What is needed is proper command and control.

Apart from inter services cooperation, MI also has contacts with R & AW. Many military officers work in R & AW and there is a Senior Officer at the level of Maj., General (designated Chief Military Intelligence Adviser) to assist the Secretary, R & AW. But in the realm of strategic intelligence, MI is at a disadvantage. For, this is the exclusive purview of R & AW. Due to the very tight controls that each intelligence agency keeps on it spheres of operations in India, a certain uneven development has taken place. All the service Intelligence Directorates must argue for clearly defined mission profiles that include both strategic and tactical intelligence. In looking at the past, be it the '62 war or the Sri Lankan experience, one has to therefore realise the overall organisational structure and role of each intelligence agency before passing judgement on the levels of success and failure.

In the overall context, the three service intelligence agencies have the requisite assets to perform their tasks., But organisationally, they still remain without proper coordination. The Army intelligence setup, being the biggest has got more attention, but the problems it faces are also faced by its sister services, though on a smaller scale. What is needed is change of setup, emphasis and functioning of Armed Forces Intelligence organisation in a manner suitable to our national security. The future will require both MI and R & AW and IB to act in-co-operation. Intelligence from all these sources can provide a reasonably balanced assessment. The reliance on one agency will then be reduced.

For the Future for MI to be revitalised, (this goes for all the service directorates) reorientation of organisation is required. Not only does India need a joint intelligence group in the MOD, but each directorate has to be given greater scope and direction. The areas for study and analysis should be-foreign countries, science and technology, armed forces, and intelligence-operation. Equally, Army HQ has to treat MI as an equal partner if it wants good intelligence. As seen in the first section of this paper greater emphasis has to be given to the various sources of MI.

For example, Air Force intelligence is usually collected by PR using Mig 25R recce aircraft, and converted Jaguars. But with advances in space technology it is important for the IAF to acquire capabilities in Imagery Intelligence from space. At the height of the Cold War, USA used its satellites to get intelligence inside the Soviet Union. Similarly, during the '71 war Russian satellite imagery gave India information about Chinese intentions thus allowing for positioning of troops on the western border. This means, that apart from the geographical area of interest. MI has to keep open for survey a wide range of issues. This could range from enemy military strength to the adversary's socioeconomic standing. Only then can long term threat appreciations be made.

Conclusions

In conclusions just two points need to be made. First, MI in India needs a drastic review and reorganisation. Second, this is not so because, as was seen above due to its failures in action, but due to its, inherent structure. That in itself is a greater problem than facing a few failures.

MAINTENANCE OF ELECTRONIC EQUIPMENT : THE IAF SCENARIO

Introduction

Maintenance of electronic equipment is now an advanced technology in which extensive use of In-Circuit Testers (ICTs), Automatic Test Equipment (ATEs), Built-In Test Equipment (BITE) is made by the maintenance staff. By the use of computers in maintenance support even further improvements are possible. The features that make avionics maintenance different from the rest are the imperative flight safety and air-worthiness, which place wide implications on the maintenance of airborne electronic equipment. This article brings out these special requirements and features and explains how the Indian Air Force (IAF) organises itself to meet the challenge.

Many references to Civil Aviation are also made. Today's fighter aircraft is aptly called Wings on Electronics. However, the IAF operates not only the modern aircraft such as MIG-29, Mirage and Jaguar but also older ones such as Hunter and Canberra. Likewise the IAF electronic equipment varies from valve versions to GaAs devices. The geographic spread of the units operating such variety of assets renders the management of maintenance activities more complex than the mere pursuit of air-worthiness and flight safety. Maintenance of avionics should not only be done but appear to have been done. Some third person must certify to the pilot or the passengers that everything is fit for happy landings. This concept is becoming more significant with the airline operators due to the increase in legislations and litigations related to flight safety. Something similar is true when it comes to military aircraft wherein inquiries are invariably ordered into incidents, accidents and crashes.

Classification of IAF Equipment

The IAF electronic equipment can be classified in a variety of ways as follows:

- Platform.
- Aircraft.
- Missiles.
- Ground systems.
  - * Static systems.
  - * Mobile and Ruggedised systems.
- Criticality of subsystems.
- Life critical such as flight controls.
- Safety compromising such as armament, fuel etc.
- Mission specific such as Bombs or Electronic Warfare.
- Applications.
- Radars.
  - o Airborne.
    - * Doppler Altimeters etc.
    - * Weather Warning.
    - * Terrain Mapping.

        * Identification Friend or Foe (IFF).
    - o Ground based.
        * Surveillance.
        * Height Finding.
        * Tracking and Fire Control.
        * Missile Guidance (MGR).
- Communications.
- Voice.
- Data.
- Electronic Warfare.
- Flight Control subsystems.
- Navigation.
- Technology.
- Frequency band dependent operations.
- High Power systems at High Frequency.
- Stealth technology.
- Infra red, Electro-optics and Laser Guidance.

Requirements for Maintenance of Avionics

Conformance to Specifications: International organisations such as International Civil Aviation Organisation (ICAO), International Air Transport Association (IATA), Joint Aviation Requirements (JAR Europe), Federal Aviation Administration (FAA) of USA, Civil Aviation Authority (CAA) of US, as well as the Indian counterparts DGCA, IAAI and NAA are continually striving to lay down requirements for safe operations of air transports.

The degree of stringency varies for light aircraft, wide bodied heavy transports and military aircraft. These are elaborated in Certificate of Air-worthiness (C or A), Permit to Fly, Air Operator's Certificate (AOC), Light Aircraft Maintenance Schedules (LAMS), CDSO schedules for military aircraft in UK and in Indian Air Force etc. Any operator, be it Airlines, Air Taxi or Air Force is expected to conform to specifications both for operations and maintenance as laid down by one or more of the above.

Operational Considerations: The effectiveness of a major system such as aircraft is defined by three considerations-availability, reliability and maintainability. Reliability and maintainability are two important subjects adequately covered in literature. Aircraft systems are designed for these attributes. However, in case of IAF aircraft the aspect of availability assumes significance due to the nature of our operations. Survivability and portability contribute towards availability and therefore, our designs and maintenance keeps these in mind. In addition to these stipulations, two other considerations direct the philosophy for maintenance.

Mission Accomplishment: It is apparent that different approaches to maintenance are required for different groups of IAF electronic inventory. Barring a few of the ground based systems the rest are all required to be maintained for mission specific commitments. An IAF aircraft is utilised for many sorties, and different levels or depths of maintenance are carried out in cycles, but in missiles, maintenance is carried out for years to achieve just one final firing. The mean time between repair (MTBF) therefore does not provide a true status of reliability of a mission oriented weapon system. A prudent moderation by another parameter such as mean time between premature withdrawal of components or unscheduled repair arising (MTBUR) is necessary.

Flight Safety. All forms of transport systems are subject to safety requirements, since they involve human life. Aviation is particularly vulnerable.

Simultaneous Serviceability: Every aircraft sortie therefore requires simultaneous serviceability of a predefined mandatory list of subsystems. A list which is fairly large. Additionally a few redundant subsystems must be fully functional. The avionics maintenance therefore involves simultaneous serviceability of a large number of components or subsystems.

Modifications: Changes made in aircraft subsystems either to remove design defects, enhance capabilities or safety etc. are all required to be approved by suitable authority. Repair and maintenance to aircraft avionics is, therefore, not open to innovations at the technician level. Similarly, the spares used must bear type approval from the concerned Organisation.

Documentation: Recording of flying as well as maintenance

work is a legal requirement since safety is now becoming more prone to litigations.. The maintenance activity is consequently required to be supported by legislation and certification. This involves two major types of documents; schedules to define the work content and log books to record whether the maintenance conforms to specifications. In IAF we have a form 700 whose sanctity for these purposes is religiously maintained. It is neither questioned nor compromised.

Maintenance Reviews: It is not feasible to inspect each and every aspect of maintenance at all its occurrences, therefore regular maintenance reviews are carried out to certify that maintenance practices are correct and directed to the laid down specifications of safety and mission accomplishment. In the IAF we have a Directorate of Maintenance Inspection for this purpose, whose teams visit each and every flying wing regularly.

Licensing of Maintenance Staff: British Civil Air-worthiness Requirements are published by CAA. This covers grant, extension and renewal of aircraft maintenance engineers licenses, and the approval and recondition of applicable training. This document also recognises CAO's licences. In the IAF the authorisation for maintenance is derived from the training imparted by the Air Force Technical College to officers and by schools to technicians.

Engineering Support for Maintenance: Requirements for engineering support necessary for grant of Air Operations Certificate (AOC) by CAA are set out in the document CAP 360 Part 11, and this covers:

- Administration.
- Maintenance.
- Contracting-out maintenance.
- Air-worthiness control procedures.
- Maintenance facilities.
- Quality control and assurance.
- Engineering manual.
- The technical log.

Maintenance Philosophy

The philosophy for maintenance of electronic equipment on

aircraft was outlined for the first time by the FAA in 1960. Before that all aircraft maintenance was based upon the theory of preventive replacements in accordance with laid down life of components and subsystems. It was a conservative philosophy in which the granted life was less than the life that was actually sustainable. Extensions were granted as the experience built up. This philosophy was not only wasteful but also hid away the premature withdrawals since these never took place.

Under the Maintenance Steering Group (MSG) programme of the FAA, the erstwhile philosophy of hardtime replacement was replaced by a logic based philosophy which provided for inspecting the sub-assemblies and overhauling them on-condition. It catered for an assessment whether a component failure would cause an immediate safety hazard or not. Whether it will abort the mission or its rectification can be deferred for a subsequent visit to the hangar.

This philosophy however, placed a greater responsibility on the maintenance staff to make GO-NO-GO decisions in connection with prematured withdrawals, life extensions, flight safety etc., during aircraft operations and maintenance. The present day maintenance philosophy of aircraft systems considers a few additional factors such as cost effectiveness, productivity and other economy oriented constraints. The main question is that of the ratio of downtime/servicing time to the flying hours logged. In such a complex environment the question of maintenance is sought to be answered by classifying the maintenance activities as follows:

- BITE and other on-board condition monitoring system.
- IRAN philosophy for expensive and rare assets.
- Mods, SITs and SIs for more formal servicing.
- I, II, III, IV line scheduled servicing.
- On-site repairs.
- Single window responsibility for complex ground based systems.
- The actual formulation of schedules.
- Support by exhaustive and distributed computerised information system.

Maintenance Organisation

The IAF carried out all maintenance classified above, by a complex setup. The I line scheduled servicing includes first sortie, turn-round and last sortie servicing and is done at the operating units under the guidance provided by CSDO maintenance schedules.

The fault rectification and II line scheduled servicing is carried out at better organised facilities at Wings. The III and IV line servicing is more detailed, requiring longer hours off-flying and is carried out at specialised repair agencies which work like production units. The repair agencies are controlled by Maintenance Command whose only responsibility is maintenance, as opposed to operational commands which control the operations of the fleet.

Spares Support

The IAF inventory comprises items procured from a number of countries which follow their own numbering systems. The identification at component level is not exhaustively provided because the suppliers do not expect IAF to undertake repairs on some of the hi-tech devices in the UHF/SHF bands of frequency. In many cases western systems are integrated on Russian platforms. This makes the spares provisioning not only difficult but it inhibits exploitation of industry standard JIT or EOQ philosophies. However, the IAF has excellent experience in managing an 8 lakh inventory, effectively.

Manpower Resources

The IAF recruits 10+2 level students and converts them to the equivalent of ITI graduates within 2 to 3 years by a carefully drafted training methodology. Technicians come from a rural background but become capable of communicating and understanding technical matters in English, by the time they undergo the specified IAF training. Inspite of the fast turnaround due to the tenure policy and an initial term of only 15 years, the quality of our maintenance personnel is something to be proud of. They are capable of undertaking rectifications at far-flung operating locations.

Conclusion

Smooth conduct of maintenance of IAF electronic equipment requires the support of specialised repair agencies which deal with specific technologies or applications. Naturally these will be geographically spread out. Much that we prefer to have these agencies communicate with each other for production scheduling and monitoring lead times, constraints such as security inhibit exploitation of modern marvels like data communication networks. There is a crying need for encryption equipment of MIL standards so that the IAF operations and maintenance can benefit from modern communication setups in the country.

There is just one more difficulty. The use of computers without inhibition. The fear of virus shies us from extensive dependence on computers, since some of the applications could be life-critical. There is also a requirement for a certification agency for software, in the country. The maintenance of software, the less said the better.

A major change in the stance of defence forces towards electronic equipment is the dilution of requirements for ruggedised systems. EMI/EMC, EMP hardening of TEMPEST technologies are being used only selectively. This has come about mainly to reduce costs, yet it helps us in two other major ways. The use of commercially off-the-shelf (COTS) equipment instead of militarised equipment enables us to use state-of-the-art technology rather than the older technologies. Secondly, it reduces our dependence on specialised repair agencies since the repair is available in the industry.

C³I-ITS RELEVANCE IN THE INDIAN CONTEXT

Introduction

The term C cubed I or C³I is an amalgam of four systems and functions. Command, Control, Communications and Intelligence. The value of C³I lies in its ability to provide a nation's executive with the wherewithal to make proper decisions affecting national security. It is also the means by which military operations are carried out in a proper manner, leading to favourable situations to one side in combat.

Definition

In general terms then C³I is everything a government uses in making decisions and ensures that they are carried out. It includes the authority accruing from his or her appointment to a position and involves people, information, procedures, equipment and the chief executive's own mind. A C³I system is a series of functions which includes gathering information, making decisions and monitoring results. A C³I system is a collection of people, processes and equipment which involves support of the overall process. In the military context, C³I is concerned with the control of events and processes through the transmission and receipt of messages. Seen another way C³I is that what brings together the staff of defence. For example, it is necessary for a General to know where his troops are positioned on the battlefield, it is this process which C³I facilitates.

Components of C³I

C³I is important both in the national and military context because it permits the decision makers to take quick decisions and the implementation at all levels is speeded up. For instance, India needs responsive systems for disaster management so that quick relief can be provided to the affected areas. Thus C³I is a system responsive both to the national and military management. Each component of C³I has a different connotation. Each component has different meanings for different people. The best way of examining each component is by studying in its context. In the defence context, command covers a whole range of levels of organisation from the President of India as Supreme Commander down to the platoon commander in charge of a platoon. Thus, the exercise of command can cover a whole range of issues from the declaration of war to deciding how many companies to send to capture a specific military objective. Another way of seeing command is that it is a mixture of example, persuasion and compulsion by which you get men to do what you want them to do, even if they don't want to do it themselves. This is the human aspect of command which is also known as leadership. In the command aspect of C³I there are three integrating elements-the commander, his HQ and staff, and officers and men he commands.

Control is a term that describes the channels or 'lines of command' through which a commander orders, advises, admonitions and queries his forces. Such lines reflect responsibility as well as of military force and technicalities of its execution. In many ways, command and control or C^2 have been in existence since the dawn of warfare. They are inseparable, but not identical. Achieving control varies from mission to mission in C^3I. In the context of modern warfare, C^2 cannot exist without a third C-Communication. Given the size of the armed forces and the geographical areas in which they operate, the role of communications becomes all the more important. They are the means by which information is carried back and forth between a commander and his forces. The term includes everything from runners, and carrier pigeons to the most sophisticated and secure electronic transmission devices. Intelligence is the acquisition, analysis and dissemination of information about an enemy or about our forces. Intelligence can be either strategic or tactical. Seen another way, it is the production of information that can give an edge to any government or military forces in peace and war.

Features of C^3I

Therefore, the intermeshing of all these systems provides a nation and its forces with C^3I a dual systems process involving man and machine. And any C^3I system will have both human automatic decision making processes. Increasingly, commanders are being flooded with information, which needs computers to process. Thus the use of electronic systems for communication and processing is making C^3I machine-intensive. This does not mean that automatic decision making will take over the command decision of a General-What is important to stress is that in the modern battlefield scenario, the flow of information back and forth has to be of real time value to be effective. The time between manual and automatic decision making in a C^3I system is determined by the nature of activity performed. From this point, a nation can have both strategic C^3I and tactical C^3I. There is little doubt that such systems can be effective force multipliers, but they are not inviolate and therefore require protection by technical and tactical means.

C^3I systems possess certain other special features. There occurs a centralised coordination of all resources and activities, which are usually scattered over a huge geographical area. The decision making process is aided by communication technology and an intelligence network. In any C^3I system, whether national or military there has to be a constant flow of real time information which will speed up execution of decisions taken. Each component of C^3I has its specific relevance. In the case of the exercise of C^2 by a commander on the battlefield, a number of communication feedback loops are used which expedite the decision making process and the execution of a task as following.

- Surveillance and intelligence is gathered through sensors, reconnaissance and other sources.
- Communication from the field to the commander (read HQ) is passed quickly and efficiently.
- The information so received is then processed, filtered and disseminated.
- A commander can make his decisions based on the above process in conjunction with his staff and advisers within a stipulated time.
- The communication network also works in reverse, wherein orders for execution are quickly passed from a commander to his force. Finally, the execution of the decision takes places.

Two points need attention here. First, the loop provides a dual communication network. Second, the feedback loop can be applied to both national and military systems.

Survey of C^3I Systems in the West

At the national level, most countries took a long time to develop the requisite C^3I systems. Due to the prohibitive costs of these systems, countries like India find it difficult to create a satisfactory infrastructure. C^3I systems in the West are big and expensive and the United States has one of the best systems, which was amply demonstrated during the Gulf war in 1991 against Iraq. The United States however requires a global C^3I system, to serve global interests. It possess C^2 platforms spread around the world and a wide variety of satellite communication systems provide linkages to various US field forces. Despite the global interest scenario. The US still has C^3I problems. The US has a worldwide military command and control system (WWMCCS) whose main constituent is the National Military Command System (NMCS) which provides the American executive with the intelligence for decision making, resource allotment and mission assignment. Apart from this the US Armed Forces have their own C^3I systems. For instance, the US Army employs the Mobile Subscriber Equipment (MSE) systems for radio network. Apart from this, the US Air Force and Navy have acquired C^3I systems which not only cater for local field operations but are also linked via satellite to the WWMCCS. It is evident that reliable and secure communication systems are an essential prerequisite for the functioning of a C^3I system.

Communication systems worldwide use micro-wave links which are based either on the chain-of-command principle or on grid trunk nodes, which are independent of the former. The US MSE, the British Ptarmigan and French Rita make use of the trunk nodes system. A grid of trunk nodes are established within which the HQ and their units are required to move when communication is required. The transfer of information today in both peace and war uses data entry devices and automation has helped to speed up the process. The required data is fed into the device 'off-line' and when the data is to be transmitted, it is done in a very short burst, much faster and secure than mere voice communication. The British use a computer network known as *Wavell*, an automated system for staffs at various levels. This system though manually fed with information, automatically collates, evaluates and processes information and periodically updates the information. The output is displayed in a series of 'formats'. All major field HQ in 1 (British) Corps are linked to each other over the Ptarmigan communication system.

C^3I in India

India's experience of national security management since 1947 shows that it has lacked coordinated and unified structures which can develop effective C^3I systems. Equally, command and control in the past both during peace and war have not worked satisfactorily. A survey of the command profile of the Indian

Armed Forces shows that immediately after independence C^2 was exercised in an ad hoc manner, and it proved effective. Later this system deteriorated further and the 1962 border war with China showed up this fatal weakness. The-1965 war with Pakistan presented a better showing of C^2 structures, but the functions of communication and intelligence still remained inadequate. The 1971 war proved that given proper C^3I management it was possible to marshal resources for war. Of course, it needs no reminding that no overall system existed as such and there were no unified channels for either communication or intelligence.

It will be worth looking at intelligence specifically. Intelligence in India has always been a scattered and overlapping affair. There exist too many organisations which hold their sources and information in a struggle for power. This has stunted the growth of unifying structures like the Joint Intelligence Committee (JIC) whose task is to keep the executive informed of all threats to national security. A similar problem is faced by Military Intelligence organisations within the services, as they do not get much help from the RAW in the realm of strategic intelligence. Thus, an effective C^3I system still eludes us.

Within the Services though, things are changing. The Army for instance now has ARENS, a command information network which should play a crucial role in future wars and in peace time too. Certain units in the army, like the Armoured Corps are studying and integrating C^3I systems which will improve their combat efficiency. Therefore, various C^3I subsystems are being devised to meet the immediate needs of its users. But for overall use, a long-term overall military C^3I has yet to emerge. Given the prohibitive cost of C^3I equipment, it may be wise to integrate existing civilian and military networks for use in peace and war. For instance, the nationwide NICNET of computers which provides a comprehensive information network using satellite communication can be upgraded for military uses. This system if integrated with C^3I subsystems, in times of conflict, will provide a national communication system. The system will obviously require considerable upgradation and expansion, but the overall improvement in the availability of information will be of benefit to all users.

One of the major problems the Indian Armed Forces face in terms of Command and Control, is the location of commands in scattered geographical areas. As each service has its forward HQ in a different location, the unity of command is not achieved. This increases reaction time and proves costly in times of conflict. As stated earlier one of the main feature-of employing C³I system is to allow for centralised coordination of resources and activities which may be scattered. For instance, the IAF's Eastern Air Command HQ is at Shillong, while the Army's Eastern Command HQ is at Calcutta. This pattern is repeated at various levels. To overcome the problem an alternative could be to install reliable and secure and integrated C³I systems. Major requirements of such a C³I system would be:

- Command, and control centres,
- Sensors, reconnaissance systems, surveillance and target acquisition systems. In other words, Battlefield Intelligence systems;
- Communications which provide reliable and secure links between the various CI centres and their respective systems.

The Indian Armed Forces also need to emphasise more on C³I at the training level. Modern warfare is a highly complex affair and the greater number of troops involved means more C³I. Much of this needs constant practice, if actual operations are to be run smoothly. One instance of an attempt to actually integrate available C³I in the case of the Army is provided by *Exercise Brasstacks.* One of its objectives was to integrate the Army's Radio Engineering Network's (AREN) automatic electronic switching facility with other tactical communication systems.

However, each service in India still has its own C³I component, and, there is a lack of overall C³I conceptualisation and usage at various stages. Our command profile shows a clear lack of appreciation, even at the training stage of the usefulness of C³I systems." Moreover none of our extant C³I systems have been tested in hostile EW environment. At times, Indian communication systems have been found prone to interception, e.g. during the initial stage of IPKF operations in Sri Lanka to capture Jaffna in October 1987. This is something that, can prove costly in a future conflict, which may be a battle for the control of the electromagnetic spectrum. To that extent, the Indian Armed Forces must look ahead and try and find adequate means of acquiring and integrating C^3I systems which will be user-friendly. As our armed forces are still manpower intensive, they require a greater amount of C^2 training at the initial stages of training. Today's young officer is intelligent and given the light kind of training to use C^3I as a force multiplier, a balanced system sensitive to change, the existing circumstances and requirements for the future can be developed.

Conclusions

In conclusion, it can be said that the relevance and usefulness of C^3I can be considered as a system which 'moulds' together the stuff of defence. In a larger, national context it signifies a system and process whereby an executive makes decisions affecting a nation's security. The above analysis shows that keeping in mind that the each component of C^3I has a different meaning to different users, it is possible to create a C^3I infrastructure for both national and military purposes. At the same time, in a country-like India, expensive C^3I systems cannot be integrated. What needs to be done is to integrate indigenous C^3I networks into our armed forces keeping in mind the need to upgrade C^3I doctrines at the training level. That this process is already going on as is evident from the efforts at, indigenous production and integration of C^3I system, is a good sign for the future.

2 Defence Planning in India

NATIONAL SECURITY, DEFENCE POLICY AND PLANNING

It is generally acknowledged that the approach to national security requires a comprehensive view of various political, social, economic, technological and strategic aspects. National security implies not only safeguarding territorial boundaries but also that the nation is able to build a cohesive, egalitarian, technologically efficient and progressive society with a good quality of life. Compared with national security, defence policy is more focused, concerned with the protection of the state and its citizens from direct and indirect (proxy) military threats and actions of other states. In defence planning, the emphasis shifts to national security concerns that are mainly military in nature. There are two concepts at this level: deterrence (including coercive diplomacy) and defence (dissuasion).

Deterrence refers to policies designed to discourage the adversary from taking direct or proxy military action, by raising the cost so that it outweighs the gains that he may wish to attain. Defence (dissuasion) policies are designed to reduce the capability of the adversary to cause damage—and own costs and risks—in the event deterrence fails. Deterrence and defence are two interwoven strands of defence policy. Defence planning involves the conceptualisation of plans and decisions for the execution of defence policy. Long-term planning for defence is essential for the following reasons:

(a) The existence of a highly fluid strategic environment, which results in continuous shifts and changing profiles of threat and power equations.

(b) To ensure judicious allocation of resources and cost effective utilisation.

(c) Revolution in Military Affairs (RMA), i.e. advances in technology, which result in weapons and equipment systems becoming obsolete at a fast rate.

(d) Lead time required to raise and prepare defence units; to produce or acquire and introduce new weapons and equipment systems.

(e) The changing nature of conflict and reduced reaction time.

(f) Coordination problems between defence, economic, science and technology, infrastructure and industrial activities, as well as among the Defence Forces.

The defence planning process attempts to match the budgetary resources likely to be made available for the requirement to establish the defence capability necessary to face the threats and challenges. This exercise is undertaken in two phases: (a) What should be the proportion allocated to the defence effort as against other areas of national security concerns and economic growth? This exercise involves a 'visionary' analysis of external and internal security threats (often linked) and challenges. In order to minimise adverse affects of high military expenditure on socioeconomic development, it is necessary to harmonise national development planning with defence planning. (b) Optimisation of allocated resources, i.e. distribution of resources within the Ministry of Defence (MoD) based on Force planning (Force and weapons mix, command and control, logistics and human resources management) by the Defence Services to combat current and future threats, and development of required capabilities by the Defence Research and Development Organisation (DRDO), defence production and other agencies concerned.

The quantum of indigenous production and the requirements to be procured from outside are decided in this phase. The objective is to achieve maximum defence capability from the given resources. Both allocation and distribution are closely linked. They need to be reviewed periodically but not so frequently that the planning process becomes ad hoc. In India's case, this is done at five-year intervals.

BACKGROUND OF DEFENCE PLANNING IN INDIA

Before independence, the defence services worked on a system of contract budget. Defence expenditure was pegged at Rs 55 crore per year, which was more than half of the Central Government's revenue. There was no serious threat from outside (except during World War II, when a fresh agreement was signed) and this amount was more than adequate to maintain the establishment.

The savings were not allowed to lapse but put away in the Defence Reserve Fund that was utilised to finance measures for re-equipment of the Defence Services, thus freeing the Government from having to provide fund money greater than the contract amount. Expenditure on defence rose steeply soon after independence. However, there was no planned effort and defence programmes consisted mainly of outright purchases from abroad, drawing heavily on available Sterling reserves. In the late 1950s, some efforts were made to initiate domestic weapons production by the Ministry of Defence when Mr. Krishna Menon was the Defence Minister. The Sino-Indian conflict in 1962 aroused a new defence consciousness in the country. After taking care of immediate postwar requirements, systematic defence planning started in 1964. Defence requirements were assessed on a five-year basis and the First Five Year Defence Plan (1964-69) was drawn up. This plan took into account the resources available and assistance which could be expected from friendly foreign countries. The plan was primarily based on an expansion and modernisation programme considered necessary by each Service in the light of the respective threat perception assessed. It also proposed a defence production base that would gradually reduce the country's external dependence, provide for improvements in border roads and communications, and a modest expansion of DRDO. The Government recognised the imperative need to synergise 'defence' and 'development' instead of planning each on a separate and unrelated level. The MoD emphasised the "inevitable need to harness all resources of the country for the country's defence and for the defence effort to derive full sustenance from the country's economic development plans".

Thereafter, the National Development Council authorised the Chairman of the Planning Commission to review the needs of both development and defence. A Planning Cell was established in 1965 in the Ministry of Defence 'to deal with the wider aspects of defence planning'. The new system was intended to facilitate medium and long-term defence planning and to maintain constant liaison with the Planning Commission and other ministries. It was expected that the MoD would derive maximum advantage from the development effort by being able to place its priorities for consideration along with the overall economic and industrial plans drawn up by the Planning Commission. The experience of the First Five Year Defence Plan showed that the development of weapons and equipment was a long drawn out process. The Government realised that there could be no forward movement in attaining self-sufficiency in weapons and equipment unless these requirements were planned over a reasonably long period, long enough to cover the span of development and production of new weapons systems and other fighting tools.

The inadequacy of foreign exchange reserves was another hindrance in planning and implementation. In order to mitigate some of these drawbacks, the Second Five Year Defence Plan (1969-74) was instituted on a "roll-on" basis. After a year, an additional year was added so that the Defence Services would have before them a revised and updated five-year plan. In this context, the MoD commented: "Opportunity is taken by this annual exercise to take note of and reflect the change in priorities, the shifts in emphasis and the latest concepts and programmes to reorient the plan within the scheme of resources so that the aims and means are most effectively balanced." This system was expected to facilitate the planning of projects that took five years or more and to revise or eliminate projects, depending on the prevailing foreign exchange situation and availability of domestic resources.

For a period of five years, firm assurances were to be given on the availability of resources. This, unfortunately, never happened. In 1971, it was impossible to adhere to the discipline and the pattern of the roll-on plan. Instead of roll-on annual revisions, immediate requirements dominated the Government's attention that pre-empted plan efforts. In its 1971-72 Annual Report, the MoD acknowledged that having a Planning Cell in the ministry was an insufficient and unsatisfactory method of meeting a crisis.

The Planning Cell was not taken seriously in the crucial stages of economic planning and the argument that defence needs would be adjusted in the over-all allocation of resources was proved wrong. In 1974, an Apex Group headed by the Union Minister for Planning again suggested that steady long-term defence programmes would be more cost effective and economical rather than fluctuating allocations due to periodic economic and security crises. In order to integrate defence planning with the overall economic planning effort, defence and economic development plans were made co-terminus.

The Planning Machinery

Most of the defence planning machinery and planning methodology was developed in the decade 1964-74. The Joint Intelligence Committee (JIC) was established in the Cabinet Secretariat to provide external and internal threat assessments. Inputs for this purpose were to be provided by all Intelligence agencies of the Government. The Service Chiefs were to assess the broad military aims and a strategy, coordinated in the Chiefs of Staff Committee, was to be approved by the Defence Minister. However, this was seldom done. Each Service ended up planning its own force level, choice of weapons and equipment, and build-up of infrastructure. In 1977, the Government formed a Committee for Defence Planning (CDP) to "undertake regular assessments relevant to defence planning in the light of all factors having a bearing on national security and defence". However, this committee could not function smoothly nor meet the desired goals.

Planning units were also established in the Department of Defence Production and DRDO. A Planning and Coordination Cell was created in the MoD to coordinate and compile various plans into a 'Defence Plan' for Cabinet approval. As the bureaucrats in the ministry had no professional knowledge or background, this cell could only compile different requirements without any analysis. In Army Headquarters, the Deputy Chief of Army Staff was made responsible for preparing the Army plan. A Perspective Planning Directorate was established in the late 1970s. Naval and Air plans were prepared in the respective Planning Directorates. Financial considerations, non-existent at this level earlier, were introduced through Finance Planning Sections attached to these Directorates.

In 1986, the Directorate General of Defence Planning Staff (DGDPS), comprising officers from the three Services, DRDO, and Ministries of Defence and External Affairs, was established under the Chiefs of Staff Committee (COSC) to coordinate and harmonise defence planning. Civilian officers from the Ministries probably did not find the job professionally satisfying and were gradually withdrawn, thus leaving the DGDPS a tri-Service set up.

All these measures enabled each Service headquarters to prepare defence plans in a more rational manner. But due to lack of clear political direction and each Service primarily planning for itself, joint planning, coordination between Services and other departmental plans of the MoD, were largely ignored.

After the Kargil conflict in 1999, the Group of Ministers (GoM) and later the Cabinet Committee on Security (CCS) approved several reforms. An Integrated Defence Headquarters (IDH) was established and the DGDPS was merged with it. The creation of the post of Chief of Defence Staff (CDS), whose tasks would include ensuring intra and inter-Services prioritisation of defence plans and improvement in joint functioning of the Defence Services, was recommended. The reforms also included establishment of a Defence Intelligence Agency and creation of Defence Equipment Production, Research and Planning councils in the IDH and MoD, respectively. Unfortunately, the CDS, who would be the cornerstone of integrated operational planning for defence, has not been appointed.

Analysis of the System

Despite several years of planning efforts, defence planning in India is characterised by seesaw bouts of frenzied activity followed by long periods of relative inaction. Five-year defence plans have rarely been formally approved before commencement. The Tenth Defence Plan, now in its third year, is yet to be accorded formal government approval. Ad-hocism is the order of the day, leading to knee-jerk responses and haphazard planning, making India a reactive rather than pro-active nation in matters pertaining to national security. Whenever India's major adversaries plan a big defence purchase, there is an outcry for similar acquisitions, resulting in piecemeal decisions regardless of long-term impact and overall requirements.

The Defence Forces are forced to follow "a case-by-case" approach to modernisation and procurement of arms, ammunition and equipment to replace obsolescent items, in many cases long after their life cycle is over and they cannot be maintained in a cost effective manner. The Army's Vijayanta tanks, MiG-21s of the IAF, and IL-38 maritime reconnaissance aircraft of the Navy are some examples. Weapons development, procurement and absorption are complex processes. A lead-time of 15-20 years is required to plan and execute major projects. Despite this, for several years, a large amount of the capital acquisition budget has been surrendered.

In the prevailing era of strategic uncertainty, the changing nature of warfare demands a judicious mix of threat and capabilities-based forces that can operate efficiently as combined arms, joint Services teams and components of multinational coalition forces.

NATIONAL SECURITY POLICY AND STRATEGY

The concept of national security rests mainly on the proposition that many foreign and domestic political, economic and military issues are interrelated, each with implications on the other. In India's case, this has been highlighted by insurgencies and other political events, particularly in border-states, and other outside pressures, which are brought to bear on the country's economy and technological progress from time to time.

A response to this type of environment calls for a highly focused national security policy and strategy. Effective guidance on national security and defence policy objectives is fundamental to the defence planning process. National security is a relative matter without a firm criteria but unless firm national security objectives are set and a defence policy evolved, there can be no military doctrine or balancing of defence effort with other national objectives and priorities such as maintaining a viable economy and supporting development of society. The lack of a cohesive national security strategy and defence policy has many implications. First, it results in the absence of clear political direction regarding politico-military objectives, which is the very basis of sound defence planning. Secondly, there is inadequate coordination of defence plans and economic development. Finally, science and technology policies for defence, general industrialisation and other development programmes are not coordinated properly to achieve security goals and objectives.

Perspective Planning

A Defence Plan has to be prepared on the basis of a 15-year long perspective planning system, such that the first five years of the plan are very firm (Definitive Plan), the second five years less firm (Indicative Plan) and the third five-year term tentative (Vision Plan). There has to be a reasonably firm allocation of financial resources for the first five years and an indicative allocation for the subsequent period. Perspective planning needs to be done in the Integrated Defence Headquarters, where military, technical and R&D experts take an integrated view of future threats and challenges. This has to be based on future battlefield scenarios, and array of forecasts, evaluation of strategic options and force mixes, and analysis of potential technical and industrial capabilities. Based on this, the respective Service should work on their perspective plans and the R&D and Defence Production/Supplies experts should spell out their requirements in terms of effort, technology and indigenous production.

Integrated Planning

As stated earlier, the CDS, who would be the cornerstone of integrated operational planning for defence, has not been appointed. India's defence planning, therefore, continues to be Service based. Often, the threat perception of one Service is at variance with that of another Service. What emerges is essentially a sum of total of Service or department wise programmes. The focus is not on overall goals or priorities but on what is required by a particular Service. In its endeavour to lay the groundwork for an increased share of the budget, each Service tends to exercise its own priorities, favouring its own plans to the detriment of joint plans.

Subjects like surveillance, air defence, electronic warfare, and amphibious operations, which relate to more than one Service, do not get adequate attention. Integrated planning for defence is essential for creating balanced force structures and for the successful execution of all military missions. In fact, it is the most effective manner of ensuring effective defence. According to Charles Hitch, "the revolution in military technology has not only changed the character of our military programmes, it has also to a significant degree blurred the lines of demarcation among various Services". Most major miiitary missions today require the participation of more than one military service. Therefore, the principal concern now must be centred on what is required by the defence establishment as a whole to perform a particular mission—not what is required by a particular Service to perform its individual part of that 'mission'. The areas of commonality in modern weapon systems are immense and growing rapidly. Communications, guidance systems, missiles, radars, lasers—even traditional equipment such as guns, fuses, ammunition and vehicles are common. Integrated defence planning is necessary in view of escalating costs of these weapons and equipment.

Self-reliance in Defence Technology

The DRDO has a network of 51 laboratories and establishments. The Scientific Advisor (SA) to the Raksha Mantri (RM) is the Secretary of this Department. The DRDO has a staff of 30,000, including 6,800 scientists and engineers. It receives approximately four to six per cent of the defence budget annually. The DRDO is engaged in the pursuit of self-reliance in critical technologies relevant to defence. It formulates and executes a programme of scientific research, design and development for the induction into the Armed Forces of state-of-the-art weapons and other equipments.

In April 1984, the DRDO envisaged a programme "to transform the Department into a leader of international class with the mission to capture and retain commanding heights in critical technologies". A 'mission mode' organisational structure and approach was approved by the Government with a view to increasing the element of self-reliance from the current 30 per cent to 70 per cent by 2005. This goal, however, is nowhere in sight.

The Department has developed more than 1,100 items of weapon systems and equipment with a production value of over Rs 6,000 crore. But it has not been able to make any major contribution to the state-of-art weapons and equipment. Most of its programmes, like Prithvi (sea borne version), Trishul (short-range surface to air missile), Akash (medium-range surface to air missile), Nag (anti-tank missile), Light Combat Aircraft with Kaveri engine, Pinaka (multiple-barrel rocket system), MBT Arjun, Electronic Warfare equipment, new radio sets for the Army, Sonar system for Navy, and many other items, are way behind schedule.

Because of the failure to deliver the required weapons and equipment, defence planning and Force structuring by the Services has suffered continuously. The DRDO's inability to deliver in time has caused a crisis of confidence and constant dissatisfaction in the Services. In order to ensure smooth progress towards self-reliance in defence technology, the Government must undertake a periodic performance audit of DRDO projects to reinforce efforts in areas of success and weed out projects that are unproductive.

DEFENCE PRODUCTION AND SUPPLY

The Defence Production Department created in 1962 and the Department of Defence Supply set up in 1965 were merged in 1984 to constitute the Department of Defence Production and Supplies. Presently, 39 Ordnance factories and eight Defence Public Sector Undertakings (DPSUs) come under this department. The Directorate of Quality Assurance, Air Technical Development and Production (Air), Standardisation, and Exhibition Organisation also form part of this Department. The Ordnance Factories produce more than 1,500 items of arms, ammunition, equipment and components.

Most of these products constitute relatively low to medium technology items. Twenty per cent of the output goes to non-defence customers. Due to the very high cost of production, delivery delays and suspect quality, it has not been possible to meet export targets and, sometimes, even orders given by the Services. Ordnance factories as well as DPSUs need to shed the manufacture of low technology items to the private sector and focus on hi-tech products. They should also be in a position to take up substantial product improvement themselves and not be dependent on DRDO.

Defence Planning Tools

In recent years, defence economics and management techniques have made an important contribution to defence planning. A number of techniques such as Operational Research and Systems Analysis (ORSA), Planning Programming and Budgeting System have been developed to make the planning process more systematic and to maximise the benefits obtained from the given amount of resources. Systems Analysis can assist in developing rational procedures for procurement of new weapons systems. Systems performance at design stage can be evaluated through computer simulation. Planners all over the world are using computerised war-gaming techniques and structure analysis. Prospects exist for a more enlightened approach that can bring together military officers, historians, technologists and quantitative analysts. In many countries, there is a growing interest in analytical realism, operational relevance and integrated defence planning. In India the Services are far behind in introducing these aids in our defence planning system. The planning directorates in Service Headquarters do not even have data banks which can provide relevant information on a specified subject. Most of the planners have high combat and command qualifications but little clue of the modern techniques.

There is an urgent need to introduce modern planning aids into our planning system. Defence planners should also learn the basic principles and techniques of economic analysis and not leave it to their 'Finance' colleagues.

Management of Defence Budget

A major lacuna in defence planning and implementation has been lack of financial commitment for the Plan period. Financially, the defence plans are treated more as annual plans rather than composite five years plan. There is a rush to spend the annual capital budget by the end of the financial year since the amount not spent has to be surrendered.

In FY 2004-05, the previous government had proposed to institute a non-lapsable Defence Modernisation Fund of Rs 25,000 crore. This was a long awaited reform in the defence-finance mechanism as budgeted capital expenditure worth thousands of crores was surrendered year after year. However, the new government, being of the view that there are no provisions in the budgetary rules and regulations to carry forward unspent funds for three years, has done away with this reform.

It needs to be pointed out that a similar procedure was being followed in the 1930s and 1940s. The provisions invoked at that time need to be studied carefully and could be used as a precedent. Action should be taken expeditiously to revive the Defence Modernization Fund.

Otherwise, funds earmarked for capital expenditure on an annual basis will continue to lapse, leading to lack of systematic defence preparedness. In the Revenue Budget, there is a need to include incentives to save and reduce annual maintenance expenditure without adversely affecting operational efficiency. It is also necessary to exploit the increasing domestic industrial capability to support the existing infrastructure and thus reduce maintenance costs and enhance the quality of maintenance.

Human Resources Management

The development of human resources must keep pace with the modernisation of the armed forces so that new, state-of-the-art equipment can be optimally exploited by well trained and motivated soldiers, sailors and airmen. The age profile of military personnel, particularly in the Army, and the age of commanders at battalion and brigade levels needs to be looked into. Currently, a soldier has to serve for 15 to 17 years to earn his pension. When he retires, besides the lifelong pension that has to be paid, a trained individual is lost to the nation. Similarly, while there is a shortage of approximately 14,000 officers, most officers retire in rank of Lieutenant Colonel or Colonel at the age of 52-54 years when they still have years of productive life ahead though they are no longer fit for active combat.

Innovative measures need to be adopted to reduce the effects of the current national loss on this account. The best method would be to institute a procedure of 'lateral induction" under which both officers and personnel below officer rank can be transferred to central police and paramilitary forces (CPMFs). The colour (active) service of jawans should be reduced to 7-10 years with no pension liability after which the volunteers are transferred to the BSF, CRPF, ITBP, CISF and other such forces. Similarly, the Shipping Corporation of India, National Port Trust and other such maritime organisations can fruitfully employ Naval personnel. Ex-servicemen will be expected to serve in these organisations till superannuation, after which they would be entitled to pension. This will improve the age profile of the Services, provide trained manpower to the CPMFs, ensure productive long-term employment for a large number of trained men till superannuation, and also reduce the pension bill of the Central Government.

The Army should increase the recruitment of Short Service Officers to make up its shortfall. Induction of these officers to the CPMFs after five years of service will improve junior leadership and effectiveness of these forces in internal security and counter insurgency operations.

Recommendations

- Given the fluid strategic environment and the rapid advances in defence technology, there is a need for judicious allocation of the limited budgetary resources. Long lead times are required for creating futuristic Forces, hence the need to make long-term defence planning mandatory. Greater synergy between defence and development plans is required.
- The lack of a cohesive national security strategy and defence policy has resulted in inadequate political direction

regarding politico-military objectives. The Government should prepare a clear national security strategy, defence policy, and review it every 4-5 years.

- In view of the time taken to create the capabilities necessary for facing future threats and challenges, it is essential for the Defence Services to evolve 10 to 15-year perspective plans with the required budgetary support.
- The Chiefs of Staff Committee has not been successful in preparing comprehensive 'integrated defence plans' due to emphasis on single Service planning and constant competition among the Services for a bigger share of resources. The civilian bureaucrats in the MoD do not have the professional expertise to decide on inter-Service priorities. Hence, the early appointment of Chief of Defence Staff (CDS) is essential as he will be the cornerstone for integrated defence and operational planning.
- A non-lapsable Defence Modernisation Fund must be expeditiously created to ensure that allocations are optimally utilised and funds earmarked for capital acquisitions are not allowed to lapse.
- The Revenue Budget of the Services needs to be better managed. Annual maintenance expenditure can be curtailed by greater exploitation of the available public and private sector industrial infrastructure capability and offering incentives to the Services to save.
- To ensure smooth progress towards self-reliance in defence technology, the Government must undertake a periodic performance audit of the DRDO plans and projects. The review should reinforce efforts in areas of success and weed out unproductive projects.
- Ordnance Factories should produce only hi-tech products and shed the production of low-tech items to the private sector.
- Integrated Defence Staff and the Services' perspective planners should acquire expertise in operational research and systems analysis, as also financial planning, for evolving complex integrated defence plans.

- In order to improve the age profile of the Services and simultaneously reduce the pension bill of the Central Government, personnel below officer rank should be transferred to central police and paramilitary forces (CPMFs) after active service of 7-10 years.
- The Army should increase recruitment of Short Service Officers to make up its shortfall. Induction of these officers to the CPMFs after five years of service will improve junior leadership and effectiveness of these forces in internal security and counter insurgency operations.

Conclusion

Defence planning has been neglected for long in India. This has led to ad-hocism in decision-making and adversely affected the modernisation plans of the Services. The key issues needing immediate attention include the need for formal prior approval for five-year defence Plans, better management of the defence revenue and capital acquisition budgets, streamlining of the defence procurement process and better human resources management. The Government of India should appoint a group of eminent experts to study the present defence planning process, identify the lacunae and grey areas in the process and recommend structural and procedural changes. The aim should be to streamline defence planning, harmonize it with national development plans, and make the process more responsive in order to deal effectively with the rapidly changing geo-strategic and regional security environment.

CHALLENGES IN DEFENCE PLANNING

Defence planning is essentially a subset of overall national level planning in the political, economic and social spheres and has to be evolved in the context of global and proximate factors affecting the nation.. It has also to take into account the philosophy and ethos animating the national psyche; in other words the historical and cultural forces which have shaped the collective memory and outlook of the people over the centuries. The Cold War, was a classic example of the factors stated above. There were fundamental philosophical differences between the adversaries –

the western bloc, advocating the virtues of free enterprise and its own interpretations of democracy, and the Soviet bloc, equally strongly asserting the merits of the socialist system as the only one genuinely meeting democratic aspirations and assuring social equality and economic well-being of the people as a whole, rather than for a few. Fifty years of the Cold War could not conclude the capitalism-socialism debate, though, in the end, it did push the socialist forces into, perhaps temporary, retreat. This was because the struggle was really for power and domination.

"The evil empire" of Ronald Reagan's description may have withered away, but the necessity for the US to target the so called "rogue states" has not disappeared. Many examples can be found of philosophical differences leading to standoffs, usually with the USA as one of the parties. The USA-Cuba divide is a long-standing one. USA-Venezuela standoff is just developing and resonating in other Latin American countries. Sometimes the differences are couched in the language of anticipated threats, such as in US-North Korea, or US-Iran relations. The true reasons and underlying causes are buried in verbiage and obfuscation. A more serious rift has developed over the selective and poorly conceptualised US war on terrorism, launched for spurious reasons in Iraq, when the real source of terror was elsewhere and far more complex.

Differing religious beliefs and rigidities are often cited as causes but do not sufficiently explain conflicts within the same religion, as between Protestants and Catholics in Northern Ireland or the Shias and Sunnis in Iraq and elsewhere. Planning for the security and defence of a vast country like India with its particular geographic location, historical experiences and associations, social, ethnic, religious and cultural diversity, political and economic structure and a large, relatively poor, democratically governed population, is a complex and challenging task. It is rendered more so in the context of the national and international situation in the last sixty years or so, embracing post-World War II de-colonisation, partition, the creation of Pakistan and later Bangladesh, conflicts with Pakistan and China, the Cold War and its aftermath, the disintegration of the Soviet Union, the re-definition of NATO's role, and of most recent and decisive significance, the September 11, 2001 terror attack on the United States mainland. This last factor is significant because it resulted in a major re-orientation in US foreign policy.

Strategic Overview

Planning for defence pre-supposes identification of threats and contingencies. Until about five years ago, the strategic situation for India was difficult but relatively clear. Pakistan was a definite threat, conventional, clandestine and nuclear. China was a strategically reducing threat, though its international power, influence and economy were growing. Uncertainties in Bangladesh and Nepal required us to be vigilant for fall-out effects. There were problems in the northeast of insurgent groups exploiting the ethnic ties and jungles in Myanmar, and the destabilising spill-over effects of the activities of the Liberation Tigers for Tamil Eelam (LTTE) in Sri Lanka. The presence in our proximate waters, of non-littoral naval forces in substantial numbers, such as those of the US, which has been traditionally supportive of Pakistan, had to be taken cognisance of. Also the fact that warfare at sea, because of its distinctive characteristics of rapidity of concentration and dispersal of forces, mobility, flexibility and speed of execution, requires a different, longer term approach to threat assessment. Strategically the global situation is now evolving in a manner less inimical to India's interests than in the preceding fifty years. Yet the end of the Cold War did not see any easing of pressures on India. On the contrary, economic sanctions and technology denials were increased so as to coerce India to conform to norms of international behaviour prescribed by dominant world powers, led by the US and the European Union on the one hand and China on the other. The reason was the desire of the P-5, the five permanent members of the UN Security Council, who are also the N-5, the self-certified nuclear powers, to preserve their monopoly power status in the face of India's challenge through the nuclear tests of 1998. Yet, the re-evaluation of foreign policies by leading powers set off by the September 11, 2001 terrorist attack on the USA, has initiated processes that are, by and large, beneficial to India. An indication of this is the US declaration of seeing India as a strategic partner for the 21st century, and its efforts to legislate exceptions to its domestic laws to allow supply of nuclear materials for peaceful civilian use to India by the cartel operated by the

Nuclear Suppliers Group (NSG).

Nearer home, the pathological hostility of the Pakistanis establishment towards India is rooted in its quest for a national identity, which no novel interpretations, distortions or reinventions of sub-continental history seem able to provide. It will be a long time before there can be normal relations with Pakistan because they are influenced more by the internal contradictions and dynamics of the Pakistani state rather than considerations of mutual benefits through good relations. Since the Pakistan army is the self-appointed guardian of the undefined "ideology of Pakistan", normalcy will come when the Army decides it should be so; or the cost-benefit equation alters.

With China, there is perceptible progress on resolving disputes and fostering economic and cultural relations. As for Nepal, Bangladesh, Myanmar and Sri Lanka, there is no significant positive change, and because of shared borders, internal problems in those countries will continue to spill over into India. Instability in Afghanistan remains a cause of concern, especially because of Pakistan's dubious role, and this will have its impact on the pursuit of India's energy and strategic interests in Central Asia.

Non-littoral naval forces in significant numbers are still present in the Indian Ocean, but there is no coercive or inimical intent as in the past. Indeed, the Indian Navy holds regular friendly exercises with them on a routine basis. China's long term plans for a naval presence in the region have to be taken note of. There are ample signs of Chinese maritime interest, starting from building and operating communications facilities in Myanmar to financing and building Pakistan's Gwadar Port on the Makran coast, collaboration in building warships for the Pakistan navy at Karachi shipyard, as well as port building in Sri Lanka. On the western rim of the Indian Ocean, China is vigorously pursuing options in Africa, underlined by the meeting of 49 heads of state/government in Beijing.

National Objectives in the Long Term

Planning for defence has to be in the framework of national objectives over a period of decades ahead, even if these are not publicly articulated. USA does not hesitate to state its intention to remain the dominant global technological, space and military power for the foreseeable future and tailors strategic policies accordingly. China has, by its actions, investments and developments over the years, demonstrated that it intends to be at least the equal of the USA, though with "Chinese characteristics". Pakistan makes no secret of its intention to be "different" from India, and to compete with and undermine India at every opportunity.

India too has shown in various ways that it intends to be in the forefront of nations in every sphere: economic, technological, industrial and human development. What about military capability? Does it wish to have only a capacity to ward off aggression by land and sea? Or does it aspire to play a larger role in the region? If it emerges as the world's third or fourth largest economy in a few years, would a commensurate military role follow? Or are national objectives to be largely achieved by a combination of diplomacy and economic policies? If it aspires for a permanent seat in the UN Security Council, is it prepared for the increased diplomatic and military responsibilities attached? Many of these seemingly philosophical issues require to be debated to facilitate meaningful defence planning for the future.

ORGANISATION FOR DEFENCE PLANNING

Planning for defence involves almost all aspects of government, not only because of the extreme seriousness of the undertaking, but also because a long duration war will require marshalling the total resources of the nation. It can never be presumed that hostilities will always be of short duration, as there is a tendency to do so in the context of India-Pakistan conflicts. Many instances in history illustrate this, for example the US misadventure in Iraq. The US-led coalition forces were injected on the assumption of a quick victory, a warm welcome by Iraqi citizenry and a glorious return home for Christmas.

They are still there nearly three years later, as also in Afghanistan, with no indications of an early resolution of the conflicts. Madeleine Albright, the former US Secretary of State has this to say about the US Iraq expedition: "We have damaged our reputation very badly.

Iraq may turn out to be the greatest disaster in American foreign policy, which by its very nature means that it is worse than Vietnam. In this context, it is worth recalling the words attributed to Fredrick the Great: "No war is accidental or unintended. The only thing unintended is the bloodiness and duration of the conflict. Defeat too is unintended". No rational planning can be done on basis of a worst-case scenario. Apart from being illogical, it is unaffordable, and therefore unachievable.

Rather, realistic defence planning requires a thorough and detailed analysis and evaluation of the security environment, threat perceptions, technological assessments, etc. and should result in an integrated defence plan. Such a plan should be linked to national capacity in the civil sector and integrate utilisation of resources such as road transport, civil aviation and technical manpower in a pre-determined manner for war.

British Example Through almost four hundred years of wars and colonial expansion and contraction, the British learnt to restructure their fleets and armies as the situation demanded and finances allowed. This was not done at the cost of contingency planning and military effectiveness, as the rapid mobilisation at the time of the Falklands war in 1982 showed. A major defence costs study, *Front Line First* was initiated in 1994, whereby the entire UK defence organisation was to be reorganised to effect economies, especially at headquarters, with maximum integration of civil and military staff at all levels, enhanced delegation of financial powers and simplification of procedures. Some of the conclusions of the Study could apply equally to Indian defence organisations: The Ministry of Defence Head Office and other headquarters at all levels were seen as being too large, too top heavy and too bureaucratic.

The process of delegating responsibility to individual budget holders was generally seen as the key to maximising efficiency. There were too many minor rules and regulations that were rigidly applied, and stood in the way of maximising value for money.

There was a need for greater cost consciousness so that costs could be linked more explicitly to output. Rationalisation of command, training and support structures on a joint Service basis could increase operational effectiveness as well as offer savings.

(Huge differences in the size of the three services and the sub-continental geographic spread would make this impractical in India).

Changes were necessary in the culture of the Department, in simplification of working practices and in placing more weight on personal responsibility and accountability. The possible savings envisaged according to the study were:

- Equipment and Logistics-51 per cent.
- Estate and Support Infrastructure – 14 per cent.
- Organisation and Management – 16 per cent.
- Personnel and Training – 19 per cent.

The reduction in Head Office personnel was to be drastic indeed, from 12,700 in 1990, to 5,200 in 1995 and finally to 3,750 by 1998. The report contains other interesting observations that have relevance for us:

- There is no single body below the Ministerial level with authority and responsibility for the full range of the Department's policy activity and management. (One may ask whether this is feasible or even desirable).
- Align single Service Chief of Staff's responsibility as professional head, with financial responsibility and accountability.

The MoD in UK is a unique *integrated* organisation in the government, as it is both a Department of State, as well as the headquarters of the Armed Forces as a whole. The Study states: "The importance of preserving clear lines of functional responsibility to Ministers for the different aspects of the business remains. We do not believe that this requires parallel, separate, military or civilian hierarchies. It was encouraging that the study found little evidence of this in the existing structure".

United States Experience

Whereas the UK defence organisation has evolved over a considerable period in a measured way, the Defence structure in the United States in its present form is largely a post-World War II creation. Due to the preponderant role of the US armed forces during and after the war, its emergence as a SuperPower with a global reach, the requirements of major wars (Korea and Vietnam), the Cold War, numerous smaller military involvements, and because of the possibility of nuclear war, the US defence organisation has become extraordinarily large and complex.

A further impetus for change and streamlining of the US, UK and other European defence organisations, was the creation of the North Atlantic Treaty Organisation (NATO) and the Warsaw Pact and the half-century long nuclear standoff between the Western and the Soviet blocs. These changes were brought about by stark necessity and were *politically driven*, often in the teeth of opposition and even sabotage by the civil and military establishments. The fear of a pre-emptive nuclear attack without warning drove the adversaries to demonstrate an organisational capability to retaliate instantaneously and overwhelmingly, and thus hope to deter the attack altogether.

Major organisational changes in the USA, such as the creation of a Joint Chiefs of Staff Committee (JCSC), and a national security setup were initiated during President Truman's time in 1947. The last major reorganisation was in 1986 under the Goldwater-Nichols Act of 1986.

Changes in UK followed, notably under Prime Minister Margaret Thatcher. It should be remembered that fear of nuclear war was very real in the minds of national leaderships and military planners during the Cold War. Extremely complex and high cost weapon systems were developed and money had to be found by curtailing duplication and waste in the armed forces and in the civilian and military bureaucracies.

Apart from operational considerations, the creation of the Joint Chiefs of Staff (JCS) in the USA and the CDS in the UK were felt to be necessary for budgetary reasons, to clarify lines of control and responsibility, and to facilitate legislative supervision. All democracies require that armed forces be firmly under civil direction and control, but there is also nagging fear that somehow they manage to evade legislative oversight. In mature democracies, these concerns are not necessarily about relative power, but about better financial management of the requirements of the state, and the apportioning of the budgetary pie. The aim is also to forestall military inspired adventures. Sometimes, however, it is the civilian political authority that goads the military into action, as the USA did in Iraq, despite sound advice to the contrary.

Delays, Cost Overruns and Failures

Despite the more evolved and refined systems of defence management in advanced countries, delays, cost overruns and plain failures of major weapons systems are not infrequent. Here is what the US Government Accountability Office has to say about the Pentagon's failure "to deliver high quality products in a timely and cost-efficient fashion", asserting that future national security is at risk.

As a result it is "not unusual to see cost increases that add up to tens or hundreds of millions of dollars, schedule delays that add up to years and large and expensive programmes frequently re-baselined or even scrapped after years of failing to achieve promised capability". The GAO also criticised the lack of accountability in the Department of Defence, and that the Pentagon "has never clearly specified who is accountable for what, invested responsibility for execution in any single individual, or even required programme leaders to stay until the job is done."

The UK experience is much the same as far as major defence projects are concerned. For example, according to the National Audit Office major projects report, the current cost estimates for the three latest Astute class nuclear attack submarines (SSNs) has risen from UK Pounds 2.6 billion to UK Pounds 3.5 billion. The project has barely survived "cost overruns and schedule delays, arising from a combination of poor project management, an immature computer-aided design (CAD) tool and a haemorrhaging of skills and experience in the submarine industry".

Planning for a future submarine nuclear deterrent platform is also not very optimistic. Assuming the UK government takes a decision in 2006, the submarine is not likely to be delivered before 2024, which according to the UK Director General Nuclear and Controller of the Navy, Rear Admiral Andy Mathews, "sounds a long way off, but is actually quite a tight timescale for something like this". If this is the fate of defence planning in mature and experienced countries such as in the UK and the USA, is it any surprise that our planning too is beset with inadequacies?

SITUATION IN INDIA

Effecting major organisational changes in the management of the armed forces has to be politically driven from a full understanding of the issues involved, the benefits to be derived, the efficiencies and savings to be achieved, without undermining operational effectiveness. A pre-condition has to be that the highest political executive be convinced of the necessity for change, has a hands-on familiarity with the management of defence issues in broad terms, and has the will, time, and organisational, legislative and people skills to see the changes through. Such conditions existed in varying degrees in the USA, UK and most European countries during and after the major wars, and urgency was provided by the people's instinct for survival in the face of possible nuclear holocaust. In India, the necessary conditions for driving change are largely absent, despite the dysfunctional nature of the organisation for defence planning and endemic delays, cost overruns and failure to meet specifications.

Planning for defence is an extremely complex matter abounding in uncertainties. Since the state is dealing with future requirements, the success of research or design effort, availability of material resources or skilled personnel, capability of the builder, manufacturer or supplier, or even assurance of funding and stability of policy cannot be taken for granted. This is further complicated if foreign governments or manufacturers are involved, introducing uncertainties of licensing, sanctions, denial regimes, end-user issues and even unrelated matters such as diplomatic pressure. There are also the complications of offsets, sweeteners, kickbacks and disinformation/misinformation by competitors and interested parties.

Integrated Defence Planning

Whatever the complications, it would seem self-evident that comprehensive integrated planning for the defence of India would reduce duplication and waste, better utilise technical and manpower resources, make for more efficient and cost-effective procurement for the armed forces, and simplify their logistics management. This is of course easier said than done. The first difficulty is the vastly disproportionate size of the Indian army compared to the Navy and the Air Force, the nature of its operational role and its special equipment requirements, very little of which is common to the other two services. Until more common platforms such as the Advanced Light Helicopter (ALH) and the Light Combat Aircraft (LCA) enter service, shared logistics will remain restricted to basic items such as ammunition, transport vehicles, rations, medical supplies and the like. Some commonality also exists in indigenously developed missiles, UAVs, radars, communications equipment etc, but the list could be expanded.

Nevertheless, there is a modest degree of integration in the Indian armed forces, starting with the common training of officer cadets at the National Defence Academy which began in January 1949 long before the concept gained favour with leading military powers. The Indian armed forces have been moving towards integration at the higher levels of the defence organisation too with deliberation, within the limitations of the security environment, the infirmities of the political system, the shortcomings of bureaucracy and the doubts within the military establishment itself.

The Service Headquarters are now styled as the Integrated Headquarters, Ministry of Defence (Army/Navy/Air Force) as the case may be, and there is limited integration of civil and military staffs on a functional basis. There is also more devolution of financial powers, the positive effect of which is discernible even at the unit level. However, despite strenuous efforts and comprehensive recommendations by a "Group of Ministers", the nettle that is yet to be grasped is that of the Higher Defence Organisation at the level of the Defence Minister, the Chief of Defence Staff (CDS) and his charter and responsibilities, and the reorganisation of the Departments of Defence, Defence Production and Research and Development. No integrated staff can function effectively unless there is a common professional superior, and none exists. All joint planning and proposals routed through the Chiefs of Staff Committee (COSC), are agreed to (or shelved) on the basis of consensus and promulgated under the authority of the rotational Chairman, COSC. Consensus is not a bad thing; it causes less frictions and has a greater chance of succeeding. But it is critically dependent on the cooperative relationship between the services, mutual accommodation, goodwill, personalities of the three Chiefs, their interpretations of parochial service interests and willingness to moderate them for common objectives. Instances are known of a single service secretively processing cases that have implications for the other two, in cooperation with some civil servants for their own ends, and together, misleading the minister. Naturally, trust is the biggest casualty, with not only administrative but operational implications.

Since budgets are always tight, no consensus is possible on the equipment plans of the three services if it entails sacrificing a major service project. Budgetary proposals are, therefore, merely aggregations of each service requirements, and no matter how justified, result only in separate rough and ready budgetary provision for the Army, Navy and the Air force in the national budget.

This by no means implies authority to spend the amounts on the proposals submitted, which have to be again justified individually up the tortuous chain for approval by the "competent authority", whosoever that might be in a given case. Delays and shortfalls are inbuilt into the system and seem to worry only the military that has to live with the consequences in terms of diminished operational capability or personnel hardship and morale. Another major deficiency is that the Department of Defence under the Defence Secretary, who is the *de-facto* Chief Staff Officer to the Defence Minister, does not participate in any meaningful way in formulating and developing the proposals received from the armed forces before they are moved for financial and executive approval, preferring instead to "examine" them for ministerial endorsement, often without being technically or professionally equipped to do so.

Because of the staffing pattern, its competence lies in procedural matters, but as "examiner", it feels obliged to raise numerous, supposedly searching queries that are often based on superficial information.

CHIEF OF THE DEFENCE STAFF (CDS)

The creation of a Chief of Defence Staff will not solve the problems associated with the defence planning process without a complete overhaul of the Ministry of Defence organization. Here the UK experience is directly relevant in conceptual terms but will differ greatly in detailed execution. The Minister, termed Secretary of State for Defence in UK parlance, presides over a ministry and armed forces, integrated on a functional basis at all levels. Thus, a largely military office could have several civilian officers; a largely civilian office could have military representatives. These would work through their respective chains, largely civilian or largely military. At the top, the CDS and the Permanent Under Secretary (PUS), a civil servant, "neither of whom is subordinate to the other", are the Principal Advisers to the Secretary of State for their respective areas of responsibility.

The services Chiefs offer their *collective advice* to the CDS in the forum of the Chiefs of Staff Committee. All four senior military officers have direct independent access to the Secretary of State and the Prime Minister. The functional integration of the Indian Ministry of Defence requires parliamentary legislation and a competent minister to oversee the implementation over a period of years. There have undoubtedly been some strong ministers in the past with sound grasp of administrative issues and the political clout to force through the desired change. But these have been rare, and, in the present era of coalition politics with a paucity of talent in individual political parties, it is somewhat unlikely that such a minister can be found for the requisite duration, assuming that the government lasts its term. There is another more important consideration.

A fundamental change of the type being contemplated has to be driven by a Prime Minister committed to the change and who understands its implications and consequences and is confident and capable of directing and controlling the process. Assuming such a Prime Minister is equipped to do all this, he must have the time for personal involvement to see the change through as it takes place. Heads of government in the UK or the USA are not beset by daily severe domestic crises, and can devote substantial portion of their day to foreign or military affairs, which, given the global nature of their involvement, are closely intertwined.

Rare is the day when the Indian Prime Minister is not rushing to put out political fires lit by "allies" or opponents. The author once asked Prime Minister, PV Narasimha Rao, how much time he could actually devote to his job of perspective planning for the nation and its vital international diplomatic, security and economic concerns. He replied without hesitation, "Not even twenty percent". Nothing more was asked or said; the Babri Masjid demolition was two days away, and thousands of men carrying so-called consecrated bricks were on the march through the roads, villages and towns of northern India towards Ayodhya.

Defence Procurement

The armed forces procure stores, equipment, weapons and systems costing billions of rupees every year after a labyrinthine process of proposals and approvals. As the experience in most other countries indicates, there are factors, which make it difficult to streamline the process. We need to import most of our defence equipment, as India does not yet possess all the advanced technologies required for modern military hardware. The navy has achieved the maximum indigenisation through its shipbuilding programmes but still has to import major weapon systems and vessels, especially submarines, from abroad or seek collaborations. Until recently, this was complicated by US and western sanctions against India that restricted the transfer of numerous technologies.

Defence procurement is the area where maximum delay is caused by our tortuous bureaucratic and financial procedures and lack of accountability and internal transparency. It is also hamstrung by allegations of corruption and resultant political paralysis. The case of the Bofors guns and the HDW (SSK) German submarines are well known and the truth is still to be made public. But while the political charades go on, the armed forces are deprived of capability build up and go into conflict without having the weapons and wherewithal, no heads roll, and no one is arraigned for any gross impropriety or crime.

The HDW SSK submarine project was to set India on the path of indigenous design capability and enable their building in India with increasingly locally manufactured equipment. Two submarines were built in Germany and two at Mazagon Docks in Mumbai — the last some ten years ago — after which the project ground to a halt because some persons were alleged to have taken bribes. The political attacks and scandal that followed ensured that no government would bite that particular bullet. Meanwhile, the HDW has changed hands several times, and at one time was owned by an American bank as a speculative investment.

Interestingly, South Korea started building similar HDW SSK type 209 submarines about the same time as India did. While our programme has floundered, the Koreans built nine of these boats and have launched the much-improved follow-on type 214 on June 6, 2006. Nine of these will be built, for a total of eighteen.

Korea is no stranger to corruption and political scandals, yet defence capability build up has not been compromised. We have now turned to the French, who have so far been supplying the Daphne and Agosta class submarines to Pakistan. The plan is to build the Scorpene class in India. No sooner plans are announced, scandals erupt about alleged dubious and shady deals. Even if the project gets going, it will be five years or more before the first Scorpene enters service. What happens to India's deteriorating submarine capability and operational readiness in the event of war? Who is the person or persons whom the nation will call to account for putting India's security in jeopardy? The country bears an enormous cost for controversies over corruption in terms of opportunity lost and diminished defence capability.

Transparency and Confidentiality

There is need for confidentiality, even secrecy, in defence procurement for reasons of security, price negotiations and vendor competitiveness. But certainly there should be *internal* transparency in the procurement process, in the formulations of proposals, their processing, recommendations at various stages and financial and political decisions. Some of this will automatically come about if an integrated defence organisation is created since much of the *procedural opacity* is in fact located in the Department of Defence and the Ministry of Finance where the political inputs are injected.

Political interventions in the national interest can be entirely legitimate if they are in consideration of vital economic, security or diplomatic issues. They are wholly improper if they are to further political party or personal interests, as has too often been the case. Transparency is a goal earnestly to be wished for but it is futile to talk of overall transparency unless there is honesty in the political system. This would appear to be a bleak prospect if former Cabinet Secretary TSR Subramanian is right. He says: "In my four decades of public service I have come across thousands of politicians... I have worked closely with hundreds of them in one context or another. I am saddened to say that I have come across only a handful of honest politicians." He is unsparing too of his own tribe, the civil servants and succinctly articulates the reasons for the collapse of the "the steel frame"-the Indian Civil Services.

Importing equipment from abroad has long-term implications for supplier reliability, costs, etc. Increasingly, as a consequence of business restructuring in Europe, companies get taken over by others, perhaps from another country or even continent, with ensuing business complications. Add to this, arbitrary restrictions on spares or support placed under NATO or US stipulations that effectively render the equipment unserviceable over time. We have experienced this with several major systems. It is for such reasons that India has hesitated to procure US equipment and Venezuela, for example, is turning to Russia and China for its defence requirements.

Moreover, hardly any country in Europe has sovereign ownership of its firms, only majority holdings, though the French try to retain substantial control over companies such as Thales and EADS. Most firms are part owned by other firms from other European countries. This is fine for buyers from the EU, NATO and western allies but has serious implications for assured supply of spares for a country like India, and also because equipment life cycles are of 15 to 20 years.

It would seem logical from several points of view to manufacture and build within India to the maximum extent. In this we should follow the Russian or Chinese model rather than be beguiled into thinking that we will have ready access to western equipment sources for the asking, despite their friendlier stance in the changed environment led by US initiatives. Besides, with their higher costs, there is always the question of affordability.

Our past experience of sanctions and denial regimes under the NPT, MTCR and other such stipulations should always be kept in mind. There have been instances of even manufacturers in India – subsidiaries of foreign firms– selling equipment to the private sector but refusing to supply to the Indian defence forces under directions from their home country. Even between western NATO allies the technology transfer relationship is not without pitfalls, and many US weapon systems are denied, even to close allies such as the UK. The policy of "buy American" and export restrictions insisted upon from time to time by the US Congress, as much due to vote bank considerations as for safeguarding technology, strains even the US-EU arms relationship. India would do well to temper its expectations on technology transfer from the USA, Europe or any other foreign source for that matter.

Public-Private Partnership

With the maturing of technology in the private sector in India, the prospects of Public-Private partnership have greatly improved. Warships being built in India are a very good example of this carefully nurtured relationship over a period of nearly 40 years. But the growing demand for privatization of Public Sector Undertakings (PSUs), should be cautiously handled in the case of strategic PSUs. Vitriolic criticism in the media of defence PSUs and the Defence Research and Development Organisation (DRDO) from an imperfect understanding of the totality of issues involved, including the historical context, ill serves India's interests for self-reliance in defence technology and weaponry.

It is vital for India to retain control over strategic PSUs as our private industry is not evolved, diversified and mature enough to handle the kind of turmoil caused by takeovers in the European pattern. We should rather consider the French model where the state continues to substantially own the asset, while granting it functional freedom. French defence firms like Thales and EADS, are some of the largest, most high-tech and competitive in the world, while being substantially state-owned.

The emerging pattern in European defence industrial structure has another uncertainty. Can we be certain that the European

Union will exist in the future? It too can disintegrate like the Soviet Union or Yugoslavia if major differences arise over, for example, the admission of Turkey or some other emotive issue, or the differing visions of powerful, charismatic national leaders. History has witnessed this over and over again. The eastward expansion of NATO and its newly conceptualised global role could provoke strategic reassessment and political retaliation from an already resentful and economically recuperating Russia that is still trying to overcome the trauma of the disintegration of the Soviet Union.

The re-assertion of national sovereignty over the defence industry in a fractured European environment will be messy indeed, and foreign customers will be the biggest sufferers. India has already experienced this in the dissolution of the Soviet Union when many manufactures located in Ukraine, Belorussia, Latvia, etc., went their separate ways, leaving the Indian armed forces high and dry for necessary spares and support. Even the re-unification of Germany disrupted supplies from East German firms that were closed down.

Conclusion

Planning for defence is one of the most complex functions of a government. It begins with an appreciation of the international security environment, the global political, social, economic and military forces at work, and takes into account long-term national and security objectives and economic factors.

We have adopted the British pattern of defence administration but have not carried it to its logical conclusion of a streamlined, functional organization, integrating civilian and military elements. The nature of the Indian state and system of governance make it difficult to make radical changes. The creation of the post of the CDS is a case in point and is unlikely to come about until the Prime Minister is freed from domestic crisis management and can be more directly involved in supervising defence through a competent minister and functionally integrated ministry. India with its size, economy and technological competencies, should design, develop and build most of its defence requirements within the country. Production assets should be substantially state-owned, but meaningful private-public partnership should also be energetically encouraged. Reliance on foreign suppliers should be greatly reduced in a deliberate, phased manner.

Defence procurement is beset with delays, high costs and dubious transactions rooted in the political process. These result in lost opportunities and lowered operational capabilities, yet no one is held to account and the public seldom gets to know the truth. In the absence of political probity, expecting transparency in the process of defence procurement appears to be optimistic. Nevertheless, apart from required confidentiality, internal transparency at staff and decision-making levels is both desirable and feasible.

3 Indian Defence Projects

INDIGENOUS PROJECTS

INS ARIHANT-ADVANCED TECHNOLOGY VESSEL (ATV)

India's first indigenous nuclear powered submarine was launched by Mrs. Gursharan Kaur, wife of Prime Minister Manmohan Singh on July 26, 2009 at Eastern Naval Command headquarters in Visakhapatnam. INS Arihant, Destroyer of Enemies, was designed and developed under the ATV project which was given a go ahead in 1984 by then Prime Minister Indira Gandhi. The ATV project became a serious endeavour in 1985 after Mazagaon docks began construction of two German HDW 209 class submarines in 1984.

Agni II

Agni-II is a two-stage solid propellant ballistic missile with a launch weight of 17 tons, a diameter of 1m and length of 20 m. It can hit targets between 1,550 and 1,860 miles away with a 2,200-pound payload. Considering that a nuclear warhead weighs around 1,200-pound, the missile could hit targets at much higher ranges. Developed by Defence Research and Development Organization (DRDO), the missile is part of the Agni series which includes Agni-I (700 km range) and Agni-III (3,500 km range).

Agni-I, and Agni-II have already been inducted by the Indian Strategic Forces and Agni-III is in the process of induction. The Agni II missile equips the Strategic Forces 555 Missile Group.

The August 29, 2004 test appeared to be a depressed trajectory test. The test on May 19, 2009, which failed, served to train the Strategic Force in independently operating the missile as well as to evaluate a new navigation system.

Both the above tests were done using rail mobile launchers. During the test on May 19, the missile wondered 180 degrees off track and plunged into the sea after 127 seconds having covered 203 km. The limited number of tests so far and the long gaps between them probably indicate that it is still under development.

Agni III

Agni-III, is a 3,500 km range missile that is 16.7-metre tall missile and has a 50 ton lift-off weight. It is reportedly capable of carrying a 1.5 ton thermonuclear warhead with a yield of 200-250 KT. The missile has been tested on three occasions in the past. The first test on July 9, 2006 was unsuccessful due to cascaded failure of booster flex nozzle controller. The second test on April 12, 2007 was a success. The missile impacted its designated target area after a flight of 900 secs. The third test flight on Wednesday, May 7, 2008 lasted 800 sec and the missile impacted its designated target area south of the equator, monitored by two IN ships.

Agni V

The Indian Government sanctioned Rs 2,500 crore to develop the Agni V missile, with a range of 5,000km in 2008. The missile is expected to be ready for testing in the 2010-11 time frame.

Mr. VK Saraswat, DRDO's Chief Controller of Missiles and Strategic Systems, told Business Standard in May 2008 that DRDO is working on a 5,000 km range Agni-5 missile, with multiple warheads (MIRVs) that can manoeuvre and send out decoys to confuse enemy anti-missile defences. The missile is being developed by adding an all composite third state to the two-stage, 3000km Agni III missile. The second stage of the missile will also use composites to save weight and allow for the addition of a third stage.

Talking to The Hindu in November, Mr. Avinash Chander, director of the Agni program and of the Advanced Systems Laboratory (ASL) said the Agni V design has been completed and the first development flight test will be conducted in 2010. The mobile missile will be capable of canister launch allowing it to be deployed and launched from any part of the country. The missile will have 60% commonality of components with Agni III, including its ring laser gyroscope and accelerometer.

The gyroscope was developed by Research Centre Imarat (RCI), sister laboratory of ASL, and is part of DRDO's missile complex in Hyderabad. The ring laser is also fitted on the Shourya tactical missile.

AKASH MISSILE

Indian Air Force has placed a Rs 1,200 crore order with Bharat Dynamics Limited (BDL) for two squadrons of medium range, surface-to-air missile Akash. Basically an upgraded Russian SA-6 system, Akash has been under development by DRDL for 25 years. The 720kg, 5.78-metre long missile has a diameter of 35 cm and a length of 5.78 meters. The Mach 2.5 missile can engage targets as far as 25 km away flying at heights ranging from 20m to 18kms.

The missile is supported by multi-target and multi-function phased array fire control radar called 'Rajendra' that has a range of about 60 km. The first test flight of the missile was conducted in 1990, and since then many development and field trials have taken place. The last field trials for the missile were conducted at Pokhran in Rajasthan in late 2007. The missile has consistently fallen short of IAF requirements, which wants a smaller, lighter missile with a longer range, greater manoeuvrability and an active seeker.

DRDO proposes to remove the shortcomings in the missile through batch-by-batch improvements. India wants to build a version of Akash for use on ships, and is already looking into a longer range (60 kilometres) version. The Akash missile system, according to a statement made by Defence Minister A.K. Antony in the Rajya Sabha, cost the exchequer Rs. 516.86 crore for its development, the highest for any of India's missile systems.

ASTRA AIR-TO-AIR MISSILE

Astra is an active radar homing, Beyond Visual Range (BVR) missile being developed by Defence Research and Development Organization (DRDO). The 154kg (340lb) Astra uses active radar homing and is reportedly capable of engaging targets at 80km in the head on mode and 20km while astern. The missile has a cruise speed of up to Mach 2.2 carrying a 20kg fragmentation warhead. It has a length of 3570 mm and a diameter of 178 mm. The missile was first launched on May 9, 2003 from the ITR. Its second and third trials were conducted on May 11 and May 12, 2003 respectively at the same range. These tests were without control and guidance systems. A second series of developmental flights to test the guidance system of the missile were carried out on March 25, 26 and 29, 2007.

A follow up ground launch of the missile was carried out on September 13, 2008. A successful developmental test of the missile was announced on Thursday, May 7, 2009. The missile was launched from the ground at an imaginary target to test its dual mode guidance. Captive flight tests of the missile are planned in 2009 during which the missile will be mated to a launch fighter aircraft. Several manoeuvres at different speeds and altitudes would be conducted and the compatibility of electronics, avionics and other systems checked. After the captive flight tests, the missile would be integrated with the Sukhoi-30 and test-fired by the middle of next year.

DRDO is hopeful of equipping the Tejas and Sukhoi Su-30MKI aircraft with the missile since they have powerful airborne radars to leverage its BVR capability. Even though the missile is in the early stages of its development, DRDO has drawn up plans to jointly develop a short-range air defence system with MBDA using a vertically launched variant of Astra.

BARAK 2 MISSILES (MR-SAM AND LR-SAM)

India has signed a $1.4 billion defence contract with Israel Aerospace Industries Ltd. (IAI) to co-develop a Air Defence System.

The contract includes a 30 percent offset clause under which Israel will procure military or aviation products and services from India, and invest in Indian defence companies. Under this clause IAI will make purchases from Mumbai based Tata Advanced Systems (TASL) which will partner with IAI to develop missiles, drones, radars, electronic warfare systems and homeland security systems– all areas of Israeli defence industry specialization.

IAI announced the deal on March 26 to Israeli business daily *Globes*, after having received advance payment. India is making part payment on the deal during the development period, and the balance during the 66-month delivery period, which is slated to begin 90 months from the date the advance payment is received. The missile defence system will be based on two missiles: A 70 km range MR-SAM and a 120 km range LR-SAM. The MR-SAM will equip Naval Ships while the LR-SAM will be shore based for use by the IAF. Project N11356 Stealth Frigates will be armed with MR-SAM which will have the long range radar and weapon control system to support the extended range missile. During the visit of the Navy Chief Admiral Arun Prakash to Israel in July 2005, Israel offered to develop the next generation Barak-II ship defence missiles jointly with DRDL. The issue was discussed during the Naval Commanders' Conference in November 2005.

India and Israel reportedly inked a deal valued at $350 million on 27 Jan 2006 to co-develop the two missiles over the next 5 years. Both the nations agreed to hold a 50/50 stake in the venture with additional funds being pumped in by both parties as needed. The February 27, 2009 contract, which is yet to be officially acknowledged by India, appears to be follow up to the 2006 deal.

Ballistic Missile Defence (BMD) System

Defence Research and Development Organization (DRDO) is developing a Ballistic Missile Defence (BMD) system to be deployed by 2015.

The system will be based on radar technology for tracking and fire control which the DRDO developed jointly with Israel and France.

In Phase I the BMD system will be implemented as a two tiered terminal phase interceptor system comprising of:

1. Prithvi Air Defence (PAD) exo-atmospheric interceptor missile for intercepting targets outside the atmosphere.
2. Advanced Air Defence (AAD) endo-atmospheric interceptor missile for intercepting targets up to an attitude of 30 kms. The seven-metre long AAD interceptor is a single stage solid rocket propelled guided missile, equipped with an inertial navigation system, a hi-tech computer and an electro-mechanical activator totally under command by the data up-linked from the sophisticated ground based radars to the interceptor, sources said.
3. 'Swordfish' Long Range Tracking Radar (LRTR). The Swordfish LRTR has been developed from the Green Pine early warning and fire control radars imported by India from Israel in 2001-2002.

BMD Tests

India has conducted three successful intercepts using the Phase 1 system against non manoeuvring targets in 2006, 2007 and 2009.

On March 6, 2008 a PAD missile successfully intercepted a modified Dhanush surface-to-surface missile fired, from INS Rajput anchored inside the Bay of Bengal at 1620 hours, towards Wheeler Island, simulating a target "enemy" missile with a range of 1,500 km.

On November 27, 2006 a PAD missile intercepted a Prithvi ballistic missile at 48 km altitude.

In December 2007 an AAD missile intercepted a target missile at an altitude of 15kms.

India is also developing two new missiles, AD-1 and AD-2, as part of the ABM system. These Phase II missiles are being developed to intercept ballistic missiles with the range in excess of 5000 km and probably represent elements of a mid-course interception system.

Upcoming Test

DRDO will carry out another test around the year end to enhance the capabilities of AAD endo-atmospheric missile, which is used for intercepting missiles at altitudes up to 15 km. Sources use composites to save weight and allow for the addition of a third stage.

Talking to The Hindu in November, Avinash Chander, director of the Agni program and of the Advanced Systems Laboratory (ASL) said the Agni V design has been completed and the first development flight test will be conducted in 2010. The mobile missile will be capable of canister launch allowing it deployed and launched from any part of the country. The missile will have 60% commonality of components with Agni III, including its ring laser gyroscope and accelerometer.

The gyroscope was developed by Research Centre Imarat (RCI), sister laboratory of ASL, and is part of DRDO's missile complex in Hyderabad. The ring laser is also fitted on the Shourya tactical missile.

AKASH MISSILE

Indian Air Force has placed a Rs 1,200 crore order with Bharat Electronics Limited (BEL) for two squadrons of medium range, surface-to-air missile Akash. Basically an upgraded Russian SA-6 system, Akash has been under development by DRDL for 25 years. The 720kg, 5.78-metre long missile has a diameter of 35 cm and a length of 5.78 meters. The Mach 2.5 missile can engage targets as far as 25 km away flying at heights ranging from 20m to 18kms.

The missile is supported by multi-target and multi-function phased array fire control radar called 'Rajendra' that has a range of about 60 km. The first test flight of the missile was conducted in 1990, and since then many development and field trials have taken place. The last field trials for the missile were conducted at Pokhran in Rajasthan in late 2007. The missile has consistently fallen short of IAF requirements, which wants a smaller, lighter missile with a longer range, greater maneuverability and an active seeker.

DRDO proposes to remove the shortcomings in the missile through batch-by-batch improvements. India wants to build a version of Akash for use on ships, and is already looking into a longer range (60 kilometres) version. The Akash missile system, according to a statement made by Defence Minister A.K. Antony in the Rajya Sabha, cost the exchequer Rs. 516.86 crore for its development, the highest for any of India's missile systems.

ASTRA AIR-TO-AIR MISSILE

Astra is an active radar homing, Beyond Visual Range (BVR) missile being developed by Defense Research and Development Organization (DRDO). The 154kg (340lb) Astra uses active radar homing and is reportedly capable of engaging targets at 80km in the head on mode and 20km while astern. The missile has a cruise speed of up to Mach 2.2 carrying a 20kg fragmentation warhead. It has a length of 3570 mm and a diameter of 178 mm. The missile was first launched on May 9, 2003 from the ITR. Its second and third trials were conducted on May 11 and May 12, 2003 respectively at the same range. These tests were without control and guidance systems. A second series of developmental flights to test the guidance system of the missile were carried out on March 25, 26 and 29, 2007.

A follow up ground launch of the missile was carried out on September 13, 2008. A successful developmental test of the missile was announced on Thursday, May 7. The missile was launched from the ground at an imaginary target to test its dual mode guidance. Captive flight tests of the missile are planned in 2009 during which the missile will be mated to a launch fighter aircraft. Several maneuvers at different speeds and altitudes would be conducted and the compatibility of electronics, avionics and other systems checked. After the captive flight tests, the missile would be integrated with the Sukhoi-30 and test-fired by the middle of next year.

DRDO is hopeful of equipping the Tejas and Sukhoi Su-30MKI aircraft with the missile since they have powerful airborne radars to leverage its BVR capability. Even though the missile is in the early stages of its development, DRDO has drawn up plans to jointly develop a short-range air defense system with MBDA using a vertically launched variant of Astra.

BARAK 2 MISSILES (MR-SAM AND LR-SAM)

India has signed a $1.4 billion defense contract with Israel Aerospace Industries Ltd. (IAI) to co-develop a Air Defense System.

HAL currently has orders to deliver 260 to 270 Dhruv, its Chairman Ashok Baweja said on Thursday, February 12, 2009, at Aero India 2009 in Bengaluru. Five Dhruvs were handed over the Ecuador Air Force chief at a high-profile media event at Aero India 2009 on Friday, February 13.

EMB-145 AEWC&S PROJECT

Centre for Airborne Systems (CABS), is coordinating the Rs.1,800-crore effort to develop an indigenous airborne early warning and control system (AEW&CS) to augment the three Phalcon AWACs being procured by the IAF.

The AEW&CS will comprise of an indigenous radar and control system mounted on a Brazilian Embraer EMB-145 regional jet. Under a $210 million deal signed with Brazilian aviation company Embraer in summer 2008. Embraer will supply India 3 EMB-145s with the system mounted on them. The choice of Embraer as the platform was made by the IAF.

The CABS is looking for an experienced partner who will be responsible for integrating the Active Array Antenna Unit (AAAU), other antennas, trans receiver modules and various sub systems being developed by Indian defence laboratories onto the three Brazil manufactured EMB-145. It has sent a request for proposal to six vendors-Israel's Elta, the European consortium EADS, France's Thales, Sweden's SAAB Erikson and the United State's Raytheon and Northrop Grumman. The vendors have time till the third week of January 2009 to submit their proposals. The first EMB-145 is scheduled to be delivered in 2011 and the complete system will be flight tested by the DRDO along with the Indian air force from 2012.

Sensors

The primary sensor will be an active electronically scanned array radar with two planar arrays mounted on top of the fuselage in a dorsal unit, and capable of air and sea surveillance. The radar has been developed based on design and technology supplied by ELTA.

The secondary radar will have an identification friend or foe function, while communication and electronic support measures will also enable the aircraft to detect and identify hostile emitters. A self-protection suite will consist of missile approach and radar warning receivers, plus countermeasures dispensers.

Interoperability

The AEW&C will feature voice and data communication over UHF voice and data channels. The system is designed to complement three Ilyushin Il-76s equipped with Elta Systems Phalcon radars and Indian navy Kamov Ka-31 radar picket helicopters. However, it is not clear if it will feature data links with the other two systems.

The modified EMB-145 will have a service ceiling of 35,000ft (10,700m), a radar operational altitude of 25,000ft and extra internal fuel tanks to allow in-flight refuelling. The IAF is looking to acquire an additional 20 such systems.

The development comes nine years after India's original indigenous AEW&C program came to a standstill after a Hawker Siddeley HS748 test bed with a prototype radar crashed. Several scientists who were integral to the program were killed in the accident, and India has been trying to resurrect the program since.

FIFTH GENERATION FIGHTER AIRCRAFT (FGFA)

Under an intergovernmental agreement signed in October 2007, Sukhoi, which is part of Russia's United Aircraft Corporation (UAC), along with India's Hindustan Aeronautics Limited (HAL), will develop a fifth-generation fighter. Russia and India will simultaneously develop two versions of the combat aircraft-a two-seat version to meet the requirements of India's air superiority policy, and a single-seat version for the Russian Air Force.

Sukhoi has already started construction of three prototypes at the Komsomolsk-on-Amur Aviation Production Association (KNAAPO) in Russia's Far East. Flight tests of the fighter could begin as early as August 2009, and the aircraft may go into production in Russia and India by 2015.

The fighter, estimated to be in the 30t category, is expected to feature super manoeuvrability, super cruise and stealth with an internal weapon bay. It is also expected to feature an advanced variant of the Tikhomirov Instrument Engineering Research

Institute developed N035 Irbis-E radar that equips the Su-35BM. India and Russia will sign a formal contract to jointly develop the fighter at the beginning of 2009, the head of the United Aircraft Corporation said on 2008, December 5. "We are planning to conclude the contract at the beginning of next year," Alexei Fedorov said. It is clear from the manner in which the contract is being negotiated that HAL inputs into the design of the fighters will be minimal.

Russia to Speed up Fifth Generation Fighter Development

Russian deputy PM has asked Sukhoi to speed up the development of the fifth-generation fighter being produced in collaboration with India. "I insist that the testing start as early as 2009, and the fifth-generation fighter must enter service with the Russian Air Force in 2015," Sergei Ivanov said at a meeting of the Military-Industrial Commission. Ivanov said the plant had almost completed the construction of a first prototype of the fifth-generation fighter, but it will undergo only durability tests on the ground at a research facility in Zhukovsky near Moscow. However, a second prototype will be built and will take to the skies by the end of this year, he said.

FGFA to be Inducted into IAF by 2017

M Fakruddin, Director-Corporate Planning and Marketing, Hindustan Aeronautics Limited (HAL) told to The New Indian Express in February 2009 that India and Russia have sorted out their differences on the Fifth Generation Fighter Aircraft (FGFA) to be jointly developed by them and are set to sign a formal contract. "There have been differences between the two Air Forces as both have specific requirements," said Mr. Fakruddin. "These issues will be sorted out soon and by the middle of the year we expect to start work so that the aircraft is inducted by 2017," he added.

INDIAN AIRCRAFT CARRIER (IAC) PROJECT 71 INS VIKRANT

India is constructing a 40,000 ton aircraft carrier with a complement of 1,600 personal will be capable of carrying a 30 aircraft comprising MiG-29K / LCA Trainer, ALH Dhruv and Ka-

31, under the Rs 3,260 crore Project 71. The aircraft carrier will feature a ski jump like the INS Vikramaditya, instead of a steam catapult, for assisted takeoffs. Cochin Shipyard Ltd (CSL) designed 70% of the ship, starting in 2001-02. It used an Italian company Fincantieri as design consultants for integrating the propulsion system, while a Russian firm, NDB, is contributing aviation technology.

Fincantieri delivered the 30,000 ton aircraft carrier Cavour to the Italian Navy in 2008, which is powered by four General Electric LM2500 gas turbines generating a total of 80 MW of power, the same engines that will power the Vikrant. Construction started in 2006 but the keel of the ship was officially laid on February 28, 2009, by Defence Minister AK Antony in the presence of Admiral Sureesh Mehta, Chief of the Naval Staff. The 260 metres long and 60 metre wide ship will have a speed of 28 knots and an endurance of 8,000 nautical miles.

The carrier will field long-range surface-to-air missile systems with a multi-function radar, a close-in weapon system, the most modern C/D band early air-warning radar and the V/UHF tactical air-navigational and direction finding systems. It will have jamming capabilities over the expected electromagnetic (EM) environment, along with carrier control approach radars to aid air operations. Integration of all weapon systems onboard will be through an indigenous combat management system.

The ship's integration with the Navy's network-centric operations will provide for force multiplication. The ship will be launched by October 2010, as per the phase I contract signed by CSL with the Defence Ministry. The phase II of the contract will end with the delivery of the ship to the Navy by the end of 2014. Work on the second aircraft carrier is expected to start before the first one is delivered to the Navy.

INTERMEDIATE JET TRAINER (IJT) 'SITARA' HJT-36

The IJT program was sanctioned by the government in 1999 with an initial budget of Rs.180 crore as a replacement for the HJT-16 Kiran. The first prototype flew in March 2003. Around 225 IJTs are to be produced for use by the IAF, IN, as well as the Air Force's Surya Kiran aerobatic team. Two prototypes of the aircraft are currently flying-PT1 and PT2. The aircraft is to be powered by Russian aero engine major NPO Saturn's AL-55I (I for Indian). The first engine was delivered to India in November 2007 and is fitted on the PT2. The PT1 is powered by a French engine. The larger size of the AL-55I mandated changes to the airframe.

As per the original schedule, the first batch of IJTs was to have been delivered to the Air Force in 2005-06. Coded the Hindustan Jet Trainer (HJT)-36, the HAL has received an order for 12 Limited Series Production (LSP) and 60 production aircraft. The revised schedule is for the Air Force to receive the 12 LSPs by 2010.

LIGHT COMBAT HELICOPTER (LCH)

The first prototype of the Light Combat Helicopter was to make its maiden flight in March 2009 but has now been postponed to mid-August. "We have completed the design. However, there was a problem with one of the vendors who was supposed to provide the tooling for the LCH, and so we have no choice but to push the first flight to August," said Ashok Baweja, HAL's chairman, during Aero India 2009.

The LCH will supplement the 22 attack helicopters that India is seeking as part of an international tender. Final operational clearance (FOC) is expected to follow within a year. The 5.5-tonne twin engine LCH, a derivative of Dhruv ALH with tandem seating, will be armed with a 20mm turret twin-barrel gun, cluster bombs, rocket pods as well as air-to-air and air-to-ground missiles. Like the Dhruv, LCH is powered by two Shakti engines jointly developed with France's Turbomeca.

Designed for anti-tank and anti-infantry roles with a maximum speed of 275 kmph (148kt), it will also be capable of high-altitude warfare since its operational ceiling will be 16,000 to 18,000 feet (5,490m). "The LCH will incorporate a number of stealth features and crash-worthy landing gear for better survivability. The LCH will have a narrow fuselage, with two crew stations," said an official.

HAL has worked with Israeli companies to develop its avionics equipment, which includes helmet-mounted targeting systems and an electronic warfare suite.

IAF has projected an initial requirement of 65 LCHs. When in service, the type will join the air force's Mil Mi-35 attack helicopters, reportedly being upgraded with new Israeli avionics and night-fighting capabilities.

MEDIUM COMBAT AIRCRAFT

The DRDO displayed a wind tunnel model of its Medium Combat Aircraft (MCA) twin engine fighter concept at Aero India 2009. The 19-20 ton category fighter will feature stealth including an internal weapon bay.

Speaking at Aero India 2009, M. Natarajan, DRDO chief and scientific adviser to the defence minister said, "Even though we don't have a project as yet, we have started conceptual work on our own for the Medium Combat Aircraft. I will not call it Fifth Generation Aircraft but it is very close provided we are able to incorporate more stealth features."

Referring to the 126 MMRCA currently under procurement, Natrajan said: "It is possible to have an MCA with a twin engine, with less weight and improved electronics. It will also have an inbuilt weapon load for stealth reasons. It is doable and it is a challenge."

The project was initiated to capitalize on the knowledge and expertise gained from the work put into the LCA project. The Air Force has shown interest in the project.

NAG MISSILE

Nag is anti-tank missile with a 4-km range and fire-and-forget capability. The missile uses a IR seeker and has a top attack capability to strike a tank where its armour is the weakest. The missile has what is called a tandem warhead. The warhead will have two stages – in the first stage the missile will make a hole in an enemy tank and in the second stage it will go inside and blow it up. The IR seeker has lock-on-before-launch capability for day and night operation. A smokeless nitramine based propellant has been developed for the Nag. The missile is carried either on "NAMICA" (Tracked ICV) or the Advanced Light Helicopter.

The missile features a high strength composite airframe with foldable wings and fins, onboard real time processor, compact sensor package and electric actuation system, digital autopilot and high immunity to counter measures. The final user trials of the missile were carried out in July and August 2008 in Rajasthan and the missile has since been approved for production by the Army. The winter trials of the missile were held in December 2008. The missile will be produced by M/s Bharat Dynamics Ltd., which will roll out 200 missiles in the first year and twice that number in subsequent years. It will replace Russian Konkours and European Milan missiles currently under license production at Bharat Dynamics Ltd.

The DRDO took over 20 years to develop the missile, the design work for which was started in 1988 with the first test having been carried out in November 1990. It is proposed to increase the range of the ground launched version of the missile to 7 km and develop a helicopter launched version in two years.

NIRBHAY CRUISE MISSILE

Nirbhay (Fearless) is an intermediate-range (1000km) subsonic land-attack cruise missile that is being developed by Advanced Systems Laboratory (ASL) in Hyderabad since 2007. The missile is being designed to match the capabilities of the US Tomahawk and its Pakistan developed variant Babur. The missile will be capable of carrying 24 types of warhead but it is not clear if it is nuclear capable. "The need was felt for a subsonic cruise missile that will be capable of being launched from multiple platforms in land, air, and sea," says the ASL director. A technology demonstration test is scheduled for early 2009.

PROJECT 15A

Three warships under this Rs 11,000 crore project are being built by Mazagaon Docks Limited (MDL) for the Indian Navy. A follow up of Project 15 Delhi Class destoyers, which were based on the Soviet Kashins with elements drawn from the Godavari and Sovremenny classes, these 6,800 tons destroyers will incorporate more stealth. The first ship of the class, INS Kolkata, was launched on March 30, 2006, and is currently being fitted for a scheduled commissioning in May 2010. The next two are scheduled for delivery at one year intervals, i.e. May 2011 and

May 2012, respectively. The commissioning of the ship was stalled because of a three year delay in the delivery of propellers and shafts by a Ukraine shipyard, which eventually forced MDL to place orders with a Russian shipyard.

The ships are powered by four Zarya reversible gas turbines from Ukraine, which have already been delivered. The engines will be installed after Russia delivers the propellers and shafts.

Displacement	6,800 tons
Length	163 m
Beam	17.4 m
Speed	30+ knots
Sensors	Multi-function radar system, Humsa-NG hull mounted sonar and a Nagin active towed array sonar
Armament	1 x 130 mm gun 2 x 8 Brahmos Supersonic Cruise Missiles48 cell Barak 8 SAM16 Barak 1 SAM 4 x 30 mm AK-630 rapid fire gatling gunstwin-tube torpedo launchersanti-submarine rocket launchers
Aircraft Carried	2 Sea King and Dhruv Helicopters

PROJECT 15B

The Defence Acquisition Council (DAC) cleared the construction of four 6,800-ton destroyers by Mazagon Dock Ltd, Mumbai (MDL) in April 2009. There was no competitive bidding for the project which is a "follow-on" to the currently underway Project 15A-, construction of three Kolkata class destroyers at MDL. Project 15B warships are expected to differ from their predecessors only in the sensor and weapon suite that they carry. MDL expects minimal design changes and hopes to freeze the design within 1 1/2 years, with the first ship being launched within four years and subsequent ships being completed at one year intervals. If the order is placed on MDL by end-2009, the first 15-B destroyer would be commissioned in mid-2015.

PROJECT 17

Mazagaon Docks Limited (MDL) is building 3 Indian designed stealth frigates for the Indian Navy under this project. P 17s are based on the Project 11356 (Talwar / Krivak IV class) ships being acquired from Russia, and were designed jointly by the Naval Design Bureau (NDB) and Russia's Severnoye Project Design Bureau (Severnoye Proyektno-Konstruktorskoye Bjuro-SPKB), the designers of the N11356 frigate. The first ship of the class, INS Shivalik, was launched on April 19, 2003. The two follow on ships- INS Sahyadri and the INS Satpura are under construction at Mazagon docks. These are expected to be finished and delivered by 2010.

INS Shivalik and its sisters are 143 metres long and 16.9 metres wide (at beam). Their stealth character diminishes physical signatures-radar, infra red and sound-making it difficult for an enemy to detect and attack them. When fully armed they displace 4,900 tonnes.

Though much smaller than the Delhi class of destroyers, their weapons package is far more potent. These include the latest surface-to-surface vertical launched missiles, surface-to-air missiles and state of the art radar and communication equipment. The ships cruise using two French-made Pielstick diesel engines. For bursts of speeds upto 30 knots they use two GE LM 25000 gas turbines.

They operate two large helicopters for surveillance and anti-submarine operations.

The armament carried includes:

- 76mm Super Rapid Gun Mount (SRGM) (Main Gun)
- 2 x AK-630 Rapid Fire guns
- 24 x CIWS/SAM systems-KASHMIR
- Barak/Shtil VLS SAM (Undecided)
- 8 x VLS Klub/Brahmos Cruise missiles
- 90R missiles (ASW)
- DTA-53-956 torpedoes
- RBU-6000 (RPK-8)

PROJECT 17A

In June 2009, the Defence Acquisition Council (DAC) cleared a Rs 45,000 crore project to build seven stealth frigates using advanced manufacturing process like modular shipbuilding. The ships will be manufactured in India by the Mazagon Dock Limited, Mumbai (MDL) and the Garden Reach Shipbuilders and Engineers (GRSE), Kolkata.

SAGARIKA

Sagarika is a submarine-launched ballistic missile with a range of approximately 700 km (435 miles). India successfully tested the 'Sagarika' missile under the K-15 project on February 26, 2008, off the coast of Visakhapatnam from a pontoon simulating the conditions of a submarine. India does not currently have a submarine capable of carrying the Sagarika and it's believed the missile will be integrated with the Advanced Technology Vessel (ATV), a nuclear-powered submarine that India has been working on for more than 20 years.

SHAURYA

Shaurya is a surface-to-surface tactical missile with a range of 600-km and a payload of about one ton for use by the Army. It can carry both conventional as well as nuclear warheads. The solid propellant, two-staged missile is little over 10 metres in length and about half-a-metre in width. It is easily transportable, user-friendly and is stored in a canister for longer shelf life.

LCA TEJAS

The Light Combat Aircraft (LCA) project was sanctioned in 1982 with a budget of Rs 560 crore to develop a state-of-the-art fighter aircraft to replace IAF's MiG-21 fighters. Close to Rs 6,000 crore have since been spent since but the aircraft, rechristened as Tejas, still remains under development. It is currently being tested with a substitute engine (F404-GE-IN20) and makeshift avionics package.

Kaveri Engine

The Kaveri Engine was to power the Tejas aircraft. DRDO's Gas Turbine Research Establishment (GTRE) has already spent Rs 200 crores ($411 million) developing the engine since 1989, but the powerplant is still overweight and does not have the 21,000-22,500lb of thrust (93-100kN) that the IAF requires. In October

2008, Defence Minister A K Antony announced that the country would purchase a total of 140 aircraft to form seven fighter squadrons of the IAF.

Air Chief Marshal FH Major said the first two squadrons of the fighter would be fitted with the American GE 404 engine. "The initial squadrons of the LCA will be with the present engine. All the remaining five squadrons will be with a new engine that we will choose."

In September 2008, it was announced that the Kaveri would not be ready in time for the Tejas, and that an in-production power plant would have to selected. The ADA plans to issue a request for proposal (RFP) for a more powerful engine in the 95-100 kilo Newtons (kN) range.

The contenders are likely to be the Eurojet EJ200 and the General Electric F414. It has been reported that Eurojet is proposing a thrust vectoring version of the EJ200 for the Tejas. The initial 40 Tejas aircraft will be powered by the GE 404. Subsequent aircraft will be powered by the Kaveri replacement.

EADS Participation

In January 2009 ADA sought assistance from EADS to redesign the Tejas undercarriage and help reduce the weight of the fighter which is already 1.5 tons heavier than envisaged. Some of the other problems that ADA needs help are fuel distribution, uneven braking, flight controls, environment controls and testing. Under a $20 million, four year deal EADS will help get final operational clearance for the LCA Tejas.

Project Status

The second and third prototypes of the Tejas aircraft, PV-2 and PV-3, conducted armament trials in November 2007 at air-to-ground firing ranges in Pokhran, Jaisalmer in Rajasthan and Jamnagar in Gujarat. The two aircraft underwent cold weather trials in December 2007 in Leh.

In March and April next year, all three aircraft, possibly joined by LSP 2, will take part in hot weather trials at Nagpur in Maharashtra.

WEAPON TRIALS

In its first live weapon trial, a LCA Tejas prototype (PV3) dropped two 25lb practice bomb on a practice range near Bangalore. LCA has completed 1011 Test Flights successfully: TD1-233, TD2-298, PV1-182, PV2-107, PV3-120, LSP1-33, and LSP2-38.

Features

Powerplant	1xF404-GE-IN20)
Thrust (Dry)	54.9 kN (12,250 lbs)
Thrust (Afterburner)	85 kN (19,000 lbs)
Internal fuel capacity	3,000 Litres
External fuel capacity	5×800 liter tanks or 3×1,200 liter tanks, totalling 4,000/3,600 litres
Radar	ELTA EL/M 2052 AESA Elta claims that the long-range AESA fire control system is capable of detecting 64 targets, and of simultaneously engaging "several" using radar-guided missiles. A prototype of the radar is currently being tested on a Boeing 737 testbed. For ground surveillance, the design is capable of generating high-resolution synthetic aperture radar imagery and of detecting moving surface targets, and can also be used to support maritime surveillance tasks.
Weight (Empty)	5,500 kg (12,100 lb)
Weight (Max Take Off)	14,500 kg (31,967lb)
Wing Loading	221.4 kg/m^2 (45.35 lb/ft^2)

LCA TEJAS MK 2

Aeronautical Development Agency (ADA) has issued a RFP for the supply of 99 engines with thrust in the 95-100 KN to power Tejas LCA Mk 2, which the agency hopes will fly in 2014. The RFP is being sent to just two contenders: General Electric (GE) for the F414 engine and Eurojet for the EJ200 engine. They are required to submit their proposals by October 12.

The RFP indicates an initial procurement of 99 engines with an optional follow-up up for 49 more. The initial batch of engines will be procured directly from the manufacturer with the rest being assembled at HAL. The Tejas will need to be redesigned to accommodate the larger engine probably triggering another weight spiral.

UNMANNED HELICOPTER

HAL is working with Israel to convert its Chetak helicopter into an unmanned air vehicle for an Indian armed forces requirement for eight aircrafts. The order size may eventually grow to 40 aircrafts.

NEW WEAPON SYSTEM PURCHASES

Active Protection System for T-90 Tanks

In April 2008, the Indian Army issued a Request for Proposals (RFP) worth $270 million to retrofit its 987 T-90 MBTs with an Active Protection System (APS). The request was issued to Israel Military Industries (IMI), Rafael, BAE Systems, Raytheon, Rosoboronexport, Saab, and Germany's IBD Deisenroth Engineering A contract would involve some 1500 systems.

Advanced Jet Trainer (AJT)

The IAF cancelled its plans to acquire an additional 40 Hawk 132 AJTs in February 2009 because of bottlenecks in the procurement of spares. Instead, the service has floated a tender to procure a new trainer type to meet its additional requirement. Six companies have been invited to bid as follows:

- UK's BAe Hawk 128
- Italy's Alenia for the M-346
- Korea Aerospace Industries/Lockheed Martin T-50
- Czech Aero Vodochody L-159
- Russian Yakovlev YAK-130
- Russian MiG AT Trainer

INS Chakra (Akula 2 / Nerpa) Nuclear Submarine

India is reported to have leased a Nerpa (Akula II) nuclear submarine from Russia under contract signed in 2004 by Russia's then-Defence Minister Sergei Ivanov during his visit to India. The price of a 10-year lease was fixed at $650 million. The submarine is earmarked to be commissioned as INS Chakra.

Antonov AN-32 Upgrade

In June 2009, India signed a $400 million agreement with Ukraine to upgrade its fleet of 100 AN-32 aircraft to extend its life and improve its avionics. The upgrades will be done in Ukraine to begin with and then at Kanpur. Defence Ministry officials said the upgrades will extend the life of the aircraft by another 10 to 15 years. The Antonov website additionally claims the upgrades will increase maximum takeoff weight and flight range. AN-32, a twin-engine turboprop, was acquired from the erstwhile Soviet Union. They were made by Antonov, based in Ukraine.

Attack Helicopters for IAF

A request for proposals has been issued to seven companies for the supply of 22 attack helicopters for the Indian Air Force. The new helicopters will replace IAF's ageing fleet of Mi-35 helicopters. The contract, estimated to be worth $500 million, stipulates aircraft in the 2.5t-class. The deal is expected to be finalized within two years and supply completed over the next three years.

The qualitative requirements are as follows:

* Twin engine
* High manoeuvrability
* Anti armour capability
* All weather capability
* All terrain capability

The IAF wants these gunships to be highly-agile, have good armour protection and a 20mm calibre turret gun, as also be capable of firing 70mm rockets with a 1.2-km range and missiles with at least 7-km range. The helicopters are likely to be equipped with an electronic warfare and self protection suite developed by EADS and India's Defence Avionics Research Establishment. Competing for the order will be:

* Boeing AH-64D Apache Longbow
* Eurocopter Tiger

* AgustaWestland AW129
* Bell AH-1Z SuperCobra
* Kamov Ka-50
* Mil Mi-28
* HAL's Light Combat Helicopter

HAL's Light Combat Aircraft, which is still underdevelopment, is expected to take to the air sometime in 2009.

BARAK MISSILES

India inked a deal in January 2009 to purchase an additional 300 Barak missiles, at a cost of about $1.6 million each, for the Barak anti-aircraft missile/aircraft systems it has already bought.

The ship-borne Barak is a short range, vertically launched quick reaction missile designed to intercept and destroy approaching anti-ship missiles. The system is built to automatically launch Barak missiles from a Rafael-made vertical launch assembly when the radar detects an anti-ship supersonic missile at a height, and sea-skimming missile at a low altitude. The Barak's fire control system made by Elbit can automatically lock onto two incoming missiles at the same time.

The Barak's defence is capable of intercepting targets not less than 500 metres away. Its Rafael-made warhead makes up a substantial 22 per cent of the missile's almost 100 kg weight, bestowing it with a wider kill envelope. Each Barak system (missile container, radar, computers and installation) costs about $24 million. The only weakness of the existing Barak missile system is its limited range of 10 km / 6 miles.

AWACS

The system comprises of a Israeli Elta EL/M-2075 Phalcon Active Electronically Scanned Array (AESA) radar mounted on a IL-76. The Elta comprises three radar antennas, providing 120 degree coverage, in a non rotating radome mounted on top of the aircraft. It is capable of simultaneously tracking 60 targets, including low flying aircraft and cruise missiles, up to 400 km around. Under a $1.1 billion deal signed in March 2004, Israel was to supply three systems with the first to be delivered in November

2007. Following a delay in the integration of the Phalcon radar to the IL-76, the delivery schedule was revised. The first aircraft was formally inducted into the IAF on May 28, 2009. The second and third ones are expected to be delivered in September 2009 and April 2010. It has been reported that India has placed a follow up order for 3 more Phalcon radar equipped IL-76 from Israel at a cost of $1.5 billion, pushing the total number to be acquired upto 6.

C-130J

India signed a deal with US DOD in 2008 to purchase six Lockheed Martin C-130Js for $596 million. The aircraft, to be used by Indian special forces, are currently under construction with the first plane set for delivery in January 2011.

EL/M-2083 Aerostat Radars

The IAF currently operates two EL/M-2083 Aerostat radars acquired under a $145 million deal with Israel in 2004-2005. The Indian Navy is set to acquire five EL/M-2083 radars from Israel to fill vital gaps in the coastal security and the IAF four more.

The tethered EL/M-2083 phased array radar is mounted on a blimp that can hover up to 13,000 feet. Developed and manufactured by Israel Aerospace Industries' Elta Systems Group (IAI/Elta), the radar is a simpler version of the Green Pine radar, made by IAI and used by the Arrow missile defence system.

Data gathered by the radar is transmitted to a central air defence command & control centre where it is used to maintain an extended comprehensive air situation picture. Each system is reportedly capable of providing 3-D coverage in a radius of 500 km, which is roughly equivalent to the coverage that would be provided by 30 ground based radars. According to IAI, the system is designed to detect hostile approaching aircraft from long ranges, especially those flying at low altitudes. Pakistan is reported to be getting six L-88 Aerostat Systems from the US.

Heron II UAV

Under a $220 million deal IAI sold 50 Heron II UAVs to India. In the past Israel has sold IAI-Malat built Searcher and Searcher II.

BOEING C-17 GLOBEMASTER

Boeing is reported to have briefed the IAF on the aircraft in October 2007. In 2008 India sent Boeing a Request For Information to which the company responded. The aircraft gave impressive flying demonstrations at Aero India 2009 in Bangalore. In June 2009, the IAF projected a requirement for 10 aircraft to the government.

The Globemaster is more capable than IL-76 in terms of payload and range. It can carry 70 tons of cargo with a crew of 3, against the 45 tons carried by an IL-76 with a crew of 6.

Boeing P-8I Poseidon Maritime Multimission Aircraft (MMA)

India inked a $2.1 billion deal with Boeing for the supply of 8 customized P-8A Poseidon Maritime Multimission Aircraft (MMA), designated P-8I, for use by the Indian Navy. It is the biggest ever defence deal between India and the US, surpassing the 2007 $962 million deal for the supply of six C-130J 'Super Hercules' aircraft for Indian special forces.

INS VIKRAMADITYA

Under a contract signed in January 2004, Russia's Rosoboronexport was to deliver the 44,570-tonne aircraft carrier, Admiral Gorshkov, to India in 2008. The $1.5 billion contract earmarked $964 billion for the Gorshkov and $536 million for the complement of 16 MiG-29K fighter aircraft on board.

The Admiral Gorshkov was laid down in 1978 at the Nikolayev South shipyard in Ukraine, launched in 1982, and commissioned with the Soviet Navy in 1987 as Bakue It was renamed after the collapse of the Soviet Union in 1991.

In 1994, following a boiler room explosion, the Admiral Gorshkov sat in dock for a year for repairs. After a brief return to service in 1995, she was finally withdrawn from service in 1996 and put up for sale.

The contract covers complete overhaul of the ship, which had remained docked at the Sevmash shipyard in northern Russia for the past 12 years, fitting a ski jump take off, and equipping it with modern weaponry, including MiG-29K Fulcrum aircraft and Ka-

27 Helix-A and Ka-31 Helix-B anti-submarine helicopters. After modernization, the carrier is expected to be seaworthy for 30 years. Press reports linked the Gorshkov deal to India's desire to lease a nuclear submarine from Russia. The Gorshkov is to be inducted into the Indian Navy as INS Vikramaditya, as a replacement for India's INS Viraat, which is now 50 years old.

The carrier has a 273m flight deck to carry up to 20 MiG-29 fighters and up to eight Kamov Ka-28/Ka-31 helicopters. Eventually, it would carry HAL Tejas trainer aircraft, Dhruv light helicopters, Kinzhal air defence missiles and Kashtan air defence gun or missile systems.

Renegotiations

In early 2008, Russia claimed it underestimated the scale and the cost of the modernization and said it would not be in a position to deliver the ship before 2012 and at an additional cost of $1.2 billion.

India termed the cost escalation exorbitant. After protracted negotiations, in February 2008 India agreed to pay an additional $800 million for the retrofit. In November 2008, shortly after the Russian nuclear submarine Nerpa met with an accident, Russia demanded an additional $2 billion for the ship, instead of $1.2 billion. "Construction of the ship will be completed in 2010 and tests will start in 2011, while in 2012 it will be transferred to the Indian Navy," said the director of Sevmash shipyard, Nikolai Kalistratov.

He, however, stressed that the ship would be handed over to Delhi only if it coughed up the additional money. "The market price of such an aircraft carrier varies between $3 billion and $4 billion. The ongoing maintenance and upgrade makes up 60-70% of the new carrier's cost. This is about $2 billion," says Sergei Novoselov, deputy general director of Sevmash.

RIA Novosti quotes a source in Russian Defence Ministry as saying that if India failed to foot the bill, the carrier could be given to the Russian Navy. "If India does not pay up, we will keep the aircraft carrier," he said. In early December, 2008, the Indian government cleared the MOD to renegotiate the price of the carrier with the Russians.

In January, a four day meeting was held in New Delhi between officials of both the sides. Later, a team of four officials left for Russian on 2009, January 26, to fix the final price. Once the team returns a final round of talks will be held at the Defence Secretary level.

In late May 2009 it was reported by the Russian media that India and Russia have reached an agreement on a revised price for INS Vikramaditya. "The negotiations were successful," Sevmash CEO Nikolai Kalistratov told ITAR-TASS. He did not specify the revised price.

In July 2009, a top Indian official expressed confidence that the renegotiated price would be pegged at $2.2 billion instead of the $2.9 billion demanded by the Russians "We are confident the total cost for Gorshkov's refit will be pegged somewhere around $2.2 billion," said a top Indian official.

Old Price; $964 million

New Price: $2.2 billion

Sea Trials

Under the renegotiated agreement, sea trials for the Vikramaditya will be completed by 2012. In addition to $2.2 billion for refurbishment of the ship, the Russians have asked for $600 million to conduct one year sea trials in the Barents Sea. India is reported to have reduced the cost by holding part of the trials in Indian waters.

Delivery of MiG-29K

Russia delivered the first four MiG-29K aircraft under the contract to India and a batch of Indian Navy pilots started six months type conversion on the aircraft in Russia in October 2008. "Indian pilots are already training to fly the MiG-29Ks from a shore-based facility. They have been doing even 15 sorties in a day during the winter. We expect the first four MiG-29Ks to arrive in India later this year, with the other 12 being delivered by 2010," said Mr. Pogosyan, who was recently appointed by Russian Prime Minister Vladimir Putin as the overall head of nearly all of Russia's defence manufacturing and designing industry, said during Aero India 2009.

He also disclosed that the MiG-29Ks meant for India would be certified by Russian pilots taking off from a Russian carrier. However there were no plans as of now for Indian pilots to train from a Russian carrier. Once the pilots return home they will keep in touch with carrier landing operations using the Shore-based Test Facility (SBTF) that has been constructed with Russian help at the naval airbase INS Hansa in Goa.

HEAVY LIFT HELICOPTERS

India invited bids for 15 heavy-lift helicopters in May 2009. Along with the 22 Attack Helicopters being procured, the bid is valued at $2 billion.

HAWK AJT

India contracted for the delivery of 66 BAE Systems HAWK Mk132s under the AJT (Advanced Jet Trainer) program. Twenty four aircraft were delivered directly from the UK, with 42 being license-manufactured in India. Plans have been formulated to purchase a second batch of 57 Hawks, 40 for the IAF and 17 for the Navy. One BAE supplied Hawk crashed in Bidar on April 29 during a formation take off. HAL was to hand over 10-11 Hawks to the IAF by December 2008 and 15 by March 2009. It has so far handed over just one. The IAF is also facing a shortage of spares.

KAMOV KA-31 SURVEILLANCE HELICOPTERS FOR NAVY

The Cabinet Committee on Security approved a deal worth Rs 950 crore for acquisition of five Russian Kamov-31 early-warning helicopters for the Indian Navy on August 4, 2009. A contract is expected to be finalized within a month.

The helicopters are equipped with the E-801M Oko (Eye) airborne electronic warfare radar mounted beneath the fuselage. A Ka-31 can simultaneously track up to 40 airborne and surface threats, with a 360 degree coverage, from 100 to 200 km away depending on the target's size. Navy already has nine Ka-31 helicopters, inducted in 2003-2004, which operate from its solitary aircraft carrier INS Viraat and three Talwar-class "stealthy" guided-missile frigates as well as shore-based air stations.

LIGHT UTILITY HELICOPTERS

India issued a request for proposals for 197 military Light Utility Helicopters (LUH) in July 2008, to replace its existing fleet of Chetak and Cheetah helicopters. "All of the helicopters will be bought directly from the manufacturers. Of these, 133 are for the army and 64 for the air force. The services will have a joint evaluation and pick the helicopter that best fits their requirements," said a Defence Ministry spokesperson.

The eventual requirement for the helicopters is projected at 384. The additional requirement for 187 LUHs (126 for the Army and 61 for the Air Force) will be met by HAL either through license production of the winning bidder's model or the manufacture of an indigenously developed helicopter. The RFP was sent to AgustaWestland, Bell Helicopter, Eurocopter, Kamov and Sikorsky. The contract, valued at up to $750 million, contains a 30% offset investment provision. Deliveries against the contract are expected to start by the end of 2010 after a one year evaluation. An earlier tender for 197 utility helicopters in favour of Eurocopter AS550 was cancelled in December 2007 following allegations of irregularities in the procurement process.

KRIVAK IV MISSILE FRIGATES (PROJECT 11356)

The Indian Navy currently operates three Russian Krivak-class stealth frigates. They are INS Talwar (2002), Trishul (2003) and Tabar (July 2004). India and Russia signed a $1.6 billion contract for the construction of an additional three Project 11356 Krivak IV-class guided missile frigates for the Indian Navy in July, 2006. The new lot, to be delivered by 2011-12, will be armed each with eight BrahMos supersonic anti-ship cruise missiles instead of the Club-N/3M54TE missiles, which were installed on previous frigates.

Russia and India are negotiating a new contract on the delivery of additional Project 11356 frigates for the Indian Navy, the head of Russia's arms exporter said on Wednesday, February 4, 2009. The Krivak class frigate have a displacement of 4,000 metric tons and a speed of 30 knots, and is capable of accomplishing a wide range of maritime missions, primarily hunting down and destroying large surface ships and submarines.

MEDIUM MULTI ROLE COMBAT AIRCRAFT (MMRCA)

The Government of India issued a Request for Proposal (RFP) for the purchase of 126 Medium Multi Role Combat Aircraft on August 28, 2007. The order is valued at approximately US$10 billion. All the aircraft are required to be of the same type with one squadron (18 aircraft) being formed of aircraft supplied by the vendor, and the rest produced under license in India by HAL.

The RFP lays down that the first aircraft is supplied within 36 months of the contract being signed and the 18th within 48 months. The 19th aircraft, the first to be assembled in India, will come within 54 months. Thereafter, there will be an incremental increase with the last aircraft to be delivered by 2020.

MI-17I FROM RUSSIA

During Russian President Dmitry Medvedev's visit to India in December 2008, the two countries inked a deal for the supply of 80 Mi-17I medium lift helicopters at a cost of $1.2 billion. The two countries had earlier negotiated a price of $650 million, but early in 2008 Russia asked for a revision of the contract price.

IAF will get the helicopters between 2010 and 2014. The deal also envisages a $405 million "offset" obligation by Russia. The new choppers, which have an 18,000 ft operational ceiling, will replace 50 Mi-8s currently in service with the IAF, some of which are over 35 years old, and boost IAF's capability to support high-altitude posts in Siachen and Ladakh sectors.

The helicopter will come with the circuitry and hard points to carry weapons. At Aero India 2009 in Bangalore Rosoboronexport, Viktor Komardin, confirmed that the helicopters would be delivered as scheduled in 2010. "We hope that the first helicopter will be delivered to India at the start of 2010," he said. He previously said the first helicopter would be delivered to India before the end of 2009.

MiG-29 Upgrade

In March 2008 Russia's RAC-MiG signed a $850 million contract with the Indian Defence Ministry to modernize 62 MiG-29 fighters (54 fighters and 8 trainers). The modernization is aimed at extending their service lives by several decades, improving their air-to-ground attack capability and giving them better BVR capability.

The upgrade will allow the IAF to extend the life of the MiG-29 from the present 25 years (and 2,500 hours) to 40 years (3,500 hours). Six aircraft are to be upgraded by RAC-MiG in Russia and the remaining at IAF's 11 Base Repair Depot (BRD) in Nasik using kits supplied by RAC-MiG.

The first upgraded MiG-29 was scheduled to fly into India in March 2010. Fourteen aircraft were scheduled to roll out of 11BRD between April 2010 and March 2011. However MIG officials told The Hindu in end July 2009 that there will be a delay of at least eight months in the arrival of the first upgraded aircraft. The Russians hold the IAF responsible for the delay saying it has not finalized the 'buyer furnished equipment.' IAF was to provide RAC MiG the list of equipment and their actual physical dimensions that they want fitted on the upgraded MiG-29's. Many of these items are to be sourced or integrated by Indian companies.

MULTI-ROLE HELICOPTER (MRH) PROGRAM

India has invited request for information for 16 Multi-Role Helicopter (MRH) to replace its fleet of aging Sea King helicopters. The program is valued at $ 1 billion. The helicopters, to be equipped for in-flight refuelling, are required to have anti-submarine and surface warfare capability as their primary mission. Capable of ferrying 15 soldiers, the 10 ton helicopters are expected to be armed with cruise missiles and lightweight torpedoes for advanced anti-ship and anti-submarine warfare capabilities Also required is a secondary mission capability of anti-ship surveillance and targeting, search and rescue, medical evacuation and logistics missions from naval vessels.

A Request for Proposal is likely to be issued in mid 2009. Amongst those bidding are:

Sikorsky: S-70B Seahawk as a commercial direct sale.

European NH Industries: NH90,

Lockheed: MH-60R as US government Foreign Military Sale

Rosoboronexport: Ka-226T

The final requirement could reach 60 helicopters.

MEDIUM RANGE MARITIME RECONNAISSANCE (MRMR) AIRCRAFT

A request for proposal (RFP) for supply of six Medium Range Maritime reconnaissance (MRMR) aircraft was floated by India's Ministry of Defence in June 2008. The new aircraft, which will replace the aging fleet of 12 Islander aircraft in service, are to be equipped with an Airborne Early Warning system. The Indian Coast Guard has an additional requirement for six MRMRs without an Airborne Early Warning system. The MRMR is required to have a range of 500 nautical miles and an endurance of 6 hours. Bids against the RFP were received from Boeing (P-8, a variant of P-8I), Russian Illyushin (IL-38 variant), French Dassault (Falcon 900MPA), EADS (Case C-295) and Israel's Elta System electronics (Gulfstream 550 mounted EL/W-2085)..

MULTI ROLE TRANSPORT AIRCRAFT (MTA)

The Multirole Medium Aircraft (MTA) project was initiated by Russia's Ilyushin in 1996. It is also referred to as Il-214 Ilyushin and "Indo-Russian Transport Aircraft (IRTA) or MRTA by its Indian partner HAL. Russia and India entered into negotiations for the co-development of the aircraft in 1999. An agreement was signed in June 2001 between Ilyushin, Irkut and HAL.

MULTI ROLE TANKER TRANSPORT (MRTT)

India's MOD issued a request for proposals (RFP) for delivery of six Multi Role Tanker Transport (MRTT) in 2007. The RFP stipulates deliveries of the new tankers to begin three years after contract signature.

EADS subsidiary Airbus has offered the A330-200-in a three-hose configuration and Russia's United Aircraft (UAC) has offered a more advanced version of the Ilyushin Il-78 Midas tanker, 12 of which are in service with the IAF.

In late May 2009, Air Chief Marshal Fali Homi Major told HT in an interview, "We have finished all evaluations and selected the A330 MRTT. The deal will come up for final approval by the Cabinet Committee on Security (CCS) very soon. The Russian platform did not meet certain requirements."

The Air Chief appeared to be piqued at the poor vendor support for equipment procured from Russia. "After the disintegration of the Soviet Union, Russia has changed the whole pattern of doing defence business. Now we are faced with issues concerning spares, vendor support and built-in delays in the structure of their centralised military corporations."

PROJECT 75

The project was approved in 2002 and is aimed at acquiring national competence in submarine building. It envisages building 24 submarines over the next 30 years.

Project 75 Scorpene Submarine Acquisition

Six Scorpene submarines, to be built at Mazagon Dock Ltd (MDL) shipyard under a transfer of technology agreement with France's DCNS, will be delivered to Indian Navy under Project 75. The submarines are being acquired under a 2.4 billion eur contract signed in 2005 and will be commissioned in the Navy from 2013 through 2018. The 1750 ton displacement Scorpene is 67 meters long and equipped with six 21 inch torpedo tubes that can launch 12 torpedoes or anti-ship missiles.

Scorpene submarines incorporate acoustic discretion and combat system performance technologies developed for nuclear-powered classes operated by the French Navy. They feature a modular design and excellent endurance. They are claimed to be one of the few medium-displacement designs suitable for extended ocean patrol duties.

In June 2009 it was reported that the project has fallen 2 years behind schedule and France has hiked up the price of some key components resulting in a per boat price increase from $500 million to $600 million. Speaking in the parliament on July 20, 2009 Indian defence minister AK Antony said: The construction of the first, second and third submarine commenced in December 2006, December 2007 and August 2008 respectively. As per the contract signed with Mazagaon Docks Limited (MDL), the first submarine is scheduled to be delivered in December 2012 and thereafter, one each every year till December 2017. On account of some teething problems, absorption of technology and delays in augmentation of industrial infrastructure and procurement of MDL purchased materials (MPM), slippage in the delivery schedule is expected. The delay in scheduled delivery of submarines is likely to have an impact on the envisaged submarine force levels.

Project 75A

India will follow up its acquisition of six Scorpene submarines under Project 75 with an additional six AIP equipped subs under Project 75A. India floated a request for information under the project in 2008, defining the scope of the order. "They will also have high degree of stealth, land-attack capability and ability to incorporate futuristic technologies. Like the Scorpenes, they will be built in an Indian shipyard, public or private, with special emphasis on full transfer of technology," said a source.

SpyDer System

India is buying 18 low-level quick-reaction missile systems, SpyDer (Surface-to-air Python and Derby), from Israel for around Rs 1,800 crore. Deliveries will start in early 2011 and be completed by August 2012. The Spyder-SR slant-launched SHORAD system and the Spyder-MR vertical-launched medium range system are designed to protect against attack aircraft, combat helicopters, bombers, UAVs and UCAVs and stand off weapons. Both systems use Rafael's Derby, air-to-air active radar, beyond visual range (BVR) missile and Python 5, air-to-air dual band imaging infrared (IIR) missile. The system is unique in that it is able to combine the use of these two missiles in any given mission.

4 India Defence Industry

A nation's military strength is determined by its economic might. Industry provides the military with the wherewithal to fight the nation's wars. Since independence, the policy relating to Strategic Defence Production has been evolving. For too long, India depended on foreign industries for its military hardware. The desire to achieve self-reliance has always been there. Constraints of technology and resources prevented the process from fructifying to the extent desired. The first phase, was characterized by the State led industrialization. Since the era of liberalization, which began in 1991, the role of private sector and also that of competition, both domestic and international is playing a much greater role in the national economy. Naturally, this also meant changes in policy for Defence production. Production of defence equipment has been under the purview of Government right from its inception. The Industrial Policy of the country had kept defence production in the public sector since First Industrial Policy outlined in the Industry Policy Resolution of 1948.

The Industries (Development & Regulation) Act, 1951 gave statutory base to the Industrial

Policy. Under this policy, the Defence Industry, which required heavy investments, strong R&D backing and on which there could be total reliance because of its criticality, remained under Government Control at all times.

The control over defence industry was exercised under the Industries (Development & Regulation) Act, 1951, which made licensing compulsory. As a consequence of the then industrial policy, a large infrastructure for Defence production consisting of 39 Ordnance Factories, 8 Defence PSUs and 50 Research & Development laboratories was created in the country. However, contrary to the common perception, the Private Sector has been playing significant role in the Defence industry sector as sub contractors and ancillary industry.

The private sector mainly has been involved in supply of raw materials, semi-finished products, parts and components to Defence PSUs and Ordnance Factories to a great extent and also to Base Workshops of Army and Base Repair Depots of Air Force and the Dockyards of the Navy. Defence PSUs and Ordnance Factories are outsourcing their requirements from private sector (mainly SMEs) in the range of 20-25%. Out of this outsourcing, about 25% requirement is met through small-scale sector. Several hi-tech equipments have also been successfully produced by the private sector.

In the quest for self-reliance in the crucial sector of defence, the Government has been continuing its efforts to indigenize defence equipment wherever technologically feasible and economically viable. It has been a part of indigenization efforts to locate and develop broad-based indigenous supply source – both in the public sector and in the civil trade for many complicated and intricate equipments.

The economic liberalization in 1991 resulted in the high degree of deregulation and allowed the private industry to progress more rapidly. With the initial difficulties encountered by the Indian Industry today one has witnessed positive impact of this liberalization. There has been tremendous growth in the private sector and today many Indian companies are global players. After considering the capital intensive nature of defence industry sector as also the need to infuse foreign technology and additional capital including FDI, Govt. decided in May, 2001 to open Defence industry for private sector participation up to 100% with FDI permissible up to 26%-both subject to licensing. Now with this policy change all defence related items have been removed from Reserved Category and transferred to the licensed category, as a result of which private sector can manufacture all types of defence equipment after getting a licence.

Consequent to the Government's announcement about the policy change, Department of Industrial Policy & Promotion (DIPP) in consultation with Ministry of Defence, issued detailed guidelines regarding the modalities for consideration of applications for grant of Industrial Licence.

After the announcement of policy changes, there has been a paradigm shift in the role of private sector in the field of indigenisation, i.e., from the role of supplier of raw materials, components, subsystems, they have now become partners in the manufacture of complete advanced equipment/system. The basic objective of allowing private sector participation is to harness available expertise in the private sector towards the total defence efforts and search for self-reliance.

Inbuilt advantages of the private sector are its reservoir of management, scientific and technological skills coupled with its ability to raise resources. The involvement of private sector with its world-class expertise and high technology would not only augment India's indigenous defence production capability but also lead to creation of employment and infrastructure in the country, giving a strong impetus to the economy.

It must be acknowledged that the policy change of May 2001 for allowing private industry to produce any defence item under licence was a logical outcome of liberalization initiated in India in 1991. The private sector industry in India is now just beginning to become significant partner in production and development of Defence items. After opening up of defence production for the private sector, the industry has shown keen interest in this field.

Many large industries have shown definite inclination to invest both in R&D and infrastructure to develop capabilities in defence production to assume the role of system integrators.

Defence Expenditure-Trend

In the union budget 2007 – 2008, Rs. 96,000 crores (US$ 23.42 Bn) has been earmarked for national Defence. Out of this sum, Rs 41,922 crore (US$ 10.22 Bn) is under the capital head and would be spent on "acquisitions", which means buying new weapons, systems and equipment. Of the remaining Rs. 54,078 crores (US$ 13.19 Bn) which is earmarked under the revenue head, a proportion would be spent on "purchases", which relate to buying of spares, general stores, fuel, clothing, food and medical stores etc. According to CII estimates total defence spending over acquisition and purchases for the next five years would be approximately Rs 1,88,000 crores (US$ 45.85 Bn) and has the potential to contribute to the economy.

Defence Procurement Organisation

The Indian Defence Procurement Organisation have the following bodies-

Defence Acquisition Council (DAC)

Defence Acquisition Council was constituted in August, 2001. DAC is the highest body headed by the Raksha Mantri (Defence Minister) which oversees the entire acquisition process for the Armed Forces. It approves the long-term perspective plans and accords the acceptance of necessity in each case of capital acquisition. This process of according the Acceptance of Necessity (AON) involves categorization of items into "Buy", "Buy & Make" and "Make". This process of approving the categorization is the starting point of the acquisition process. Decisions that follow from here are implemented under the overall supervision of DAC by the Defence Procurement Board, Defence Production Board and the Defence R&D Board.

Defence Procurement Board (DPB)

The Defence Procurement Board is the body which oversees all activities related to procurement on capital account in the Department of Defence flowing out of the "Buy" and "Buy & Make" decisions of the DAC. It functions mainly as a coordinating, supervising and monitoring body for the procurement process undertaken by the Acquisition Wing of the Department of Defence for the "Buy" and "Buy & Make" categories. In this process, it has the responsibility of approving the Annual Acquisitions Plans for the three Services. It essentially accords approvals to all major projects which are beyond the powers of the Raksha Mantri and require the approval of CCS or the Minister of Defence and Minister of Finance. Its functioning is governed by the Defence Procurement Procedure (DPP), which was modified in the year 2006. The Defence Secretary is the Chairman of this Board. Its Members include representatives from the various Departments in the Ministry of Defence, the three Wings of the Armed Forces, Chief of Integrated Defence Staff and the Member Secretary is the Financial Advisor in the Acquisition Wing of the Department of Defence.

Defence Production Board

Defence Production Board is a body, which is tasked to oversee indigenous manufacture and it derives its powers from the direction given by the DAC in respect of the categories of "Make" and "Buy & Make". It is expected to closely monitor the "make" projects, advise the DAC on policy issues regarding licensed production, ToT and new development projects. Its membership is very similar to the Defence Procurement Board with the exception that the Chairman OFB and some CMDs of the DPSUs are also included. The Member Secretary of the Defence Production Board is the Director, Planning & Coordination, in the Department of Defence Production.

Defence R&D Board

The Defence R&D Board has been constituted essentially to monitor and report on indigenous R&D proposals flowing out of the "Buy & make" and "Make" decisions of the DAC. It is a body that is expected to work closely with the Defence Production Board and to ensure that the transfer of technology from the laboratory to the factory is done in the most effective manner. The Chairman of this Board is the Scientific Advisor to RM and Secretary, R&D. Its Members are similar to the other two Boards with the exception that certain distinguished scientists have been included. The Member Secretary of this Board is the Chief Coordinator, R&D, in the DRDO Headquarters.

The Acquisition Wing of MOD/DOD

The Acquisition Wing of the Deptt. of Defence is the main secretariat that provides the necessary inputs to the Defence Procurement Board. This wing is headed by an officer of the rank of Special Secretary or Addl. Secretary and is assisted by Financial Adviser (Acquisition) in the rank of Addl. Secretary and three Acquisition Managers, three Technical Managers and three Financial Managers, dealing with Land systems, Air and Maritime & Systems respectively, all in the rank of Joint Secretary. The Acquisition Wing essentially deals with cases, which have been categorized as "Buy" or "Buy & Make". The guiding principles of procurement through the Acquisition Wing are contained in the notified Defence Procurement Procedure 2006.

Current Acquisition Practices

Presently Acquisition in MOD can be clearly demarcated into two separate sections. Firstly, the proposals being dealt with by the Acquisition Wing of the MOD, which is essentially functioning as a Procurement (Buying) Agency of MOD and therefore deals only with "Buy" and "Buy & Make" category of items. The second section is dealing with the "Make" category, which is essentially an acquisition process, akin to the acquisition procedure followed in major weapon producing countries.

DEFENCE PROCUREMENT PROCEDURE (CAPITAL PROCUREMENT)

It has been the constant endeavour of the Ministry of Defence, Government of India to introduce increased levels of transparency and accountability in the Defence Acquisition process. In this effort, the first step was the Defence Procurement Procedure-2005, which has now been reviewed and revised along with the Fast Track Procedure-2001 and the Procedure for Indigenous Warship Building. In addition, most importantly, a procedure for the development of systems based on indigenous research and design, categorized as 'MAKE', has now been formulated. This bridges a critical gap that existed hitherto, and would provide the requisite framework for increased participation of Indian industry in the defence sector.

Some of the important features of Defence Procurement Procedure-2006 include:

- all major decisions pertaining to the procurement process to be taken simultaneously for reducing the timeframe for acquisitions;
- enhanced transparency by placing the generic requirements of the Services on Ministry of Defence website and generating vendor registration through Internet;
- increased transparency in the conduct of field trials;
- 'Integrity Pact' made compulsory for all contracts above Rs. 100 crores;
- an 'Offset' obligation for all contracts above Rs. 300 crores.

The Defence Procurement Procedure-2006 provides comprehensive policy guidelines for all Capital acquisitions for the Armed Forces. The Defence Procurement Procedure 2006 is available at the Ministry of Defence Website www.mod.nic.in.

DEFENCE PROCUREMENT MANUAL

Defence Procurement Manual – 2006 (DPM 2006) is an updated version of DPM – 2005 which was promulgated to provide transparent requests for proposals, uniformity in interpretation of various contracting clauses and issues, clear timeframe for each stage and process of procurement to cut down on delays, general guidelines for assessing reasonability of prices and summary of CVC guidelines and banking instruments. In DPM 2006, further measures taken by the Ministry of Defence in the light of the experiences gained during the last one year have been incorporated to make it a more effective and transparent document. Major highlights of DPM – 2006 are:-

- Incorporation of GFR – 2005 provisions relating to Limited Tender Enquiry, Cash purchases limited, purchase through Propriety Article Certificate, price valuation clause and limits for advance payment.
- Apportioning quantity to L2 and L3 when L1 does not have capacity to supply as per RFP requirement, at L1's rate in line with CVC's guidelines.
- Re-floating tenders, when the Tender Evaluation

Committee shortlists only one vendor, after reformulating Services Qualitative Requirement to ensure competitive bidding.

- Providing level playing field to indigenous vendors vis-à-vis foreign vendors by comparing CIF price with indigenous vendor's offer without Excise Duty, Sales Tax and local levies
- Rate contract for common user items for three years to ensure economy of scale while providing safeguard provisions like fall clause and short closure in the event of fall in prices.
- Reduction in repeat order quantity to 50% with such orders to be placed within six months while certifying no downward trend in prices. The updated DPM is available at MoD website www.mod.nic.in to ensure wide publicity and complete transparency in the defence procurement. With enhanced delegation of financial powers to the Services, the document seeks to strike a fine balance between pragmatism in the procurement process with compliance to basic financial and propriety norms, Services' Quality requirements and timely supply of revenue stores.

DEFENCE OFFSET FACILITATION AGENCY

The Ministry of Defence has established a 'Defence Offset Facilitation Agency' (DOFA) under the DDP as a single window agency to:

- Facilitate implementation of the offsets policy
- Assist in vetting of offset proposals technically
- Assist in monitoring the offset provisions
- Suggest improvements in the policy and procedures
- Interact with Headquarters Integrated Defence Staff and Service Headquarters
- Advise, in consultation with the Headquarters Integrated Defence Staff, Services and Defence Research and Development Organisation, areas in which offsets will be preferred
- Promote exports of defence products and services

- Provide advisory clarifications on the policy and procedures (in consultation with the Acquisition Wing wherever necessary).

The DOFA will assist potential vendors in interfacing with the Indian defence industry for identifying potential offset products/ projects as well as provide requisite data and information for this purpose. The agency will function under the supervision of a designated Joint Secretary of the Dept of Defence Production, and have representatives from the Service HQrs, HQ IDS, DRDO, DPSUs, and OFB as well as from CII, FICCI and ASSOCHAM and other agencies as deemed necessary. DOFA may set up committees and sub groups as considered necessary or based on the inputs received from DRDO.

DOFA may also engage, following a fair, rational and transparent process, reputed independent professional expert bodies, as suggested by DRDO, to assist in its functions and commission studies by such bodies on offset policies, their implementation, utility and impact.

Acceptance of Necessity Stage

While being considered by the Services Capital Acquisition Plan Categorization Higher Committee (SCAPCHC), Capital Acquisition Projects of the 'Buy' or 'Buy and Make with TOT' categories whose indicative cost is Rs 300 crore or more, will be recommended for application of the standard 30% offset clause. However, based on detailed examination of the capability of the defence industry to absorb the offset value available and its strategic importance, the SCAPCHC may recommend increased offset percentages in selected cases. The DOFA may also advise on areas where offsets will be preferred. The DAC will consider the recommendations and take the final decision. This offset condition will form a part of the RFP and, subsequently, of the contract.

RAKSHA UDYOG RATNAS (RURS)

As mentioned elsewhere, for too long, India depended on foreign industries for its military hardware. The desire to achieve self-reliance has always been there. Constraints of technology and resources prevented the process from fructifying to the extent desired. Even so, much has been achieved in creating a large infrastructure for defence production in the Government sector. The 40 Ordnance Factories, eight Defence PSUs and over 40 Defence R&D laboratories are testimony to this effort.

In a rapidly expanding military technology environment, these existing R&D and manufacturing facilities are proving inadequate to meet the total requirements. Imports continue to dominate Indian defence procurements, in value as well as volumes. The private industry, which could not participate in defence production earlier, has grown in size and reach. It has acquired modern manufacturing capabilities and the resources to match many traditional defence production agencies. There has been a general consensus that the private sector merits a rightful role in national Defence.

In the last decade – disruption in military imports from traditional sources such as Soviet Union, demonstration of advance technologies in Iraq and Afghanistan, concerted efforts by several developed countries to impose restrictions on technology / weapon transfers, have only highlighted the need for self-reliance. The only way forward is to involve the Industry in defence technologies and manufacture in a manner very different from what we are used to so far. There are positive signs of a vibrant economy. It is now up to the nation to harness these energies.

There are levels for participation of private sector in Defence Production. These are at the level of major systems, at the level of assemblies and at the level of requirement of spare parts and components. To ensure effective participation by the Industry, both public and private, at various points of interaction and subsequent long-term association in product development and productionisation, can be only done through those firms of proven excellence and which are capable of contributing, depending on their technical, managerial and financial strength. The Dr. Vijay Kelkar Committee has termed these firms as "Raksha Udyog Ratna" (RUR. These companies (RURs) are essentially platform producers and system integrators and the ones, which earlier described as "first level" of Defence Industry. The most pertinent question is therefore the process for identification of these RURs/ Champions. The committee recommended that this could be a form of 'Accreditation' and that once a private firm is accredited and put into the category of 'RUR'/ 'Champion', it should be treated at par with the Defence Public Sector Undertakings. It is necessary that the identification of Raksha Udyog Ratna is done on an objective criterion and on a transparent basis.

In conformity with the recommendations of the Dr. Vijay Kelkar Committee, Ministry of Defence, had earlier announced formation of Raksha Udyog Ratnas (RURs) for India Defence Industry. Dr. Kelkar Committee was constituted in 2004 to examine and recommend changes in the acquisition process in order to synergize the efforts of various stakeholders, improving the prospects of indigenous production and utilizing the resources available both in the Public and Private Sector with the objective to strengthen self-reliance in Defence preparedness. For identification of RURs, the Ministry of Defence had constituted a Selection Committee under the Chairmanship of Shri Prabir Sengupta, IAS, Former Director, Indian Institute of Foreign Trade and Secretary, Defence Production and Commerce.

The RURs, which have been identified, based on their managerial and technical capabilities, would be the key drivers towards raising indigenous defence technological base and world-class manufacturing capabilities in India.

5 DRDO: Providing the Technological Edge to the Indian Defence

Defence Research & Development Organisation (DRDO) works under Department of Defence Research and Development of Ministry of Defence. DRDO dedicatedly working towards enhancing self-reliance in Defence Systems and undertakes design & development leading to production of world class weapon systems and equipment in accordance with the expressed needs and the qualitative requirements laid down by the three services. DRDO is working in various areas of military technology which include aeronautics, armaments, combat vehicles, electronics, instrumentation engineering systems, missiles, materials, naval systems, advanced computing, simulation and life. DRDO was formed in 1958 from the amalgamation of the then already functioning Technical Development Establishment (TDEs) of the Indian Army and the Directorate of Technical Development & Production (DTDP) with the Defence Science Organization (DSO).

DRDO was then a small organization with 10. Today, DRDO is a network of more than 50 laboratories which are deeply engaged in developing defence technologies covering various disciplines, like aeronautics, armaments, electronics, combat vehicles, engineering systems, instrumentation, missiles, advanced computing and simulation, special materials, naval systems, life sciences, training, information systems and agriculture. Presently, the Organization is backed by over 5000 scientists and about 25,000 other scientific, technical and supporting personnel. Several major projects for the development of missiles, armaments, light combat aircrafts, radars, electronic warfare systems etc are on hand and significant achievements have already been made in several such technologies establishments or laboratories. Over the years, it has grown multi-directionally in terms of the variety of subject disciplines, number of laboratories, achievements and stature. Some major contributions to strengthen the IAF are: (i) The DRDO is responsible for the ongoing Light Combat Aircraft program. As 5th generation jet fighter, the LCA is intended to provide the Indian Air Force with a modern, Fly by wire, multi-role fighter, as well as develop aviation industry in India. (ii) The DRDO provided key avionics for the Sukhoi Su-30MKI program under the "Vetrivel" program. (iii) The DRDO is part of the Indian Air Force's upgrade programs for its MiG-27 and Sepecat Jaguar combat aircraft upgrades, along with the manufacturer Hindustan Aeronautics Limited. (iv) The DRDO has also developed two unmanned aerial vehicles-the Nishant tactical UAV and the Lakshya Pilotless Target Aircraft (PTA).

In the area of missile systems, the DRDO has made some amazing contributions to the Indian Defence Forces by the Integrated Guided Missile Development Program (IGMDP). The IGMDP was launched by the Indian Government to develop a local missile design and development ability, and manufacture a range of missile systems for the three defence services. The IGMDP has seen significant success in its two most important constituents-the Agni missile and the Prithvi missile systems, while two other programs, the Akash SAM and the anti-tank Nag Missile are nearly completion.

The Trishul missile, a program to develop a tri-service short range SAM has faced persistent problems throughout its development, and is likely to be shut down unless the Indian Air Force places orders for the system.

DRDO, BEL and the Indian Navy have developed and productionized a range of Sonars and related systems for the Navy's frontline combat ships. These include the APSOH (Advanced Panoramic Sonar Hull mounted), HUMVAD (Hull Mounted Variable Depth sonar) and the HUMSA (follow on to the APSOH series; the acronym HUMSA stands for Hull Mounted Sonar Array) sonars, Nagan Towed Array Sonar, Panchendriya Submarine sonar and fire control system, sonobuoy Tadpole and its airborne signal processor Simhika. Other sonars such as the airborne sonar Mihir, are in trials, whilst work is proceeding apace on "New Generation" sonars.

Sonars may be considered one of DRDO's most successful achievements, with the work begun under the leadership of a young Naval officer decades back. Today, the Indian Navy's most powerful ships rely on Indian made sonars. The standard fit for a frontline Naval ship would include the HUMSA-NG (New Generation) hull mounted sonar, a HUMVAD variable depth sonar and the Nagan towed array sonar. The Mihir, is a dunking sonar meant for use by the Naval ALH, working in conjunction with its Tadpole sonobuoy. The Panchendriya is in production for the Kilo class submarine upgrades. Some ships, such as the INS Beas field a mix of local (HUMSA and HUMVAD) and imported sonars (towed array), till the local towed array was developed. Research and Development in Other areas: DRDO has worked extensively high speed computing given its ramifications for most of its defence projects.

These include supercomputers for computational flow dynamics, to dedicated microprocessor designs manufactured in India for flight controllers and the like, to high speed computing boards built around Commercial Off The Shelf (COTS) components, similar to the latest trends in the defence industry. Starting with a modest design aim, the DRDO has steadily increased its radar development footprint across a range of systems. The result has been substantial progress in India's ability to design and manufacture high power radar systems of its own design and with locally manufactured components and systems. The path began with the development of short range 2D systems (Indra-1) and has now extended to high power 3D systems intended for strategic purposes (LRTR). Several other projects span the gamut of radar applications, from airborne surveillance (AEW & C) to firecontrol radars (land based, and airborne). The key aim, as far as DRDO is concerned, is self reliance, both in terms of design as well as manufacture. In this respect, the DRDO has built up a network of suppliers from across India who assist it on these projects.

DEFENCE RESEARCH AND DEVELOPMENT ORGANISATION (DRDO)

The Department of Defence Research and Development formulates and executes programmes of scientific research, design and development in the fields of relevance to national security leading to the induction of new weapons, platforms and other equipments required by the Armed Forces. It also functions as the nodal agency for the execution of major development programmes of relevance to Defence through integration of research, development, testing and production facilities with the national scientific institutions, public sector undertakings and other agencies. It functions under the control of Scientific Advisor to Raksha Mantri who is also Secretary, Defence Research and Development. Research and development activities at DRDO cover important demarcated disciplines like aeronautics, rockets and missiles, electronics and instrumentation, combat vehicles, engineering, naval systems, armament technology including explosives research, terrain research, advanced computing, artificial intelligence, robotics, works study, systems analysis and life sciences including high-altitude agriculture, physiology, food technology and nuclear medicine.

In addition to undertaking research and development activities, DRDO also assists the Services by rendering technical advice regarding formulation of requirements, evaluation of systems to be acquired, fire and explosive safety and mathematical and statistical analysis of operational problems.

DRDO has made significant achievements in its efforts to meet the requirements of the three Services. The notable developmental successes include flight simulators for aircrafts, 68mm reusable rocket pod, brake parachute for fighter aircrafts, mini remotely piloted vehicle, light field gun, new family of light weight small arms systems, charge line mine clearing vehicle for safe passage of vehicles in battlefield and illuminating ammunitions for enhancing night fighting capabilities.

Cluster weapon systems for fighter aircraft, naval mines, next generation bombs for high speed aircraft and low-level hombing, mountain gun, 130 mm SP gun, low-level tracking radar Indra-I and II for Army and Air Force, light field artillery radar, battlefield surveillance radar, secondary surveillance radar have also been achieved. Bridge layer-tank Kartik, military bridging systems capable of withstanding tank load, advanced ship sonar systems, advanced sonobuoys, naval decoys, naval simulators, torpedo launchers, advanced materials and composites for military applications and parallel processing computer for aerodynamic computations have also been developed.

Several high-technology projects are in various stages of design and development.

The main battle tank Arjun, incorporating state-of-art tank technologies with superior fire power, high mobility and excellent protection has been developed. A limited number of tanks are being produced as pre-production series which are in final stages of evaluation by the Army. A light combat aircraft which would be lighter than any other combat aircraft and would incorporate modern design concepts and several state-of-the art technologies, is under full scale engineering development.

The Integrated Guided Missile Development program is in progress. The program comprises of five missile systems: Prithvi-surface-to-surface tactical battlefield missile, Akash medium range surface-to-air-missile systems, Trishul-a short range surface-to-air missile and Nag-third generation anti-tank missile, and Agni, an intermediate range ballistic missile.

DRDO offers specialised training at its two premier training institutions called Institute of Armament Technology, Pune and Defence Institute of Work Study, Mussoorie. The courses at these institutions have been evolved primarily to meet the needs of DRDO, Department of Defence Production and Supplies and the three Services.

Establishments/Labs Of DRDO

The Department operates through a network of around 47 laboratories and establishments located nationwide and manned by over 34,000 personnel, including about 16,000 scientific technical persons

1. AERIAL DELIVERY RESEARCH AND DEVELOPMENT ESTT. (AIRDEL)
   Station Road, Post Box No.51, Agra Cantt. 28,.1 001
2. VEHICLE RESEARCH &;DEVELOPMENT ESTABLISHMENT (VAHANVIKAS)
   Ahmednagar 414 001
3. DEFENCE AGRICULTURAL. RESEARCH LABORATORY
   Almora 263 601
4. COMBAT VEHICLES RESEARCH AND DEVELOPMENT ESTT. (VEHICLEDEV)
   Avadi, Madras 600 054
5. PROOF AND EXPERIMENTAL ESTT. (PROOF)
   PO Chandipore, Balasore 756 025
6. AERONAUTICAL DEVELOPMENT ESTT. (LABAIR)
   Suranjan Dass Road, Jiwan Bima Nagar PO, Bangalore 560 075
7. GAS TURBINE RESEARCH ESTT. (TURBINE)
   Suranjan Das Road, CV Raman Nagar PO, Bangalore 560 093
8. ELECTRONICS &;RADAR DEVELOPMENT ESTT. (DEVELECTRONICS)
   DRDO Complex, Byrasandra Village, Jivan Bima Nagar, Bangalore 560 075
9. DEFENCE BIO-ENGINEERING AND ELECTRO-MEDICAL LABORATORY (DEBEL)
   High Grounds, Bangalore 560 001
10. CENTRE FOR AERONAUTICAL SYSTEM STUDIES AND ANALYSIS (CASSA)
    Suranjan Das Road, Jivan Bima Nagar, Bangalore 560 075

11. MICROWAVE TUBE R &;D CENTRE (MTRDC)
    Ministry of Defence, BEL Complex, PO Jalahaiii, Bangalore 560 013
12. CENTRE FOR ARTIFICIAL INTELLIGENCE
    LRDE Campus, Jivan Bima Nagar, Bangalore 560 075
13. NAVAL CHEMICAL &;METALLURICAL LABORATORY (NAVYLAB)
    Naval Dockyard, Bombay 400 023
14. DEFENCE RESEARCH AND DEVELOPMENT UNIT (DEFUNIT)
    S-212, Commissariat Road, Hastings, Calcutta 700 022
15. TERMINAL BALLISTICS RESEARCH LABORATORY (BALLISTICS)
    Sector 30, Cliandigarh
16. NAVAL PHYSICAL &;OCEANOGRAPHIC LABORATORY (INPHYLAB)
    Naval Base, Cochin 682 004
17. DEFENCE SCIENCE CENTRE (DEFSCCENT)
    Metcalfe House, Delhi 110 054
18. SOLIDSTATE PHYSICS LABORATORY (SOLIDSTATE)
    Lucknow Road, Delhi 110 007
19. INSTITUTE OF NUCLEAR MEDICINE AND ALLIED SCIENCE (DEFSCIENCE)
    Lucknow Road, Delhi 110 007 NMAS
20. DEFENCE INSTITUTE OF PHYSIOLOGY AND ALLIED SCIENCES (DEFSCIENCE/DIPAS)
    Delhi Cantt. I 10 010
21. INSTITUTE OF SYSTEMS STUDIES &;ANALYSIS
    Metcalfe House, Delhi 110 054
22. DEFENCE INSTITUTE OF FIRE RESEARCH (FIRERESCH)
    Probyn Road, Delhi 110 007
23. DEFENCE SCIENTIFIC INFORMATION AND DOCUMENTATIONS CENTRE (DESIDOC)
    Metcalfe House, Delhi 110 054

24. DEFENCE TERRAIN RESEARCH LABORATORY (DEFSCIENCE/DTRL)
    Metcalfe House, Delhi 110 054
25. SCIENTIFIC ANALYSIS GROUP (DEFSCIENCE/SAG)
    Metcalfe House, Delhi 110 054
26. DEFENCE INSTITUTE OF PSYCHOLOGICAL RESEARCH (DEF SCIENCE/DIPR)
    West Block No. 8, Wing No. 1, R.K. Puram, New Delhi 110 066
27. INSTRUMENTS RESEARCH AND DEVELOPMENT ESTABLISHMENT (IRDE)
    Rajpur Road, Dehradun 248 008
28. DEFENCE ELECTRONICS APPLICATION LAB (RAKESHELECTRONIK)
    Rajpur Road, Dehradun 248 008
29. DEFENCE RESEARCH &;DEVELOPMENT ESTT. (DEFRES)
    Tansen Road, Gwalior 474 002
30. DEFENCE RESEARCH &;DEVELOPMENT LAB (MISLAB)
    Kanchanbagh PO, Hyderabad 500 258
31. DEFENCE METALLURGICAL RESEARCH LAB (DEFMETLAB)
    Kanchanbagh PO DMRL, Hyderabad 500 258
32. DEFENCE ELECTRONICS RESEARCH LAB (DEFELECTRONICS)
    Chandrayanguntta Lines, Hyderabad 500 005
33. DEFENCE LABORABTORY (DEFLAB)
    Ramada Palace, Jodhpur 342 001
34. DEFENCE MATERIALS AND STORES RESEARCH AND DEVELOPMENT ESTT. (LABDEV)
    DMSRDE Post Office, G.T. Road, Kanpur 208 013
35. DEFENCE INSTITUTE OF WORK STUDY (WORKSTUDY)
    Landour Cantt., Mussoorie 240 179

36. DEFENCE FOOD RESEARCH LAB (RAKSHAKHADYA)
    Jyotinagar, Mysore 570 011
37. ARMAMENT RESEARCH &;DEVELOPMENT ESTABLISHMENT (AYODH &;ARMAMENTS)
    Armament Post Pashan, Pune 411 021
38. EXPLOSIVE RESEARCH AND DEVELOPMENT LABORATORY (MEXDEV PASHAN)
    Pashan Pune 411 021
39. RESEARCH AND DEVELOPMENT ESTT. {ENGRS} (ENGIVIKAS)
    Pioneer Lines, Dighi, Pune 411 021
40. INSTITUTE OF ARMAMENT TECHNOLOGY (ARMINST {E})
    Simhagad Road, Girinagar, Pune 411 025
41. DEFENCE RESEARCH LABORATORY (TEZLAB)
    Post Bag No. 2, Tezpur, Assam 784 001
42. NAVAL SCIENCE &;TECHNOLOGICAL LABORATORY (ENESTIEL)
    Vigyan Nagar, Visakhapatnam 530 006
43. SNOW AVALANCHE STUDY ESTT (MANALIEX CHANGE)
    C/o 56 APO
44. FIELD RESEARCH LABORATORY
    C/o 56 APO
45. RANGE CENTRE &;INTERIM TEST RANGE
    Balasore
46. ADVANCE SYSTEMS INTEGRATION EVALUATION ORGANISATION (ASIEO)
    Bangalore
47. DRDO COMPUTER CENTRE
    Metcalfe House, Delhi 110 054

HOW DRDO FAILED INDIA'S MILITARY

The difference between India's failure against Pakistan's success in their respective missile programmes is based on the purist mindset of the Defence Research and Development Organisation to develop indigenously all complex weapon platforms and Islamabad's intelligent alliance with China and the approach to achieve its goals 'by any means, fair or foul'! While Pakistan was pragmatic in its approach, India was merely pompous. Therefore, it should not come as a surprise that India's Integrated Guided Missile Development Programme has been finally shelved. This marks an unceremonious end of an ambitious technological misadventure by the DRDO — country's premier defence R&D agency.

For nearly two-and-a-half decades, it doled out mere promises to the country's armed forces — delaying their much-needed modernisation plans. The armed forces were forced to resort to off-the-shelf 'panic buying' whenever they realised that the strategic balance was tilting in favour of their adversaries. Besides missiles, there are other equipments such as the Main Battle Tank Arjun, Unmanned Aerial Vehicle Nishant, Light Combat Aircraft Tejas, INSAS rifles which have been thrust on the end users despite unsatisfactory performances during trials. In the bargain, the military lost 25 precious years and the taxpayers' nearly Rs 2,000 crore by keeping the IGMDP programme under wraps to hide its inefficiency from the nation. Even when the IGMDP was embarked upon, many pointed out that to successfully complete such a high-end technological programme, foreign collaboration would be needed.

But the DRDO's obduracy prevailed and the programme dragged for so many years. It is wasteful to try and 'reinvent the wheel', but that is precisely what the DRDO backed by New Delhi did for all these years — trying to develop every system and sub-system indigenously and ending up developing practically nothing of substance.

The IGMPD started in 1983 after India failed to reverse engineer a Russian missile in the seventies, with A P J Abdul Kalam as the head. However, 25 years later the DRDO missiles remain off target. The army cannot rely on Prithvi, a battlefield support missile, unless technological issues affecting its launch readiness are resolved. Trishul, the quick reaction anti-aircraft missile, turned out to be a dud and is now being resurrected with the induction of foreign technology as a stopgap arrangement for the air force, till the Spyder missile systems from Israel finally arrives. Meanwhile this delay for the navy meant importing Israel's Barak missile. While Akash, the medium range surface to air missile with 27-km range, had its first user trial in end 2007, Nag, the anti-tank missile with 4-7 km range, is yet to begin user trials.

Meanwhile, the Air Force with depleting fleet of obsolete Russian SA-3 Pechora and OSA-AK missile systems, is in a quandary as to how to plug holes in its air defence system in the western sector as the DRDO has failed to deliver.

AGNI –I and AGNI-II with a range of 700 km and 2,500 km respectively, have been tested five times, which is inadequate to generate confidence in a nuclear capable missile. The end users of these ballistic missiles are army and the air force with 8 and 24 missiles in their arsenals but lack confidence in the quality of the product even as AGNI-IV is readied for trial in mid-2008 with a range of 6,000 km.

The tacit admission of the DRDO's inability must not be limited to the missile programme alone; a review of all projects under its aegis is needed for a reality check and course correction. The DRDO fault-line primarily is a result of lack of accountability, focus, and failure to develop scientific disposition. The director general of DRDO wears three hats. He is also, Secretary Defence R&D and scientific advisor to the Defence Minister. These three inter-linked hats on one individual destroy the basic principal of accountability. Therefore, he is not answerable to anyone.

DRDO scuttled a contract that was on the verge of being signed by India in 1997 for the import of a Weapon Locating Radar as the latter promised to produce it indigenously within two years. Due to this negligence, the Indian Army could not neutralise Pakistan's artillery fire effectively in the Kargil conflict and suffered heavy causalities. Of course, the DRDO to date is not in a position to produce WLR and ultimately India bought it from the previously selected producer in 2003. In my view, DRDO should be held directly responsible for these unwarranted war causalities.

The DRDO actually produces in its Tezpur laboratory orchids and mushrooms, identifies the sharpest chili in the world with pride, while its lab in Pithoragarh develops hybrid varieties of cucumber, tomato and capsicum. It spends merrily from the defence budget on developing new strains of Angora rabbits and 'Namkeen Herbal Tea'! DRDO by indulging in such irrelevant activities lost its focus and sight of its primary responsibility.

Instead of building a scientific temper, DRDO from its inception indulged in empire building, spending a major part of its budget on world-class auditoriums, convention centres, conference halls, and hostels, while neglecting research work.

To remove DRDO's fault-line, New Delhi should rapidly transform India into a low cost, high end R&D centre of the world without neglecting its manufacturing sector. Fairly ideal demographic conditions exist along with favourable geo-political factors whereby international actors are willing to invest, as well as, set up shop in India. To maintain their technological lead, the West finds India as a logical destination for their defence industries, both as a potential market and also a base to develop low cost high-end research projects.

On the other hand, we need to leapfrog as well as piggyback technologically, as reinventing the wheel is not necessarily an answer to the yawning technological gap that exists between the western countries and India. Therefore, there are synergies that should be exploited. Enormous mutual benefits can occur to both, if New Delhi can develop itself as a world-class R&D centre and a global hub for manufacturing sensitive military equipment.

Due to the rapid march of technologies and huge costs involved in R&D, no single player is in a position to deliver next generation weapon systems. Whether it is Boeing, Lockheed Martin, DCN, Airbus, or HDW — all of them sub-contract different assemblies and subsystems globally to the most competitive and competent companies. The other interesting trend is the formation of trans-national consortiums of nations and companies to manufacture superior platforms like the Euro fighter or the Euro copter. The game, thus, is global as it is not feasible for a single player to manufacture or develop each item.

In the development Sukhoi SU-30 MKI, the major player was the Russian corporation IRKUT but without the help of France and Israel, the fighter aircraft could not have developed the decisive technological edge that it displays. Therefore, India needs to shed its inhibitions, diversify, and form international industrial alliances to leapfrog technological gaps, boost export revenues from its military industrial complex, and leverage this strength as a strategic asset in Asia.

In any case, defence technologies become obsolete by the time a country can reinvent the wheel. Therefore, radical shifting of strategic gears to a more advantageous position by opening up the field to private sector will stimulate self-sufficiency. Companies like Tatas or L&T can enter into joint ventures and where necessary import CEO's and employ foreign scientists to kick start complex projects.

In fact, to improve performance of the Public Sector Units there should be competitors making fighter aircraft, missiles, and warships in the corporate world. Such farsighted policy shifts will improve India's self–sufficiency in the shortest possible time frame. This in turn, will increase the stakes of multi-nationals in India's well being and marginalise sanction regimes.

The Indian Foreign Office took 58 years to grudgingly acknowledge the criticality of military diplomacy in international affairs. If DRDO can appreciate that a technologically advanced and vibrant defence industry is equally critical for India's security and its global aspirations, we will not replicate this mistake. In other words, it should be made to realise that it solely exists to support the armed forces and not vice versa. Therefore, New Delhi should force ruthless accountability, create focus and development of scientific temperament within DRDO and ensure fruitful collaboration with the Indian and international private sector, instead of permitting them to fritter away the defence budget on irrelevant and peripheral activities.

INDIA'S DRDO LOOKING FOR LOCAL VENDORS TO SOURCE COMPONENTS FOR CRITICAL PROJECTS

In a bid to cut costs and the long gestation periods for many of India's military projects, the Defence Research and Development Organisation (DRDO) has, for the first time, decided to use components sourced from commercial suppliers in large, critical projects, three people familiar with the development said. The research agency typically relies on parts designed and developed by its own teams to ensure that these can stand rugged use in military equipment, such as tanks, and are reliable in harsh conditions ranging from the desert of Rajasthan to the Himalayas.

Greater efficiency: Rustom, the unmanned aerial vehicle being built by the Defence Research and Development Organisation, uses components sourced from commercial suppliers in the flight control systems and avionics.

The radars of the airborne early warning and controls system, or Aewacs, a surveillance plane to monitor Indian skies, will be the first large defence system to be built mainly using so-called commercial off-the-shelf (COTS) components and microprocessors, an official with the Centre for Military Airworthiness and Certification, or Cemilac, said. Cemilac is the certifying authority for all military aircraft and its systems. The official didn't want to be identified.

The Aewacs radars, being built by Centre for Airborne Systems, are to be integrated on Embraer aircraft, manufactured by Embraer SA of Brazil, by 2011.

DRDO is also using such commercial components in the flight control systems and avionics for Rustom, the medium-altitude long endurance unmanned aerial vehicle being built indigenously.

Normally, the defence research agency designs systems from critical components it builds on its own to ensure what is known in defence parlance as the military-grade standard, but the designing and development of some components could take as much as five years.

DRDO also buys military-grade parts from foreign suppliers. Military-grade standard requires the components to be rugged, durable and be able to withstand extreme vibration, heat and temperature. DRDO has now found this ruggedness in locally made components as well, with the domestic electronics industry designing products to withstand the country's extreme and varied climate and infrastructure conditions. "You see a television installed in a bus that runs even in rural towns. How much more rugged can you get," said Prahlada, chief controller of research and development at DRDO. "Radars are the first systems where we are using commercial components." Use of off-the-shelf components could lower the price of building a system by as much as half and reduce time needed for its development by up to two years, he added. Prahlada, who goes by one name, however, could not put a number to the savings expected.

India began experimenting with commercially available components for its military equipment after the 1998 nuclear tests, when the US imposed sanctions, prohibiting supply of components that could be used for both commercial and defence purposes.

Projects such as India's first indigenous light combat aircraft Tejas and passenger plane Saras were hit due to the ban. Since then, though, with India's economy on a rise, the country has become a huge market for component suppliers, who bring in advanced chips and systems around the same time they are introduced in developed markets. "It will be more difficult to apply trade barriers (now). Because of the COTS, there are more players from whom you can source," said P.S. Krishnan, director of the Aeronautical Development Agency, the DRDO unit building unmanned aerial vehicles. He did not name the commercial suppliers DRDO is sourcing components from.

Defence experts, however, warn that buying such components should be done judiciously, factoring not just the cost but also lifetime support as military equipment is normally used for at least two decades. "The ruggedization for use in military has not been waived. You can't have all components off the shelf; you need precautions and those you buy should be put to tests for military grade," said J.K. Sharma, former chief executive (airworthiness) of Cemilac. "As the confidence grows, we will see more large systems that use them."

INDIAN ARMY TO INDUCT NAG MISSILES SOON: DRDO

With the third generation anti-tank Nag missile proving its lethality in the final user trials being conducted in the deserts of Rajasthan, a top missile scientist of the Defence Research and Development Organisation (DRDO) expressed optimism about its induction into the Army soon. The Army, which conducted winter trials of the missile's land version in December 2008, began the summer trials earlier this week. While four flight tests were completed by Thursday, three more were slated for Friday night. Talking to reporters on Friday, V. K. Saraswat, Chief Controller, R&D (missiles and strategic systems), DRDO, described the Nag as a modern and "very potent weapon system with high reliability in performance and damage." With the all-weather system proving its capability in the latest round of trials, he hoped its production and induction would begin by the year-end.

Successful Trials

The hit-to-kill missile, designed to take a unique trajectory resembling that of a moving cobra, smashed stationary targets (derelict tanks) in the four trials. While two targets were of medium range, one each was of shorter and longer range (four km). Using an Imaging Infra-red (IIR) seeker, the missile, with fire-and-forget capability, acquired the targets and caused extensive damage to them.

Description

Nag is an all weather, top attack missile with a range of 4 to 7 km. The missile uses an 8 kg tandem HEAT warhead capable of defeating modern armour including ERA (Explosive Reactive Armour) and composite armour. Nag uses Imaging Infra-Red (IIR) guidance with day and night capability. Mode of launch for the IIR seeker is LOBL (Lock On Before Launch). The missile has a complete fiberglass structure and weighs around 42 kg.

INDIA'S DRDO RETHINKING THE WAY IT DOES BUSINESS

We looked at the various organizational pathologies that were creating repeated failures for Indian defence procurement efforts, to the point that billions of dollars were being appropriated and not spent. We have also followed projects like India's Kaveri jet engine, its missile programs, the Arjun tank, etc. which have consumed a great deal of time (over 20 years in many cases) and many crores of rupees without fielding operational weapons systems.

The changes required are wide-ranging and complex – but in a democracy, these things eventually come home to roost and reform efforts begin. There have been a few signals lately that these changes may begin at last. Where are they going? Will they succeed?

With China taking significant steps to improve its defence industry, while funding that industry at levels far higher than a democracy like India can, something clearly has to be done. Opening India up to foreign defence manufacturers, which has been the *de facto* result of many of DRDO's project failures, can be an effective solution – viz. the PJ-10 BrahMos missile – but it is not a panacea.

Scientific Adviser to Defence Minister Shri M. Natarajan's concerns are: the "triple trap" of relying on foreign defence procurement are well stated:

1. What is developed abroad may not suit local requirements
2. What is suitable may be denied
3. What is not denied could be unaffordable

Which means India's defence industry must retain some local capabilities, and work to increase them. To that end, he is correct to note that business as usual won't suffice. India Defence now reports that The Government is looking at "substantial changes" in the existing model of developing advanced defence products. At present, India's DRDO has to do a lot of the sub-component development work that would be done by Tier 2 and Tier 3 suppliers in America or France.

Unsurprisingly, Defence & Research Development Organisation (DRDO) chief M. Natarajan said recently that they have:

"...proposed greater involvement of stakeholders by sharing project expenditure and management. DRDO is not a manufacturer. Its primary job is to create capacity. The industry is also realising that this would be possible if there is some mechanism of assured minimum quantity and there is some partnership with foreign entities."

The Indian MoD release is more specific. Natarajan suggested a pattern of funding with DRDO contributing 70%, Industry 20%, and the user Services (Army, Navy, Air Force etc.) 10% for better stakeholding in long term projects. That may not be the right ratio, or even the most important step, but note the direction of his thinking. Which brings us to other recent statements from various officials at the International Seminar On Defence Finance & Economics. On the one hand, External Affairs Minister Shri Pranab Mukherjee has called for greater synergies between public spending and private enterprises with regard to defence production. What he appears to mean by this is the traditional pursuit of industrial offsets as part of defence contracts, plus expanded auditing.

At the same conference, Sir Kevin Tebbit of U.K. presented Britain's work in the area of 'Smart Acquisition' to manage time, cost and performance, while Dr. Elisabeth Wright of the U.S.A. made an presentation on Life Cycle Management of defence acquisition costs. All are well and good. None of them appear to address the root issues.

Techniques like life-cycle management, outcome budgeting and accrual accounting may offer limited help in specific areas, and could become part of a drive to greater accountability for results if used properly. On the other hand, the kind of "oversight" much beloved of politicians can contribute to waste and delays as easily as it prevents them. The core question is, "what is the real problem?"

Unless that question is answered correctly, such measures as are proposed above can easily become a substitute for real diagnosis, and the opposite of help. Further damage is especially likely if one's biggest problem is a cultivated environment in which people won't take risks and paperwork is seen as more important than production, all in a heavily state-owned and run sector. In that environment, even Natarajan's proposal to shift some project funding away from the state can be seen as a simple offloading of risk and expense onto other entites, while maintaining a controlling share.

On the other hand, there are currents afoot that could leverage the ideas of synergies with the private sector and a move away from the state as a manufacturer, using industrial offsets to help expand India's private defence industry, all done in conjunction with expanded use of modern management tools. For instance:

"Addressing the seminar the Union Finance Minister, Shri P. Chidambaram said that Defence PSUs needs to improve their comptitiveness by reducing costs and enhancing productivity. He said,

"The argument that the Government in all circumstances must support loss making undertakings or inefficient ordnance factories because of their strategic importance or surge capacities is difficult to sustain in an increasingly globalised world with many more efficient alternatives. Efficiency, productivity and true competitiveness have to be the underpinning of a strong and vibrant Defence Industrial Base."

Shri Chidambaram said that optimal allocation and utilisation of resources is the challenge before Defence Finance & Economics. Referring to the many positive aspects of India's economic growth in the last few years, he stated that policy changes are already in place to allow private sector participation in the Defence sector with up to 100% equity ownership. Shri Chidambaram said the partnership has to be further strengthened and taken to higher levels with greater outsourcing by Defence PSUs, Ordnance Factories, R&D Labs etc. The Minister said Defence Accounts Department must constantly review their systems and procedures for faster service delivery. Shri Chidambaram was of the opinion that Cash Management Systems, Management Information Systems, Migration to International Accounting Standards are some of the important aspects in this context."

India's software development community, which boasts more Level 5 CMMI firms than anywhere else in the world, shows that Indian firms are well acquainted with the demands of quality, development of new technologies, and performance to specifications. As this very pro-DRDO but well-referenced entry on Wikipedia documents, the DRDO has also shown the ability to succeed with a number of its own projects. Even within that sample set, however, note the patterns in DRDO's bigger successes like the Pinaka MLRS and BFSR-SR short range 3D battlefield surveillance radar – and also the pattern of failures like the 125mm FSAPDS tank ammunition.

As DID has noted in our coverage of India's annual Ministry of Defence report, however, large segments of India's arms industry are government-owned. Given the number of jobs (read: votes) dependent on these enterprises, the political reality is that closing these firms or even substantially reducing their workload is extremely difficult. The result is an environment of non-accountability. One that won't be fixed by changing the accounting methods.

There are many other reforms that will be necessary in order to create a defence industry and capability level that matches India's ambitions – but if the core issues revolve around culture and performance, greater involvement by the growing private sector in India's state-run defence industry and projects is a fine place to start. Most of the other items discussed, from greater use of modern management tools, to increased focus on performance, to a growing private sector capable of partnering effectively with foreign firms and producing key sub-components, can then begin to improve of their own accord. Will India succeed? It is impossible to know. One may begin to say, however, that they are headed in the right direction at last.

6 India: New Policy on Defence Contracts Offsets

India's policies on defence-related acquisitions from abroad and production within India are believed to have been directed not only at ensuring India's security interests but also at promoting self-reliance and indigenous capability in this vital sector often involving advanced technologies. Whatever one's opinions about intentions, questions have often been raised, as to whether these goals have actually been achieved. Again, while the point may be debated, clearly there are major problems going by the evidence in the past two decades. India has been buying ever larger quantities of increasingly sophisticated military hardware from foreign suppliers, while its Defence Forces have not been able to acquire necessary comparable equipment from Indian state-sector manufacturers due to inadequate performance, inordinate time delays and massive cost overruns.

Fighter aircraft such as the Light Combat Aircraft (LCA), jet trainers, helicopters, main battle tanks, submarines are all military equipment in which India has had active indigenous or collaborative R&D or manufacturing programs over several decades. But, as inventories have reached the end of their life cycles calling for replacements, India has repeatedly been forced to go in for costly foreign acquisitions while requisite indigenous capability has continued to languish even for the next generation of technology. This has not only increased India's dependence on imports, and vulnerability to technology denial regimes, in such a vital sector, it has also meant huge lost opportunities for enhancing science and technology capabilities, and downstream spread effects, in important sectors of national industry. Very belatedly, India had set in place over the past two years a policy of "offsets" in major defence contracts worth over Rs 300 crore in value.

Under this clause, a party securing such a contract was obligated to plough back to Indian parties at least 30 per cent of the contract value by way of buy-back of products and services, with a provision for a higher percentage in special cases. Of course, there still remained the danger that even such offsets may amount to little more than some sub-contracts or assembly-line operations, not resulting in any upgradation or absorption of know-how or capability, but it least it was a beginning. Unfortunately, under pressure from major manufacturers in the US and some other western countries, there are moves to dilute even this offset clause in important ways to the detriment of the long-term Indian interests. Defence Ministry officials have confirmed that a modified DPP will be notified by April 2008.

OFFSET POLICY

The policy on offsets, first enunciated in 2005, was further elaborated along with rules and procedures in the Defence Purchase Policy (DPP) of 2006 under which a new Defence Offset Facilitation Agency (DOFA) was also set up to work with vendors on implementation and monitoring. Offsets could include buy-back of products or services, foreign direct investment (FDI) in Indian public or private companies for such products or services or co-development and infrastructure, or even FDI in Indian entities engaged in defence R&D. All these were envisaged to be "direct offsets" that is directly related to the contract, the procurement of items under it, and their cost. In the short period DPP-2006 had been in operation, two major contracts had been concluded with offset clauses.

Israeli firm ELTA System had been awarded a contract worth Rs 900 crore for supplying radars. Under the offset provision, ELTA signed contracts with two Indian firms for purchase of components, with Astra Microwave securing a contract worth Rs 100 crore. Similarly, in the $1 billion (Rs 4000 crore) contract awarded to the Russian manufacturers of the Mig-29 for upgrades of the IAF's fleet, the vendor has agreed to offsets of $300 million. Several other pending deals such as for refuelling tankers also contain offset clauses.

Interestingly, even the controversially cancelled deal to purchase 196 military helicopters from the French-led European conglomerate Eurocopter had contained offset provisions with Eurocopter having agreed to 30 per cent offsets as required. Two points must be noted here.

First, such offset clauses are not unique to India nor are they some archaic leftovers of an earlier "socialistic" self-reliance policy incommensurate with the contemporary realities of globalization. Many countries have, and continue to successfully enforce, such offset clauses in the interests of their economies and in order to boost their knowledge base and industrial capabilities. Israel, Malaysia, Thailand to name a few are among many other countries in Asia and South America having even more stringent offset conditionalities than India.

Take for instance Israel's $2.5 billion order for 50 F-16 fighter aircraft from the US giant Lockheed Martin which had lost out to its American rival Boeing (both now pushing aggressively for the Indian 126-aircraft deal).

Israel secured an offset package of $850 million or about 35 per cent of the contract value spread over 10 years. Within 3 years of signing the deal, Lockheed Martin had already invested over $250 million in 12 Israeli firms for sourcing various components, assembly and post-production services. Israel not only enhanced their capabilities in these sectors it also ensured that it acquired new knowledge in advanced areas. Lockheed Martin was made to invest and participate in co-development of flight simulators and helmet-mounted display systems, as well as other technologies relating to space applications and electronics. Israel also made full use of its option clause for acquisition of a further 50 F-16s to add pressure on the US vendor.

Offsets for What?

Second, as also brought out by the above example, offsets should not be seen merely as commercial propositions by which India could earn additional money thus reducing capital outflows in defence contracts.

Merely obtaining orders for some components, or securing servicing and overhaul contracts, or even assembly and license-production is not sufficient to ensure absorption of know-how and building up the capacity to independently develop and manufacture equipment using the next generation technology. Indeed, India's own experience of serial license-production agreements clearly reveals the yawning gap between certain types of licensed manufacture and development of indigenous capability. India manufactured the French Alouette helicopter (Cheetah) and its engine at HAL, Bangalore, in the '70s and '80s but, not having absorbed the technology, was forced to go for imports of the next generation helicopters such as the Eurocopter.

HAL's bottom line was certainly boosted, its turnover substantially increased for several years, but this does not appear to have translated into capability to develop and make its own helicopters, forcing the government to go in for another sequence of imports and license arrangements.

Similarly, India is now in the market reportedly for 200 howitzer artillery guns building up through licensed manufacture towards an inventory of 1500 guns worth an estimated $2.5 billion (Rs 10,000 crore), and even had to buy howitzers on an emergency basis during the Kargil conflict, despite having had full access to the Bofors technology since the '80s. Therefore, in working out offsets, quite apart from the commercial angle, it is very important to see that offset arrangements are properly planned and channelized to projects and institutions with a clear vision of what is required in the short and medium term in terms of developing independent indigenous capability and know-how.

NEW POLICY

Despite this past experience, and in spite of some success in pressurizing vendors into more meaningful collaboration through the policy of direct offsets under DPP-2005/6, the Defence Ministry is in the process of modifying the DPP particularly is respect of offsets. It is no coincidence that this process has been initiated at a time when major western military hardware vendors are salivating at the $30 billion Indian acquisition budget, and especially the massive $10 billion deal for multi-role combat aircraft, in the tender for which India has specified a 50 per cent offset condition, much to the open displeasure of US aviation majors Lockheed Martin and Boeing.

It is also no surprise that Defence Ministry spokesmen confirmed the advent of a new offsets policy just prior to the opening of the large arms expo in Delhi on 2009 February 18. The revised policy proposes three major departures all leading to a framework of "indirect" offsets in contrast to the earlier system of direct offsets. The first allows for "banking" of offsets wherein offsets accumulated under one project can be shown against any subsequent project too. The second, although apparently an extension of the first, allows companies engaged in civilian contracts to "bank" such offsets and show them against offset requirements in military contracts.

Clearly, this is purely a commercial consideration and makes no allowance for the fact that the main purpose of offsets is, or ought to be, building capability and know-how in the defence technology sector albeit with spin-offs in the civilian sector. It is also a measure that will clearly favour Boeing which can show offsets and "bank" its sub-contracts to Indian parties making fuselage parts for the passenger jets being bought by Air India and Indian Airlines while tendering for the combat aircraft order. The third modification and perhaps the most dangerous is to allow vendors to charge for technology transfer, show these charges as part of the offsets and deduct these charges from the actual offset payments. This is a specious provision and opens the door to all sorts of underhand manipulations, will render the entire offsets mechanism useless and make its processes completely non-transparent.

Who is to define what constitutes transfer of technology and what price to attach to it? In any sub-contracting or license production, there is some technology transfer involved. Under the direct offset clause operational hitherto in India, and practiced elsewhere in the world, licensed production includes technology transfer for manufacture. Under the modified provision, it can be charged separately, and an arbitrarily determined technology fee can be subtracted from any buy-back arrangement! With a 50 per cent offset provision for the fighter deal, about Rs 20,000 crore worth of business was expected to come to Indian firms but, with the new technology transfer clause, this could easily be reduced to half or even less!

Vested Interests Vs National Interests

It is significant that pressure has been brought on India to change its offsets provisions particularly by US companies especially in the aviation sector. The US Defence Department has always opposed offset clauses, but has not stood in the way of contracts including such clauses when it serves US policy or when US companies push for them, as with the Israeli case cited above.

In the case of India, the US India Business Council (USIBC) constituted and empowered under the US-India Strategic Partnership has been pushing hard for precisely such modifications in offsets policy as are now being made in the soon-to-be-revised DPP. At the Bangalore air show in 2007 when US aviation companies made a big show of their various offerings, Nikhil Khanna, Director of Policy Advocacy at USIBC in Washington said: "We have encouraged the broadening of the definition of offsets to include indirect offsets, so other areas of India's economy may gain from the massive investments that are sure to flow from aerospace and defence contracts." and added that this would credit for technology transfer, limitation of liability, and the ability to "bank" the value of current projects as offsets for future defence contracts. At that time Khanna stated that new Delhi was "considering the suggestions". Defence Minister A K Antony stated that "if there is scope for improvement, we will adjust and make minor changes to the policy." It now seems that he has! Only thing is, the changes are not minor!

Indian industry has reason to feel deeply aggrieved. The Confederation of Indian Industry (CII), through a Committee chairmanship of Rahul Bajaj had advocated an aggressive offsets policy as far back as 1999. CII had strongly recommended that "direct offsets be implemented as a matter of National Policy for Defence Procurement [so as to] get state-of-the-art technologies for both Public and Private Sectors [and] give major thrust to Self Reliance."

The proposed modified offsets policies, being instituted at the instigation of US companies backed by political pressure, will negate these aims. It is, therefore, imperative that pressure be brought upon the UPA government to abandon these changes, stay the course with direct offsets and ensure that the offsets are properly directed and monitored so as to reduce India's dependence on imports and consequent vulnerability to technology denial regimes while simultaneously leading to significant enhancement in science and technology capabilities, as well as a spread effect in important industrial and research sectors of the national economy.

7 Democracy and Defence Policy

Democracy influences both the process and the content of defence policy. Thus, in a democratic setup, defence policy is based on a consultative process. Its goals and objectives, as well as many finer details, are often debated in Parliament, the media, by think-tanks and during election campaigns. This process ensures a more participative, inclusive and transparent defence policy. This indeed is the case in India and other democracies. An important outcome of this process is that democratic governments cannot concentrate on militarisation alone.

They have to balance the needs of other sectors like the economy, health and education, with the requirements of defence. This ensures that there is no emphasis on militarisation and on an aggressive defence policy. It is well known that democracies do not go to war with each other. The reason for this is that ordinary people want peace and prosperity and democratic governments have to reflect this aspiration in their defence policy. On the other hand, dictatorial regimes have compulsions to spend large amounts on military to take care of both domestic instability and regime survival against external intervention. History is replete with such instances in the past and there are many contemporary examples today. This indeed is the case with democratic India's defence policy which has always focused on its own defence and has never contemplated aggression, even against its smallest neighbour. India's defence expenditure in early years of its independence was below two per cent of GDP.

Even now, it is less than 2.5 per cent, despite many real threats it has to face. Compare this to the amounts that some of our neighbours spend on military! Another important outcome of defence policy making through a democratic process is that such a process enables nations to develop comprehensive national strength. The concept of comprehensive national strength includes economic strength, technological strength, infrastructure and other important aspects that help to build up a nation's power. A country cannot be defended by its military power alone. Recent history shows that even great powers with huge militaries can face serious difficulties in achieving their goals and can even disintegrate due to the weight of their own internal contradictions. In India, we have been able to develop comprehensive national strength and, today we are counted amongst the world's most important powers. This is not only on account of our military but also due to our economy, our science and technology, our knowledge power, our sunrise industries and our democracy. Given its vigilant citizens with a stake in the security of the nation, the genuine requirements of defence are taken care of in democracies.

Thus, despite the fact that India has been peace-loving, it has always made an effort to keep pace with the latest defence technologies. In its initial years, India had opposed nuclear weapons tooth and nail and favoured complete disarmament. But, when the powerful nations of the world did not give up nuclear weapons and when our neighbours developed their own nuclear weapons, the Indian democracy showed enough dynamism and flexibility to change its policy and develop nuclear deterrence. However, our nuclear doctrine affirms that India will not resort to first strike and never use nuclear weapons against non-nuclear weapon states. Thus, even India's nuclear doctrine has a purely defensive orientation. India's nuclear policy has evolved over time and is based on its essentially consensual approach in matters of national security. India's defence policy is flexible enough to respond to changes in the international strategic environment.

The primary task of the Indian Armed Forces has been to provide security for our citizens and to defend our vital interests at home and abroad. Democratic India also wishes to play a friendly and responsible role in the international arena. India has always been in the forefront of UN peace-keeping missions. It has been an important actor in international fora, particularly the United Nations. In accordance with its growing profile and role, it deserves a place in the United Nations Security Council. India also seeks to provide an adequate military capability for operations to promote international stability, and humanitarian missions after natural or other disasters, providing assistance to the civil authorities at home, and maintenance of essential national services. India has worked for regional peace and stability and rendered exemplary service to provide relief in times of disaster. A recent example is that of relief operations following the Tsunami disaster. We are also ready to cooperate with the nations of the region to provide maritime security and participate in disaster management and disaster forecasting mechanisms.

In its external dimension, India has always sought a cooperative relationship with all nations. It has also made continuous efforts towards peace at the international level. It was in this background that in the Cold War era, India had refused to side with one bloc or another. India led the Non-Aligned Movement to mitigate tensions at the international level and to play a positive role in resolving conflicts. However, its proximity to the Soviet bloc for defence supplies was misinterpreted. Due to the configuration of the Cold War era, India and some western nations were unable to come together and form a strong partnership. Now that the Cold War has ended and India is rapidly integrating with a globalising world, it has entered into either a strategic partnership or a strategic dialogue with all important powers of the world. Our growing friendship with United States, Russia, European Union and Japan is a testimony to this positive development. India and China have set aside their boundary dispute to come together in the area of economic cooperation. Earnest efforts are also being made by the two sides to resolve the boundary issue but this does not allow our growing cooperation to be affected. We are trying to develop close and cooperative relationship with all our neighbours, including Pakistan. Our future vision of South Asia is a region which is stable, at peace with each other and cooperating to accelerate economic growth and prosperity of its people. We want our neighbours to take full advantage of our growing market and a rapidly globalising economy.

India has suffered from terrorism for many decades and has been able to cope with the problem effectively. In doing so, it has respected human rights. It is an important player in the war against terrorism which is seen as an assault on our secular, inclusive and democratic polity. Countries which are undemocratic in their orientation are often a heaven for terrorists and even pursue terrorism as a part of state policy. This is an important distinction between the defence and security policies of democracies and autocratic rulers. Because democracies do not favour draconian measures and respect the rule of law, they are some times perceived to be soft or weak. The process of debate and consultation also can be a stretched out process at time. However, democracies are inherently strong and tend to promote defence policies which are conducive to the welfare of their own people and to peace and stability in the world.

What is Wrong with India's Defence Industrial Policy?

Defence industrial policy in the initial years after independence was guided by the simple phrase called 'self sufficiency'. This was subsequently modified to 'self reliance' in defence production and has become a matter of varied interpretation. While for some it means the ultimate objective of complete non-dependence on imports for defence hardware, for others it means selective self-sufficiency in certain critical technologies. And for some others it is a simple reduction in the ratio of imports to indigenous sources of supply to the armed forces.

However, one can say that India's defence industrial policy broadly consists of three components: (i) maximisation of indigenous manufacturing and production (ii) License production of what could be obtained from abroad and (iii) direct purchase of those equipment not covered by the other two categories but considered essential for ensuring security. Another important unspoken element was that everything, whether indigenous production, license production or direct purchase, was done within the government setup in line with the general industrial policy. The recent policy change, of course, demonstrates the intention to involve the private sector in defence R&D and production through licensing and the indirect opening of the defence industrial sector to foreign companies through equity participation and the offset arrangement.

The moot question is: was there something wrong with the past policy objectives? On the face of it, the policy components and objectives appear quite sound and logical for a country like India. In simple terms, it means that indigenous production should be maximised; what could not be produced indigenously should be produced under license arrangement; and those that could not be obtained through these two routes should be acquired by direct purchase. A sound policy indeed. But the soundness of a policy has to be judged from tangible outcomes. Arguably, the problems might not have been in the contents of the policy per se. It is due to the nature defence technology and limitations of vision as embedded in the policy.

The policy objective was essentially to substitute imported equipment with indigenous production in the hope of attaining 'self-sufficiency' or 'self reliance'. Unfortunately, the security imperatives of a country translated into defence equipment are like 'moving targets'. Neither the technological capability of the defence sector nor its policy instrument as highlighted above was able to catch up with the targets.

The increasing quantum of defence imports from year to year, the country's inability to upgrade the imported equipment held for significant period under license production, and, indirectly, insignificant defence exports amply testify to this situation. The general industrial policy wherein defence items and their productions were kept strictly within the government setup further compounded the problem. In this context, two aspects of the policy – indigenous production and license production, merit detailed analysis.

Maximising indigenous production would imply more than one thing. It would mean meeting the quantitative requirements in terms of the existing demands of the Armed Forces for equipment or items at any point of time. It would also mean increasing the varieties of items and equipment required by them. Most importantly, it would mean the ability to meet the challenges of supplying their ever-changing demands of technology specific equipment and items. India's defence industrial policy has conspicuously failed in this respect. In fact, the implication of this policy is that the country should be able to indigenously produce the challenging demands made by the Armed Forces. Its logical extension is that defence research and development efforts have to be strengthened through policy focused research and development and adequate resources allocations thereto. It is a known fact that the defence research and development organisation has 50-odd laboratories and establishments. However, its lack of focused research and development is equally well known, though of late it has been able to achieve break-throughs in certain strategic technologies. Moreover, its budgetary allocation has been quite modest even within the overall defence budget and until recently it was part of 'Army Demand'. In fact, the Parliamentary Standing committee on Defence recommended that defence R&D budgetary allocation should be at least 14 to 15 per cent of the total defence budget so that indigenous production to imports in the ratio of 70:30 could be achieved. This recommendation was in line with the projected target of the report of the self-reliance committee entitled '10 year plan for self reliance in Defence systems'. But the fact remains that there is no evidence of adequate policy back-up to attain this desirable but difficult goal. The DRDO does not seem to be suffering from lack of funds per se since only 8 to 10 per cent of its total budget is reported to be spent on fundamental research. Perhaps, the solution to this issue lies somewhere else.

How about production under license, another important pillar of the policy? The normal assumption is that production under license would enable the country not only to acquire the capability to produce a particular equipment or product but also help it gain the technical know-how for subsequent upgradation and further technological innovations. For the last fifty-odd years, India has been producing a number of defence equipment under license. Good examples in this regard are the Vijayanta tank and the MIG series of fighter aircraft. But this does not seem to have helped in the development of the Arjun Main Battle Tank and the Light Combat Aircraft. Moreover, India has not even been able to upgrade certain fighter aircraft held and operated for a long time by its Armed Forces. Thus, the above assumption is definitely not correct.

A closer examination of license production arrangements reveals certain interesting features. License production arrangements are more of an 'institutional framework' under which various types of contractual agreements could be entered into between the supplier and the buyer. It is not necessarily a proven mechanism of technology transfer as such. It may envisage the setting up of a simple production line or facilities in the buyer country for assembly of the finished parts and components for the final finished product. In such cases, hardly any technology transfer takes place and the supplier does not part with any technical know-how. In fact, the supplier agrees to sacrifice only a small portion of his economic interest. It is also not possible to discern under these circumstances whether the supplier has compensated itself for this marginal loss by way of increasing the cost of the technology or equipment and components thereof. On the other hand, there could be a situation where license production involves an intensive process of technology transfer within and beyond the physical production of the equipment in the host county. This is rare rather than routine. The truth of the matter is that since technology is know-how, it is the function of human understanding. The focus of active mechanisms, implicitly or explicitly, is people. However, the truth is that no foolproof prescription could be given for the effectiveness of technology transfer. It all depends on the nature of technology to be acquired. Perhaps, India has learnt it by the hard way the limitations of licence production for attaining the objective of self-sufficiency or self-reliance in defence production.

The fact that defence technology needs long term investment, its obsolescence is high and economies of scale are difficult to attain unlike in other areas of civilian technology are well known.

This is essentially because higher capability tends to drive downward the scales of production. In the context of a limited number of customers, this trend is more regressive. On top of this, contrary to logical expectation, the production of the next generation of an equipment or of a different variant does not bring down the cost of the equipment. It has been the British experience that a new generation could cost between one and a half times to four times of the previous variant. This is due to the fact that production of the next generation is not a simple straight line trajectory work but involves the integration of various systems, which sometimes may involve a number of companies and agencies, that were not partners earlier.

This leads to the conclusion that the policy of maximising indigenous production without a strong R&D policy back-up would not bring tangible results. License production is more of an economic compromise between the supplier and the buyer, and it does not and cannot bring about significant technology transfer without an inbuilt specific and suitable mechanism. Every country at one point of time or the other will attain a saturation level when it comes to supplying certain categories of equipment for its armed forces. Therefore, the ultimate defence industrial policy goal must be to foster defence exports without which it is difficult to sustain the economic base of a country's defence industry.

India's defence industrial policy seems to be lacking in all these important ingredients. Since the industrial base has to be sustained for technological and economic reasons, exports are an essential element of defence industrial policy. This is why many countries and their companies are aggressively competing in the global defence market for exports under different arrangements including license production. It is reported that way back in 1995, the United States government spent more than $7.6 billion in subsidy to help export defence equipment to sustain the economic base of its defence industry. It is a matter of fact that strategic depth in defence production can be increased only by aiming at being 'internationally competitive' through the policy objective of defence exports. In the absence of such an approach, India's defence industrial policy is unlikely to take off in the foreseeable future.

Is India on the Path to Vibrant Defence Industry?

Every major power aspires to build a vibrant defence industrial base. This status is however not easily attainable. Apart from the United States and to some extent Russia and France, all other countries are in the state of struggling to arrive at such a defence industrial position. Certain countries like the United Kingdom may be able to attain this, but due to strategic or economic preferences may deliberately choose not to consider the enormous costs involved as against the perceived security requirements. India's aspiration for this is well documented wherein it has publicly pronounced its goal of 'self sufficiency' soon after political independence and now graduating it to 'self-reliance'. The unfortunate part is that India is still far from nearing that level even after fifty years of this laudable policy. One of the identified ongoing policy drawbacks is its weak linkage with the civilian sector of industry.

The thrust of the new policy initiative therefore is participation of the private sector in defence industry for both research and development as well as production purposes. It has also opened up the defence sector to foreign equity participation up to 26 per cent, with the government recently expressing its willingness to consider even up to 49 per cent on case-to-case basis. Together with this is the initiation of the 'offset policy' for major foreign procurement of defence equipment of Rs.300 crores and above. The big question is: will all these initiatives contribute to the growth of a vibrant defence industry in India?

The immediate effect of these initiatives is that significant numbers of licenses have been applied for and issued to major Indian companies for production of varied components and systems. In fact, according to CII sources alone, as of date, more than 140 companies are involved in about 345 defence items/ products. Complete systems/platforms/weapons systems constitute the majority of the licenses issued, which demands higher financial investments and technical capability. This reflects the ambition and confidence of the private sector in their new ventures. On the other hand, there is a flurry of partnership agreements/collaborative ventures by these industrial companies with major global defence industrial giants from the United States,

Western Europe and Israel. This is, of course, not to ignore the existing and ongoing collaborative projects of Defence Public Sector Undertakings (DPSUs) and Ordnance Factories (OFs) with companies from these countries at the governmental level. An analysis would reveal that India's defence industrial scene now is moving on two distinct parallel lines. The first is equipment and technology emanating from Russia and Eastern Europe, which represent approximately 70 per cent of the country's defence industrial setup. The new addition is Western technology or modified/upgraded technology through private sector companies that are poised to enter India's defence market. The moot question is: Will these different technologies eventually strengthen India's defence industrial base or add further complexities through highly mixed inventories?

In this emerging situation, a few logical things are bound to happen. First, due to the emerging competition from Western technology largely through the private sector, the Russians or other traditional suppliers are likely to at least scale down their often-repeated business behaviour of project delays, delay in supply of spares and parts, and unwillingness to transfer technology. Moreover, the tendency to jack up costs midway while implementing agreements may also get tempered with the arrival of new competitors. However, the fact remains that the domination of Russian origin technologies and their grip on the Indian military establishment will sustain for quite some years to come particularly given that they are largely embedded through the defence public sector undertakings and other government agencies. The major positive impact of the new situation is, however, that the government agencies/DPSUs are likely to wake up from their slumber at least in those areas where they are producing items of common use, which can be easily produced at a competitive level by the private sector. This will be the immediate benefit brought in by the private sector.

While the above may be the likely positive impact, it is unlikely that western technology will be able to easily challenge the existing market structure through the private sector. This is due to the peculiarity of defence technology and its market structure. First, given that control of technology is the essence of the growth and expansion of MNCs, the global western defence giants may not easily part with high-end technology, whereas the Indian establishment would be looking for sophisticated weapons and equipment to supplement what has already been acquired from existing sources. The private sector's ability to enter the market will depend on its capability to supply the components, parts and subsystems of the new equipment in the initial period. Secondly, opportunities for the private sector would largely depend on the government decision to opt for higher and complete major systems of western origin technologies such as the MMRCA. If such a decision goes in favour of any of the fighter aircraft of western origin, the private sector would definitely have significant scope to capture the market through the offset channel or through normal business dealings. Thirdly, the ability and willingness of western technology to supplement the defence technology requirements of the Armed Forces would be the decisive factor. As of now, the Armed Forces are already in possession of a certain level of defence technology. What they are looking for is conceptually of a higher level, which would be supplementary in nature to bridge perceived security gaps. Will the western powers through their MNCs be willing to part with this level of technology to fill the gap, which, though may be lower than the high-end strategic technology that they possess? If the answer is in the affirmative, the prospects of their capturing the Indian market are very bright. So is also the market potential for the myriad private domestic defence companies in the next five to ten years.

The challenge for Indian industry as a whole would be the will and ability to integrate the two major technology streams in the coming years. This demands the need for dedicated and focused research leading to the capability to integrate existing systems with incoming systems. While the major platforms may continue to be of Russian/Soviet origin, the genius of Indian industry would be tested in its capability to build armaments and other subsystems and integrating them at higher levels. This is the core challenge and the capability to do it would eventually make the defence industry genuinely vibrant. This will usher in the 'Indian brand of defence technology' even for export purposes free from possible objections on accounts of violations of intellectual property rights. The role of the Government of India as patron and principal customer shall be very crucial for success in achieving the above objective.

INDIAN DEFENCE POLICY IN MAJOR TRANSITION

Recently the US journal Defence News reported that the Indian government is working on a program whereby Israel would replace Russia as India's largest supplier of weapons and defence equipment by 2008. Since Russia now supplies some 70 percent of India's weapons imports, this report, if true, would mark a major transformation in Indian defence policy. Under the terms of the program, India would identify the products it wants and ask the Israeli government to negotiate with domestic firms on its behalf as Jerusalem does with regard to its own weapons.

Israel is already the second-largest supplier of military systems to India, so this program could affect a major transformation in India's security relationships. The potential repercussions of this project, which would clearly show a serious break with Moscow's arms salesmen, are immense. Given the deep ties between the US and Israeli defence industries, if this program does materialize it will also probably enhance the United States' competitive position in the Indian defence market and result in further substantial increases in the already rising amount of US arms sales and security cooperation with India. Those sales could either be bilateral or brokered through Israel, such as weapons made jointly by Israel and the United States, including missile defence systems that India reportedly is interested in acquiring.

This program would then also strengthen the developing tripartite relationship among Israel, India, and the US in regard to defence sales. We can see this already occurring, because the United States has brushed aside Pakistan's objections to India's receiving the Israeli Phalcon radar, made with US technology and thus subject to US veto on its transfer to a third party.

Realization of the projected Indo-Israeli project would also simultaneously symbolize and express India's rising continental Asian status as a great power with interests and capabilities across the continent, allowing it to break free of its confining chains as merely a major South Asian power if not the regional leader, something that both Indian and foreign observers have labeled as a prerequisite for a full partnership with the United States.

Not only would those trends strengthen Indo-Israeli ties, they would provide fuel to the oft-reported desire on the part of at least some US elites to create a tripartite alliance with India and Israel against terrorism (if not for other, broader objectives that would emerge later). Joint Indo-Israeli defence collaboration on a scale envisaged above would also, or so these advocates hope, tie into the US alliance and Israeli partnership with Turkey, creating a kind of pan-Asian bloc. The new program grows out of India's difficulty in negotiating a US$10 billion multi-year defence acquisition program with Russia. Three areas in particular seem to have caused some anxiety in New Delhi.

In March 2002, The Times of India reported that the Parliamentary Standing Committee had urged the government to avoid overdependence on Russia for armaments and spare parts. The committee reportedly acknowledged Russia's previous contributions and reliability as a provider of defence equipment to India but cautioned that the current dependence on Moscow for almost 80 percent of its arms imports is unhealthy. It also observed that Russia was not providing military hardware on the same beneficial financial terms that it had during the Soviet era. Therefore the committee also urged the Indian government to cease making advance payments for weapons acquisitions from Russia, and that in the future it seek to put more defence contracts up for competitive tender. Russia also has come under criticism because of India's difficulty in obtaining and negotiating speedy delivery of spare parts for these weapons systems. At the same time it became clear that given its worsening relations with Pakistan, India is seeking to diversify its foreign purchases and use foreign partners to develop its own defence industrial capability, eg by conditioning purchases on obtaining offsets from the sellers to develop its own indigenous capability.

The alliance, if it were to materialize, would build on the already greatly improved Indo-Israeli relationship that has led to large-scale military sales from Israel and to India's rapprochement with the United States as well. As the Phalcon deal suggests, it could become possible to envisage tripartite collaboration among these states on missile defence, especially if India's great goal of securing the end to all US sanctions on the transfer of both civil and military technology is realized.

Moreover, the broadening of India's ties and reach in political-military terms through the acquisition of top-quality defence systems would enable it to play the kind of role that analysts in both India and the US postulate as being essential to any serious strategic partnership with the United States. And that role also accords very much with some of the deepest aspirations of India's foreign and defence policy elites, thus highlighting a congruence of visions concerning India's future international position.

In effect India's aspiration to play a major role "from Socotra to Sumatra" would have been both realized and blessed by the United States, as Secretary of State Colin Powell implicitly suggested in 2001. India would then become not just a South or even Central Asian power but a major player in the Persian Gulf, the Middle East, and Southeast Asia.

At the same time, India's search for new vistas in defence acquisition and production relates very much to its rising economic, technological, and military-industrial capabilities as well as to its desire to strengthen existing long-standing partnerships, eg with Russia. For example, beyond the existing $10 billion weapons sales from Russia to India, India is collaborating with Russia on joint production of a fifth-generation fighter that Russia feels vital to its military future. Both are also collaborating on research that is probably tied to missile defence and nuclear systems as well. More broadly, India is the only country with whom Russia is collaborating on joint production of sophisticated and futuristic weapons systems. Likewise India, not China, gets the best weapons currently being produced in Russia, systems that not even Russia's armed forces can obtain. Moscow offers offsets in the form of technology transfer of production skills and know-how to India, one of its largest customers. Although India obviously seeks to diversify its sources of foreign procurement, Russian producers have until now been confident of their ability to obtain the bulk of Indian defence contracts.

Whether or not this confidence is misplaced, time will tell, but diversification and strengthening of India's own capabilities surely would increase India's scientific-technological and manufacturing capabilities for weapons production. This objective also appears to be a major goal of the deals now being made with Russia, Israel, and presumably the United States. We see similar deals with Italian and French firms for joint manufacture of weapons systems.

India's leading defence firm, Hindustan Aeronautics Ltd (HAL), is also pressing an outsourcing program whereby it would help private Indian companies find and choose foreign partners to undertake such high-tech projects as avionics integration, weapons-system integration, and other related efforts to "lay the foundation for a credible domestic aerospace industry base that could meet the majority of India's military aerospace requirements in the next 10 years". And it is no less logical to assume that India would be thrilled to duplicate this particular kind of relationship with Washington, especially as India already has a large space program with military applications and very much wants US conventional-weapons systems and technology transfer.

Indeed, a Pentagon-commissioned study of Indo-American perceptions reported that on the basis of many interviews, a uniform conclusion was reached that "for Indians, technology transfer from the United States is military cooperation's touchstone". Other Indian assessments confirm the great importance that India attaches to transfer of both civil and defence technology as a critical and essential element in any partnership with the US. While India's aspirations in the defence industry are common to other countries that seek the capability for indigenous production of most, if not all of their weapons, it is nevertheless clear that this deal, if it materializes, would utterly transform defence relationships among major players in the defence business: India, the US, Israel, and Russia. The major transformations in Asian security that accelerated after September 11, 2001, have clearly not yet run their course. Nor is it clear when the overall Asian situation will stabilize or when also the rising tide of weapons sales will abate.

But there can be no doubt that major changes are in the offing and that the future holds many more surprises and jolts for all of those who seek to play a key role in the security and defence of Asia.

8 India's Defence Purchase Policy Attracts Global Attention

Reflecting industry aspirations, India Defence Procurement Procedure-2008 broadly incorporates measures to improve domestic industrial supply, besides encouraging foreign direct investment (FDI) and intensifying R and D in defence industry. The policy has been revised four times since its inception in 2002 and India Inc. should remain hopeful that shortfalls in the policy would be accordingly reformed, said Shashikant Sharma, Director General (Acquisition) in the Defence Ministry. He was speaking at the second India Regional Offsets Conference organised here by the Confederation of Indian Industry (CII) in association with the Defence Manufacturing Association (DMA) of Britain and the US Global Offsets and Countertrade Association (GOCA).

Sharma specifically mentioned operational and policy challenges in defence offsets. Pointing out the need for universality of offset credit transaction, policy issues with technology transfers, desire for development, growth of indigenous defence manufacturing capabilities and the likes, Sharma's address 'reaffirmed that the government is considering a more dynamic defence procurement policy structure', a CII statement said. Sharma also pointed out that an offsets partner is now not required to hold a defence ministry licence to associate with India's military hardware manufacturing sector. This had increased the scope manifold from 37 to 2,000 industries that can now consider associating with the offset programmes, the official said.

The Defence Ministry was also studying the offset policies of global economies to gather provisions for inclusion in India, he added. The conference has attracted over 300 participants, including 130 international offset professionals, officers from the Indian government, the Defence Ministry, the Armed Forces and India Inc. 'The conference saw a clear understating of India targeting the global defence market,' the CII statement said. The Defence Ministry envisages spending over $30 billion for acquisition of military hardware and software over the next five years, 30-50 percent of which will have to be reinvested in India through the offsets route. This 'will intensify new acquisitions, adoption of futuristic projects, upgrading of equipment, support services, and joint ventures, amongst others'.

The overseas companies will be required to fulfil mandatory offsets obligation to the tune of 30-50 percent of such procurements. According to Maj. Gen. (retd) Mrinal Suman, Project Director for CII's defence technical assessment and advisory services, 'India is observing exciting times in defence market with a huge shopping list.' 'An ideal proportion of military equipment balance observed in the developed world is 30-40-30 which is spread over state-of-the-art technology, mature technology and obsolete technology.'

'Whilst India's military equipment balance proportion is 15-35-50, attempting to match up its defence infrastructure to world, India will be spending $100 billion by 2020,' Suman pointed out.

Rear Admiral Rees Ward of Britain's DMA said: 'Like most policies, DPP-2008 is an initial phase of the policy which will evolve with time. We have to overcome disagreements as challenges occur when we get into details.'

9 New Defence Modernisation Challenges and Strategies

Military technological differential is the key to competitive advantage in wars of today and tomorrow. And whoever controls superior military technology in the 21st century would dominate in war and peace, on the battlefield and in the market. Force multiplication is no substitute for force where technological differential become low. Defence modernisation is one area where trends in weapons manufacture and markets abroad have a major influence on not only costs and technology, but also access to them. We had relied heavily on Soviet weapons and equipment since the mid-1960s, and the European industry provided an alternative, supplying one-fifth of our total needs.

We have had negligible access to American weapons systems and military technology over the decades. But things are changing and it is necessary to look at them carefully to work out our defence modernisation strategies. The end of the Cold War resulted in contraction of defence industry worldwide.

Smaller production runs increased the unit costs of weapon systems; and rapid advances in technology have pushed costs further. Defence establishments worldwide have resorted to upgrades to enhance the operational capabilities as a via media to replacements. But this remains a partial solution in modernisation strategies. Meanwhile, collaborations and mergers became the norm in defence manufacturing, with an obvious strengthening of American hold over military industry worldwide. While some access to American weapons systems has opened with the sale of the artillery Firefinder radars to India, this process still could only amount to a marginal opening of a small window. The European option for weapons acquisitions remains.

But the European defence industry is in a difficult situation for a variety of reasons that we need not go into detail here. Its consolidation has resulted in deeper linkages to US industry. We faced its implications after the 1998 sanctions, when naval aircraft and helicopters which we had purchased from the UK were held back while being overhauled at the manufacturers. It took a couple of years before the problem could be resolved, and the costs obviously went up. The disintegration and collapse of the Soviet Union, which has been our primary source of defence equipment since the mid-1960, resulted in serious disruption and decline in the output of the former Soviet defence industry. What Russia retained in reasonably good shape were the Soviet Union's outstanding design bureaus. We must also note that the comprehensive self-reliance model put into place during Prime Minister Jawaharlal Nehru's time underwent change since the 1960s.

This was based on three parallel tracks: Buy weapons, licence manufacture as much as possible, and undertake design and development (with foreign collaboration to build our own expertise). Unfortunately, as licence manufacture increased, providing significant indigenous capabilities and a degree of independence from imports, this also led to a sort of strategic complacency in that the key area of our needs for future modernisation, design and development of weapon systems, started to suffer. Notable examples are combat aircraft where the LCA design was started 30 years after we had undertaken the design and development of an excellent multi-role combat aircraft, the HF-24 Marut, while technology galloped! Similarly, the design and development of the Mainbattle Tank Arjun, started just after the 1971 War, has yet to enter operational service. Meanwhile techno-operational environment has changed substantively forcing us to buy the T-90 tanks.

The Indian Navy has fared better, although resource crunch delayed its shipbuilding programmes, forcing us to now buy the Gorshkov aircraft carrier when the indigenous Air Defence Ship should have been in service by now. Other examples abound. But the point that we need to note is that a comprehensive strategy for modernisation has been practically absent since the 1970s.

Our weakness since then actually lies in design and development of weapons systems. The DRDO has made valiant attempts, but seems to have shied away from collaborative projects. Scientific professional pride decried collaboration on grounds that it would hamper indigenous development; politically, foreign collaboration aroused negative passions; and the defence establishment was looking to immediate needs rather than long-term capacity building in defence industrial capability. Acquisition of military technology, therefore, has been localised to import of production technology rather than building design capabilities.

It is in this context that a unique historical opportunity opened up just at the time the most severe crisis for defence modernisation occurred with the collapse of the Soviet Union. The former Soviet Union looked for collaboration in design and development of military systems. The West plugged in where it suited them. But it was China, not India, which took advantage of the situation. By mid-1990s over 3,000 Russian engineers and mechanics were reported to be working in Chinese defence industry, upgrading and working on design and development of numerous systems which China had not been able to achieve for decades. China is investing in military R&D programmes in Russian institutions and in collaborative programmes where our recent attempts at joint development of the Brahmos missile pale in comparison.

It is still not too late to plug into Russian design base and capabilities, although as it picks up economic strength it may seek to apply tougher terms. Similarly, we have been the largest customer of British Aerospace's weapons and equipment for five decades. But there is little in the country in the shape of joint production, leave alone joint design and development programmes.

Regardless of the level of budget being allocated in any particular year, the backlog of modernisation and the needs of future high-technology weapons systems would require investment of the order of $20 billion over the next decade. And that is why most of the global arms manufacturers are setting up shop in India in the hope of selling arms. But this also provides us with a powerful bargaining chip to build indigenous design, development, manufacturing and export capabilities through joint collaborative programmes. What we need is to be clear on our strategy for modernisation that goes beyond mere procurement and licence production. This is also where the private sector can play a crucial role.

In a developing country like ours, there are additional complicating factors in the modernisation processes. First, a large proportion of our defence equipment is still purchased from abroad. Our traditional supplier, the former Soviet Union, disintegrated and landed up in serious socioeconomic crisis. Bilateral trade also suffered heavily. The negative impact on supplies of weapons equipment and spares created additional complications for us. Also, many inefficiencies and complexities had crept into our procurement system and decision making for modernisation. Some of these have been sorted out by implementing the decisions of the Group of Ministers taken three years ago to improve the management of national security. But the result has been that with a system that allocates funds on an annual basis, with a review half-way down, large amounts of funds budgeted for defence and modernisation have been lapsing at the end of the financial year for the past few years.

For example, for the three-year period ending March 2003, a total of Rs 25,699 crore remained unspent out of the total budgeted figure of Rs 1,85,587 crore. The effect has been that while defence modernisation had suffered earlier due to lack of resources, now the inability to spend available resources within the stipulated financial year has adversely affected defence preparedness.

Establishing a DMF of Rs 25,000 crore would go a long way in assuring that modernisation processes do not suffer due to procedural delays and other unavoidable reasons. Both the National Security Advisory Board and the bipartisan Standing

Committee on Defence of Parliament have been pressing the issue for years. The actual functioning of the DMF, of course, must be evaluated carefully over the coming years, since this is a deviation from the traditional budgetary approach. Its utility may remain less than optimal if the five year plans are not finalised well before the Plan period commences. Also, we need to redefine the budget heads to clearly indicate the resource allocation and utilisation under three functionally different heads of modernisation, maintenance and operating costs of the defence forces separately rather than the current system that does not indicate functional segments of a large amount of the tax-payers' money in an area so crucial to our security and defence.

INDIA'S MILITARY PREPAREDNESS

India has a penchant for blacklisting foreign arms producers without considering negative effects it has on India's military preparedness. This is the reason why recent reports of irregularities in the procurement of seven Barak anti-missile defence systems and 200 missiles from Israel Aircraft Industries Ltd (IAI) have caused serious concern to the Indian Armed Forces. They fear that the Government may get-forced to blacklist IAI as per the provisions of defence procurement procedure. Should that happen, India's defence modernisation plan would suffer irretrievable damage.

Having seen the adverse effects of banning Bofors, HDW and Denel, they dread a similar fate for a large number of ambitious plans under implementation. IAI is deeply involved in most of the major modernisation plans of the three services. In addition to the upgradation of fighter aircraft (Jaguar, MIG-21, MIG-29 and Mirage-2000), transport aircraft (AN-32) and all helicopters of MI series, it is supplying three Airborne Early Warning and Control System (AWACS) systems to India. It is also the prime supplier of unmanned aerial vehicles to the three services. Most importantly, IAI is involved in a number of developmental projects. India simply cannot afford to cut off all dealings with it. The saga of banning Bofors, HDW and Denel cannot be repeated.

Bofors

After carrying out trials of various guns on offer, India opted for Bofors 155 mm FH-77B towed artillery system. A contract for 410 systems was signed with the Swedish firm in 1986 for Rs1437.72 crore. The contract included transfer of technology for subsequent manufacture of guns in India. India had planned to produce 1,840 pieces within the country to equip 92 artillery regiments. However, with the exposure of kickbacks, the Government banned Bofors for all future dealings. It had the following effect:-

- Although India had paid for transfer of technology, it failed to utilise it. India lost an opportunity to create a base for further development of artillery weapon systems. As a result, indigenous competence to manufacture and maintain guns remained stunted.
- As spares could not be procured from Bofors, middlemen thrived making huge profits. In the absence of adequate spares, the Army had to cannibalise parts from some guns to keep other guns functional. Essential maintenance also suffered.
- Without help from Bofors, India is struggling to carry out overhauling of guns in the stipulated time frame. It is feared that delay in overhaul will adversely affect extension of useful life of the gun systems. Indigenous capacity installed with a Base Repair Workshop is far too less and it will take unacceptably long to overhaul the complete inventory.
- The Navy was already using Bofors guns on some ships and they faced difficulties in ensuring regular supply of spares.
- Indian inventory of 84 mm Carl Gustav Rocket Launchers suffered as Carl Gustav subsequently became a subsidiary of Bofors and thus, came under the ban.

Denel

Discussions were in final stages with Denel of South Africa for 155 mm howitzers (both towed and self-propelled) when it emerged that Denel had employed unacceptable means to grab contract for the supply of NTW-20 Anti-Material Rifle. It was alleged that Denel had engaged middlemen to offer bribes to obtain sensitive information about the internal proceedings of the

Commercial Negotiation Committee. The Government decided to blacklist Denel in 2005 and cancel all orders placed on it. The development was highly unfortunate. Bhim project was almost concluded with Denel's T-6 155mm turret from the G-6 being mounted on Arjun hull.

An initial order had also been placed on a public sector undertaking. With the blacklisting of Denel, Indian Army's Field Artillery Rationalisation Plan suffered a crippling blow. The total requirement envisaged by 2025 is 3600 artillery guns of 155mm/52 calibre. The current inventory is of 410 Bofors guns only. Therefore, India desperately wants to procure 400 additional gun systems (220 wheeled and 180 tracked) on priority to meet inescapable minimum requirement.

Field trials in respect of wheeled systems were carried out in 2003 to ascertain compliance of Services Qualitative Requirements. Three competitors participated-Denel, Soltam Atmos 2000 and FH77 of SWS Defence. All the three systems failed to meet specified standards. Retrials of duly improved versions were held in 2004. With the blacklisting of Denel, the choice got limited to Soltam and FH77. As per the press reports, FH77 emerged far superior to Soltam and was the choice of the Army. However, due to politically sensitive reasons, the Government incorrectly termed the case as a single vendor situation and decided to float fresh tender enquiries with reformulated Qualitative Requirements. Tender for wheeled guns was floated in March 2007 and the second tender for tracked guns followed soon thereafter. It is learnt that 12 producers of guns have been invited.

Nearly 20 years have passed since the induction of Bofor guns; no new gun system has been procured. Due to ban on Bofors and Denel, India has shut doors on two major producers of guns and thereby limited its choice. Continued shortage of suitable 155mm/52 calibre gun systems implies major gaps in India's defence preparedness. Additionally, India's quest for indigenous production of 155 mm ammunition also suffered a major blow. Work on a new ordnance factory in Nalanda to manufacture 155mm ammunition for Bofors guns has got stalled, as Denel was to provide technical know-how. Hundreds of crores of rupees have also gone down the drain.

HDW

The case of HDW makes instructive reading. A contract was signed with the German firm in December 1981. India was to get two HDW 209 class fully built submarines and sub-assemblies and components for assembling two other submarines in India. HDW was also to provide required training to Indian personnel.

HDW delivered two submarines in 1987 and two more were assembled in India in due course. As allegations of bribery and kickbacks became public, the Government decided to blacklist the company. It was also decided not to build any more submarines of the same class. Marlog, a company jointly owned by HDW and Ferrostal, took over the responsibility to fulfil all contractual obligations.

There are just a handful of competent submarine manufacturers in the world. By blacklisting HDW, India antagonized one of the leading producers and thereby deprived itself of the benefits of latest technological advancements. HDW is the world leader with the most advanced air-independent propulsion system. Continued collaboration would have given a boost to indigenous submarine building competence. Additionally, India would have acquired wherewithal as regards maintenance, overhaul and repair support.

As India had not received the complete drawings and NATO identification numbers for all spare parts of the submarines, it faced immense problems in procuring them from other sources. Middlemen made huge profits. The Navy wanted to increase the offensive punch of the submarines by mounting Exocet missiles on it. As HDW could not be engaged, others laid unacceptably harsh conditions. Indian plans for the upgradation of the submarine entailed an increase in their length and that could be done only by HDW. To sum up, by blacklisting HDW India deprived itself of maintenance support, upgradation opportunities and development of indigenous skills.

DEFENCE PROCUREMENT PROCEDURE

Defence Procurement Procedure-2008 (DPP-2008) has laid down clear guidelines for all foreign vendors. They are warned not to resort to any unethical practice to influence the decision makers. A 'Pre-Contract Integrity Pact' has been made mandatory for all schemes exceeding Rupees 100 crores. The vendors are required to sign and submit it separately along with the technical and commercial offers. It is a binding agreement in which the procurement agency promises that it will not accept bribes during the procurement process and bidders promise that they will not offer bribes. It also includes an undertaking by each bidder to disclose all payments made in connection with the contract in question to anybody (including agents and other middlemen as well as family members of officials).

The Government can enforce the following sanctions for any violation by a bidder of its commitments or undertakings:-

- Denial or loss of contract.
- Forfeiture of bid security and performance bond.
- Liability for damages to the principal and the competing bidders.
- Finally, debarment of the violator by the principal for an appropriate period of time.

While signing the final contract, every vendor (irrespective of the contract value) is required to give an undertaking that he has not given, offered or promised to give, directly or indirectly any gift, consideration, reward, commission, fees, brokerage or inducement to procure the contract. Any breach of the aforesaid undertaking by the seller or any one employed by him shall entitle the buyer to cancel the contract and all or any other contracts with the seller and recover the loss arising from such cancellation. Should the Government desire to ascertain if any unauthorized payments have been made, a vendor has to allow inspection of his account books.

It will be seen that debarment of a vendor is the last resort and has to be taken only in extreme cases.

Appraisal of the Issue

Before initiating any action against a company, the Government must weigh pros and cons of all alternatives open to it. While punishing a defaulting vendor, own interests must be fully safeguarded. India must consider the following points while taking decision on blacklisting foreign vendors:-

- There are limited manufacturers of major high-tech defence systems in the world. Additionally, world defence trade is circumscribed by embargoes on technology export. Thus, there are very few manufacturers who possess and are willing to offer advanced weaponry to India.
- To develop indigenous defençe industry, India needs imported technology and reliable foreign partners with long term commitment. Blacklisting nullifies all transfer of technology agreements, even if paid for.
- India needs to modernize its armed forces expeditiously and its shopping list spans a vast canvas, including all major systems. As most major defence companies produce a large array of equipment, blacklisting in one contract will have a ripple effect on all other purchases as well.
- India possesses a huge inventory of weapon platforms which are in need of immediate upgradation to increase their useful life. This task can be undertaken by a handful of companies. Banning any will reduce own options.
- No company produces a complete defence system. Most major producers are in fact mere integrators. They outsource major assemblies from varied sources. Blacklisting of an assembly supplier can also jeopardize major acquisition proposals.
- One of the stated aims of DPP-2008 is to 'demonstrate the highest degree of probity and public accountability, transparency in operations, free competition and impartiality'. Blacklisting of vendors reduces competition and forces the Government to resort to single vendor procurements with related cost penalty. This is also contrary to Government's declared policy.
- Every time a finalised contract is suspended, the earmarked funds remain unexpended resulting in their surrender.
- Most importantly, the services get deprived of the essential equipment. It may have critical effect on nation's war preparedness. Fresh floating of tenders entails major delays and cost overruns.

In every irregular transaction, there are always two parties-the bribe giver and the bribe taker. Action must be taken against both and in equal proportion. It is unfair to apportion the entire blame to bribe givers and take no action against those who demand and extract bribes. It conveys an impression that the Government is reconciled to the fact that procurement functionaries are bound to fall prey to temptations, if offered to them. It amounts to a tacit admission by the Government of its inability to find officials with unimpeachable integrity and to exercise control over them. The Government thus, feels that the onus of keeping all transactions clean is entirely on the vendors-they should decline to pay bribes even if demanded by the decision makers. This is a strange logic. Instead of putting its own house in order, India holds foreign vendors accountable for all wrong-doings.

The Way Forward

The Government must have conclusive proof that a major breach of probity provisions has taken place. Media reports and rumours cannot be the sole basis. As has been seen, a majority of media reports are subjective, biased and even planted to sabotage a deal. This could be done either by a losing vendor or even by entities inimical to India's interests. As has been seen earlier, every blacklisting of a foreign vendor puts back India's defence modernisation plans by decades. Undoubtedly, it is the most cost effective option available to adversaries to impede India's defence preparedness.

Retaliatory action must always be well considered and commensurate with the degree of misdemeanor. It does not have to be blacklisting at the outset. It is prudent to follow a phased and graduated approach for two reasons. One, the defaulting vendor gets unambiguous message that the Government means business and the vendor should exercise due caution in further dealings. Secondly, should blacklisting become inescapable, the Government can time it to suit own requirements. In the case of HDW, hasty action to ban the company deprived India of catalogues and drawings. India could have easily waited for a few months.

India must also remember that banning a major foreign vendor may have little effect on his business and India may suffer more. Thus the whole exercise of punishing a foreign vendor for his alleged misdemeanor may become counter productive and end up boomeranging on India. In fact this is exactly what has happened in all cases. We have ended up shooting in our own foot. There cannot be another example of immature and reckless decision making. While trying to fix a vendor for his misconduct, we put our own defence modernisation plans in disarray, with consequent critical capability gaps and cost overruns.

The Government seems to have realised the foolhardiness of its policy. It has decided to tread cautiously. Blacklisting of Bofors has been revoked as the company is now owned by SWS Defence with considerable equity being held by a US based company. The Government should similarly allow HDW to do business with India. Nearly 20 years have lapsed and India has not been able to collate conclusive proof of wrong-doings. It is time to close the old chapter and start afresh. Although Denel has been proscribed recently, the Government should offer a way out by asking it to make good financial loss with stiff penal deduction. For generating maximum competition to obtain best deals, the Government has to show maturity, practicality and adroit handling. Outright blacklisting is the easiest and the most imprudent way of managing a delicate and highly critical issue.

A sustained and inspired media campaign was carried out by a small section of press to sabotage Scorpene submarine deal. It is to the credit of the Government that it resisted all demands to reopen the case. It is similarly hoped that the current reports against IAI would be looked into judiciously and an objective view taken. In case any misdemeanor is proved, appropriate and balanced action should be taken against both the vendor and the functionaries involved. Blacklisting, however, must remain the last resort. Cutting off your nose to spite your face can never be considered a prudent policy.

10 Indian Army's Modern Plans

Future conventional conflict on the Indian sub-continent will in all probability result from the ongoing low-intensity limited war on the Line of Control (LoC) with Pakistan or the unresolved territorial and boundary dispute with China and will be predominantly a land conflict. The Indian Army seriously lacks a potent firepower punch, especially in the mountain sector. Precision-guided munitions (PGMs) have still to enter service in numbers large enough to make a real difference. The reconnaissance, surveillance and target acquisition (RSTA) assets necessary for the optimum exploitation of even the existing firepower assets are grossly inadequate.

Automated command and control and decision support systems have been on the drawing boards for several decades but are yet to mature. In a future conventional war that will be fought under the nuclear shadow, manoeuvre will be extremely limited. This restriction will lead to much greater emphasis being placed on firepower to achieve the laid down military aim. Hence, it is imperative that artillery modernisation is undertaken with alacrity so as to generate firepower asymmetries on the future battlefield. After a long spell of keeping the powder dry, action on modernisation of the Indian artillery is livening up once again. Since January 2008, the Ministry of Defence (MoD) has issued three global tenders for 155mm guns and howitzers for the mountains, the plains and self-propelled guns for the deserts.

Summer and winter trials are expected to be held over the next one year and, red tape permitting, contracts may be awarded as early as in the first half of 2010. Artillery firepower had paved the way for victory during the Kargil conflict. Despite the lessons learnt in Kargil, modernisation of the artillery had continued to lag behind. The last major acquisition of towed gun-howitzers was that of about 400 pieces of 39-calibre 155mm FH-77B howitzers from Bofors of Sweden in the mid-1980s. This gun had proved its mettle in the Kargil conflict. Just when a contract for 120 tracked and 180 wheeled self-propelled (SP) 155mm guns was about to be concluded after years of protracted trials, South African arms manufacturer Denel, a leading contender for the contract, was alleged to have been involved in a corruption scam in an earlier deal for anti-material rifles (AMRs). The other two howitzers in contention, from Soltam of Israel and BAE (Bofors) of Sweden did not meet the laid down criteria according to the COAS and Army HQ recommended fresh trials, setting the programme back at least three to four years.

Another key issue was that the howitzers that had been offered were technology demonstration models and not guns that were in actual service with the home country armies. The probability of the next conventional war breaking out in the mountains is far higher than that of a war in the plains. With this in view, the artillery recently conceptualised a requirement for a light-weight towed howitzer of 155mm calibre for employment in the mountains. Neither the present Bofors howitzer nor its replacement will be capable of operations in the mountains. A light-weight 45-calibre 155mm howitzer weighing less than 5,000 kg, with a light but adequately powered prime mover, is ideal for the mountains. The gun-train should be capable of negotiating sharp road bends without the need to unhook the gun from the prime mover.

The two British 45-calibre 155mm howitzers that competed for the US contract for a similar howitzer some years ago – the

UFH (Ultra-lightweight Field Howitzer) and the LTH (Light-weight Towed Howitzer) – could be considered for licensed production with transfer of technology. In January 2008, the MoD floated a Request for Proposal (RfP) for 140 pieces of ultra-light 39 calibre 155mm towed howitzers for use by the Indian Army's mountain formations and, presumably, by its rapid reaction divisions – as and when these are raised as it will be easy to transport by air. 140 howitzers will be adequate to equip seven medium artillery regiments and will cost approximately Rs 3,000 crore. The RFP has been reportedly issued to UK's BAE Systems (which now owns Bofors), for the M777 howitzer claimed to be the lightest in the world at under 4,220 kg, and to Singapore Technologies for the Pegasus SLWH.

India has floated a global tender for the purchase of 400 155mm towed artillery guns for the Army, to be followed by indigenous manufacture of another 1,100 howitzers, in a project worth a whopping Rs 8,000 crore. The RFP was issued to eight prospective bidders including BAE, General Dynamics, Nexter (France), Rhinemetall (Germany) and Samsung (South Korea). An RfP has also been issued for 180 wheeled self-propelled guns for around Rs 4,700 crore for employment by mechanised forces in the plains and semi-desert sectors.

Since the Bofors 155mm Howitzer was introduced into service, the indigenously designed and manufactured 105 mm Indian Field Gun (IFG) and its (not so) light version, the Light Field Gun (LFG), have joined the 75/24 Indian Mountain Gun, the 100mm Russian field gun and the 122mm Russian howitzer on the obsolescence list. Approximately 180 pieces of 130mm M46 Russian medium guns have been successfully "up-gunned" to 155mm calibre with ordnance supplied by Soltam of Israel. The new barrel length of 45 calibres has enhanced the range of the gun to about 40 km with extended range ammunition.

A contract for the acquisition of two regiments of the 12-tube, 300mm Smerch multi-barrel rocket launcher (MBRL) system with 90 km range was reported to have been signed with Russia's Rosoboronexport in early-2006. This will be a major boost for the long-range firepower capabilities of the army. If this weapon system had been available during the Kargil conflict, Pakistan's brigade HQ and forward airfield at Skardu and other targets deep inside POK could have been hit with impunity. Extended range (ER) rockets are being introduced for the 122 mm Grad MBRL that has been in service for over three decades. The ER rockets will enhance the weapon system's range from 22 to about 40 km. A Rs 5,000 crore contract has also been signed for the serial production of the Pinaka MBRL weapon system, another DRDO project plagued by time delays and completed with help from Larsen and Toubro and the Tatas.

Modernisation Plan

The modernisation plan of tube artillery alone is likely to cost Rs 13,000 crore. The major acquisitions will be of initial lots of 400 towed howitzers of 155mm calibre, with a barrel length of 52 calibres, costing about Rs 4,000 crore, 140 ultra-light weight 155mm towed howitzers, with a barrel length of 45 calibres, costing Rs 3,000 crore and 180 SP 155mm howitzers costing Rs 5,000 crore. The "Shakti" project for a command and control systems for the artillery, called Artillery Combat Command and Control System (ACCCS), has reached the stage of maturity and is now being fielded up to the regimental level. The BrahMos supersonic cruise missile (Mach 2.8 to 3.0), with a precision strike capability, very high kill energy and range of 290 km, was inducted into the army in July 2007.

It is a versatile missile that can be launched from TATRA mobile launchers and silos on land, aircraft and ships and, perhaps in future, also from submarines. Fifty BrahMos missiles are expected to be produced every year. Efforts are underway to further increase its strike range. BrahMos Aerospace has orders worth Rs 3,500 crore from the army and the navy, which has opted for the anti-ship as well as the land attack cruise missile (LACM) versions. These terrain hugging missiles are virtually immune to counter measures due to their high speed and very low radar cross section and are far superior to sub-sonic cruise missiles like Pakistan's Babur. Chile, Kuwait, Malaysia and South Africa have shown interest in acquiring this missile.

The Indian army is extensively engaged in ongoing internal security (IS) and counter-insurgency operations (CI) and simultaneously needs to prepare itself for a future border conflict that may spill over to a larger conventional war in the plains. In keeping with these twin requirements, Army HQ have apparently decided to upgrade the IS and CI capabilities of infantry battalions as well as enhance their Infantry firepower-mobility-EW (electronic warfare) punch for a possible war in the plains against Pakistan or in the mountains against China. The Army Chief's modernisation vision is to "adapt to high-end technology, improve night-fighting capability... (and) information technology, information warfare and network centric warfare."

Despite its large-scale employment on border management and extensive commitments in Internal Security and Counter Insurgency operations, infantry modernisation had been languishing for several decades when the Ministry of Defence (MoD) finally cleared a visionary plan to modernise the army's infantry battalions by according "in principle" approval in the form of Modification 4B to the war establishment (WE) of a standard infantry battalion in 1998. However, no funds were specially sanctioned for this purpose till the BJP-led NDA government approved the expenditure of Rs 3,500 crore in September 2003. Thereafter, approval had to be sought on file for each new weapon system or piece of equipment on a "case-by-case" basis as has become the norm. It is by now well-known how each such case chronicles the saga of an uphill struggle to get approval first from the MoD, then MoD (Finance) and, finally, the Ministry of Finance (MoF). All this is only possible after the DRDO has first certified that the weapon system or equipment in question cannot be developed and manufactured indigenously and such a certificate is hard to come by.

While 250 Kornet-E anti-tank guided missiles (ATGMs) with thermal imaging sights have substantially increased the anti-tank capability of infantry battalions, most efforts to modernise the equipment held by infantry and Rashtriya Rifles (RR) units are aimed at enhancing their capability for surveillance and target acquisition at night and boosting their firepower for precise retaliation against infiltrating columns and terrorists holed up in built-up areas. About 200 hand-held BFSRs with practical ranges up to seven to eight km where clear line of sight is available, 2,000 hand-held thermal imaging devices (HHTIs) with ranges up to 2,000 metres for observation at night and stand-alone infra-red, seismic and acoustic sensors with varying capabilities have enabled infantrymen to dominate the Line of Control so completely that infiltration has come down to almost a trickle.

The newly acquired weapons, which complement these surveillance and observation devices, include: 1,500x84 mm rocket launchers, including some disposable ones; 1,000 AMRs (anti-material rifles); 8,000 UBGLs (under-barrel grenade launchers); 4,000 new generation carbines; 300 bullet proof vehicles; and, several hundred accurate sniper rifles. However, the numbers acquired and the ammunition stocks are still inadequate and need to be made up more rapidly. While the INSAS 5.56 mm assault rifles have now been in service for almost 10 years and proved to be effective, the light machine gun (LNG) version is still facing teething problems and the carbine version for close quarter battle has not found favour with the army. New 5.56 mm assault rifles of bull-pup design with an integrated laser range finder and grenade launcher are under development. Efforts are also being made to provide infantry platoons and sections with integrated GPS-based navigation system, secure light-weight walkie-talkie radio sets and better protective gear with a helmet that incorporates a built-in head-up display.

The mechanised infantry is now equipped with the BMP-2 ICV Sarath of which over 1,000 have been built since 1987. A new variant is the 81 mm Carrier Mortar Tracked Vehicle (CMTV) that is based on the chassis of the Sarath ICV and has been indigenously developed to enhance the integral firepower available to mechanised infantry battalions. Other variants include a command post, an ambulance, armoured dozer and engineer and reconnaissance vehicles. Mechanised reconnaissance and support battalions need better surveillance radars, fire-and-forget ATGMs and effective night fighting capability. However, their capabilities can be upgraded on a lower priority compared with infantry battalions that are engaged in border management and IS/CI operations.

The army's infantry battalions also need their own mini or micro UAVs like Elbit's Skylark or Rafael's Skylite, among others, to partly reduce the extent of patrolling necessary in internal security environment and to improve their surveillance capability in conventional conflict. These UAVs should have a range of about 10 to 15 km, should be light-weight (less than 10 kg), hand-launched, carry a single payload, e.g. a daylight video camera or infra-red camera for night operations, and should be inexpensive enough to be dispensable. A mini ground control station should be authorized at battalion HQ for planning and control. Ideally, these should be indigenously designed and developed and locally manufactured.

New DRDO Project

A new DRDO project, that is reported to be ongoing, aims to equip future soldiers with lightweight force multipliers. Soldiers of the future will have miniaturised communication and GPS systems, small power packs, weapon platforms and smart vests with fibre-optic sensors. The soldiers will also have better and lighter combat fatigues, boots, belts, ammunition pouches, rucksacks and rations in the form of meals-ready-to-eat. Though somewhat akin to the US Army's Land Warrior programme, the Indian Army programme for modernisation of infantry battalions will result in only incremental changes. However, these would be significant enough to make a difference on the battlefields of the Indian sub-continent. The infantryman's average combat load is approximately 27 kg, including the 3.06 kg 5.56 mm INSAS assault rifle and its "on weapon" ammunition. If this can be reduced by even a few kg, it will enable the soldier to improve his agility in battle and counter-insurgency operations. Ultimately an infantryman has to be prepared to engage in hand-to-hand combat and agility can make a difference between life and death.

For over 350 infantry battalions, plus about 150 Rashtriya Rifles, Assam Rifles and Territorial Army battalions, these major changes will be extremely costly to implement and will spill over at least 10 to 12 years – that is, if the funds can be found. What is certain is that there is no alternative to making the financial commitment that is necessary to enhance the operational capabilities of the army's infantry battalions. Without modernising this cutting edge of its sword, the army will soon begin to resemble the armies of India's lesser neighbours.

The indigenously designed Arjun main battle tank (MBT) has been in the pipeline for over two decades. Though the tank has many good features, it has consistently failed to meet the army's GSQR for an MBT and orders have been placed for only 124 tanks to be manufactured. The lack of progress on the Arjun MBT had slowed down the pace of armour modernisation. India then signed a deal with Russia to acquire 310 T-90S tanks in the year 2000. Subsequently, India began to assemble these tanks at Avadi. It has recently been reported that in addition to these, India has decided to acquire another 347 T-90S tanks and assemble them within the country.

The first Indian assembled T-90S (Bhishma) rolled off the production line on January 8, 2004. While T-90S Russian tanks have provided new teeth to India's strike formations in the plains and corrected the imbalance that had resulted from Pakistan's acquisition of T-80 UD from Ukraine and the Al Khalid tanks jointly designed with China, a large number of T-72 (Ajeya) tanks are still awaiting modernisation. The lack of a suitable fire control system and night fighting capability are major handicaps. As soon as the obsolescent Vijayanta tanks are phased out of service, it will be time to also discard the old T-55s as well as they can no longer be either upgraded or modernised. Armour modernisation is now proceeding apace and can be classified as a success story.

The air defence (AD) of mechanised forces is another area that is crying for attention. The Kvadrat missile system that has been the backbone of AD for strike formations since the early 1970s are now ageing and need urgent replacement. With the DRDO's indigenous Akash medium-range and Trishul short-range missile projects not making major headway, it is time to start looking at import substitutes. In fact, the assets of Army Air Defence corps of the army are grossly inadequate to provide effective protection against enemy aircraft during war. This young corps requires substantial capital infusion to really come into its own.

Another DRDO project that is way behind schedule is the Nag anti-tank missile system. The antiquated Jonga-mounted SS-11 B1 anti-tank guided missile (ATGM) system has been replaced in missile battalions by MILAN shoulder-fired ATGMs. However, a vehicle-mounted missile system like the Nag is definitely necessary for reconnaissance and attrition tasks. The experimental Plan AREN tactical communications system for strike formations needs early replacement. The ability to carry broadband data needs to be enhanced in particular. Even the more recent static communications network called ASCON lacks ISDN capability for the real-time transmission of maps and streaming video.

While some Stentor long-range BFSRs have been in service for over a decade, medium-range radars are still to be acquired. At least about 30 to 40 weapon locating radars (WLRs) are required for effective counter-bombardment, especially in the plains, and only a few have been procured so far. Israeli Searcher-I unmanned aerial vehicles (UAVs) have been introduced into service but these are few in number and it will be a long time before these will really make a difference by providing a real-time surveillance capability so that ground forces can initiate action even as a fresh input is received. Only a small number of Searcher – II UAVs, with an upper ceiling that makes them suitable for the mountains, have been acquired.

An automated command and control and decision support system for use by the General Staff is still a far cry and so are supporting systems like the battlefield surveillance system and air space management system. The urgent requirement of real-time satellite reconnaissance systems has still not been accepted despite the nuclear overhang under which the armed forces now operate. Even though the cameras on India's remote sensing and cartographic satellites now have sharply enhanced resolutions, less than one metre, military-grade photographs of still better resolution are needed to be purchased from the open market. These sources may dry up quickly during war.

A "system of systems" approach must be followed so that scarce RSTA and communications resources can be synergistically configured and optimally exploited. The war in Iraq fought in March-April 2003 was based on the concept of "network-centric warfare" in which surveillance sensors, targeting systems and "shooters" are fused together in a seamless "system of systems" that reduced response time between the acquisition of a target and its destruction to 15 to 20 minutes. While such a system may take over a decade to establish, a beginning must be made right away.

PGMs are increasingly gaining currency as weapons of choice in conflict on land, both to accurately destroy critical hard targets quickly as well as to avoid or at least minimise collateral damage. During the Gulf War I in 1991, despite all the CNN-generated hype of smart bombs flying unerringly through ventilators, PGMs formed less than 10 percent of the total high explosive dropped over Iraq and were rather inaccurate. The "collateral" destruction of an air raid shelter harbouring women and children has been too well documented to bear recounting. The coalition forces did not destroy a single Iraqi Scud missile launcher. In Kosovo, PGMs accounted for about 30 per cent of the ordnance dropped and accuracies had improved considerably by 1999. In the post-September 11, 2001 retribution inflicted on the Taliban militia and its al Qaeda supporters in Afghanistan, the share of PGMs had risen to nearly 60 percent. In Gulf War II in Iraq, the ratio of PGMs went up to nearly 70 per cent. The Indian artillery does not have any PGMs worth the name. Only limited quantities of the Russian Krasnopol PGM have been imported for the Bofors 155 mm howitzer. Among others, the Bofors Bonus PGM is a suitable candidate, subject to successful trials in the deserts and the mountains.

Finally, the approach to army modernisation must be more focused; the priorities must be clearly established and then adhered to. The government must give a firm commitment in terms of funds and the Ministry of Defence must streamline its procedures and processes for speedy procurement of high priority weapons and equipment. It is time to institute a rolling, non-lapsable defence modernisation fund of Rs. 25,000 crores as a viable method of ensuring that defence procurement is not subjected to the vagaries of annual budgets. The present situation is disturbing and, if allowed to go on indefinitely, will seriously compromise the army's preparedness to fight the next border war that inimical neighbours like Pakistan can be expected to thrust on India.

MODERNISING THE INDIAN INFANTRY

Why has it taken the Army so long to conceive an upgrade package for the oldest, most potent and intensely employed fighting arm, the Infantry, even after the so-called revolution in military affairs? The foot soldier, the original and most versatile weapon system that is always taken for granted, has emerged from the dubious shock and awe strategy of recent campaigns as its ultimate arbiter. India has paid dearly for the neglect of its infantry in terms of cost, casualties and over-stretch of battle. But the Infantry has never let us down. Kargil was its finest hour. Gen VP Malik, the Army Chief of the time, wryly noted: "We will fight with what we have." So when for the first time an international conference of Army and defence industry was launched last week to put the forgotten soldier centre-stage, some misgivings were natural.

While Army Chief Gen JJ Singh outlined his vision for the soldier system of the future, the conspicuous and total absence of Government-MoD-robbed the conference of any sanctity. In sharp contrast, for a MoD-sponsored defence finance seminar earlier in the month, Government officials and ministers were stepping over each other at Vigyan Bhavan. Free India's Army came into being in 1947 and within weeks, the Infantry soldiers landed in Srinagar to save J&K from being gobbled up by Pakistani tribal raiders.

Since then, the Infantry has not ceased fighting proxy wars there and later, elsewhere too. A former Army Chief, Gen SR Choudhury, who was not from the Infantry, described the Infantry as the Army and vice versa. Field Marshal Montgomery said: An army is considered only as good as its Infantry. The experience of four wars, several border skirmishes, two out-of-area missions, the ceaseless campaign to counter cross-border terrorism in Kashmir, numerous other insurgencies in the North-East, internal stability operations elsewhere in the country and UN peace keeping operations make the Indian Infantry the most battle-hardened and combat rich force in the world.

The simple and uncomplaining infantryman has given so much to so many for so little. The modernisation of the infantry was first attempted-halfheartedly-in the mid-1980s by the Perspective Planning branch of the Army Headquarters. The bias for mechanised warfare, zealously pursued by Gen Sundarji, was so pronounced that the Infantry modernisation plan was skipped altogether. Guns, tanks, APCs were the weapons in demand. The Infantry was ignored. Had a modest upgrade package been undertaken at that time, infantry would have been more combat contemporary and effective. Instead, till recently, some soldiers were still using World War II equipment and clothing.

Shameful as it was, soldiers had to buy rucksacks and other accoutrements from the market. DRDO is still to come out with a light bulletproof vest. The Army failed to accurately visualize the nature of combat it would fight in the future. Pakistan-sponsored insurgency in Punjab did not alert the nation and the Army to the proxy war brewing in J&K. We defaulted on both counts-anticipating low intensity conflict and cross border terrorism and preparing the Infantry for it. Despite the sustained counter-insurgency and counter-terrorism campaign in J&K and the North-East since the 1990s, the Army was sluggish in investing in the infantry.

The first Gulf War reintroduced the fiction that wars could be won from the air. The air campaigns in Bosnia and Kosovo temporarily turned fiction into reality. But 9/11 broke the myth of supremacy of air power. Operation Enduring Freedom in Afghanistan lasted 76 days; 65 of these were air operations. The 11-day land offensive secured a temporary and incomplete victory against the Taliban. Operation Iraqi Freedom on the other hand, fought for 20 days was bereft of any preparatory air campaign though a secret air war preceded it. Unhappily for the US/NATO-led coalition forces, despite their pyrrhic military victories, low intensity wars in Afghanistan and Iraq are continuing in full blaze.

The recent 34-day war in Lebanon and the ongoing campaign in Gaza demonstrate the limits of Israel's military power. Used to decisive victories in less than 10 days, Israeli Defence Forces (IDF) were badgered by Hassan Nasrallah's jihadi militia. Reliance on air power, tanks and guns in Lebanon as substitute for ground troops-infantry-was motivated by casualty aversion. We too have to be sensitive to casualties.

The wars in Lebanon, Iraq and Afghanistan spurred by the growing cult of Osama bin Laden and Hassan Nasrallah require a redefinition of the concept of power and military success. Success would necessarily be an inclusive military victory encompassing post-conflict stability and reconstruction. For this we need Infantry.

The Indian Army should not get overly seduced by high-sounding warfare like 'netcentric' that the West is being diverted into. This is not to suggest we ignore the strides in high-tech warfare. But as a former US NATO Commander noted recently: "This netcentric stuff is great but our men in Baghdad are being blown up with their Humvees by IEDs." He suggested that we address the battle we are fighting before switching to the one we will fight in the future.

India's supreme operational challenge is and will be the maintenance of internal security. Just last month, Prime Minister Manmohan Singh stated this ground reality. The Infantry is at the heart of counterinsurgency and counter-terrorism operations and may well get sucked into anti-Naxal operations as well. Keeping the Army operationally ready for both conventional and unconventional missions is imperative but the emphasis has to be on the business of the day: CI and CT.

The Indian Infantry is belatedly embarking on a modernisation programme to enhance its combat skills through increased lethality, communications, surveillance, mobility and suvivability. These force multipliers will enable the soldier to fight all-weather, 24x7 and on any terrain in the right battle-configuration albeit with the accent on LOC.

The GSQR for the Future-Infantry-Soldier-As a System (F-INSAS) must empower not encumber the soldier. DRDO must compete with domestic and international industry. DRDO has one more chance to make amends for its omissions and commissions. F-INSAS must strike the right balance between the surge of technology and sensibility of the soldier keeping the battle of the future in mind. Defence Minister AK Antony should accord F-INSAS the highest strategic priority.

11 The Indian Navy in 2020

The Indian Navy of 2010-20 is already being built – the Air Defence Ship at Kochi, the Vikramaditya (Ex Gorshkov) in Russia, along with its complement of MiG 29K, the Naval LCA at Bangalore, the Scorpene submarines at MDL, and at last count about 22 Destroyers, Frigates, corvettes, LSTs, OPVs, and FACs at various shipyards around the country. We must, therefore, look at what is needed, and what is possible, for the time frame of 2020-2030, and what else is needed to fill the voids prior to 2020. In arriving at the final figures we must take into account the probable security challenges and maritime threats that we will need to counter and the maritime interests that we will need to protect, preserve and indeed promote; India's stature and position in the comity of nations; our economic potential; and finally our design, industrial and ship-building capability.

A little "crystal ball gazing" is, therefore, an essential part of the planning process – never an easy thing to do at the best of times. Security Environment and Challenges Geo-strategic Location. Geography, they say is the handmaiden of strategy – and geography has indeed been very kind to us. It has bestowed on India many strategic opportunities, options and indeed advantages some of which are:-

- A coastline of 7516 Km, which includes the mainland as also the Island territories.
- 12 major, 21 intermediate and 164 minor ports.
- A total of 1197 Islands, which provide Defence in Depth and also give us a huge EEZ. At 2.01 million sq km our EEZ is 2/3rds of our land area. After demarcation of the continental shelf our EEZ is likely to be 2.54 million sq km.
- A very favourable geo-strategic location astride the vital East-West trade routes, which enables us to control, when necessary, this energy/trade lifeline. Position matters – on land as on the Sea.
- Moreover, the ocean that laps our shores is itself unique. Unlike other oceans, it is not "open-ended". It is closed to the North by the Indian sub-continent and has a few "choke points" that afford entry into it.

Unregulated Ocean Space. Speaking to the press at Singapore on 12 Nov 2003 I had described the Oceans as "the largest unregulated space in the world", a quote that has appeared in the editorial of the 2005 edition of "Jane's Fighting Ships". As the editorial points out, this may seem strange considering that the UN Convention on the Laws of the Sea is now in place. But the fact is that while the UNCLOS has given various rights to nations, the right to freedom of navigation has not changed, nor have the attributes and essential characteristics of the oceans that constitute 70% of the surface of the globe. These attributes are:-

- Large parts of the Oceans remain Unowned. While nations have sovereign rights over their territorial seas and commercial rights to all the resources in their EEZ, no nation "Owns" the "High Seas".
- Because the High seas are largely unowned, they are uncontrolled. It's a case of "No Policeman-No Law". On the high seas there is nobody, but nobody, to control your movements.
- Because the High Seas are unowned, there are No Boundaries at Sea. This is what makes the Navy different

to all other Services, which work within the confines of national boundaries. The Navy works in an International arena on a daily basis. Twelve miles out of port and we are in International waters.

- Because of these attributes of the Oceans, the Sea is One.

Thus, all nations with a coastline are maritime neighbours.

Maritime Terrorism. The new scourge of terrorism has taken the world by storm. So far major acts of terrorism have by and large been restricted to land areas. But as security on land is tightened, the ease of access and movement across the world's ocean areas will tempt terrorists to take their "trade" to sea. The war on terror at sea cannot be fought by individual nations. It will have to be a worldwide effort that will require Navies of the world to work together – as countries are doing ashore.

Nuclear Backdrop. We are now a declared nuclear weapon state (NWS) and, after some hiccups, the world has accepted this reality. Our nuclear doctrine clearly states that we will maintain a "Credible Minimum Deterrent" based on a triad of weapon delivery systems. We are also a declared "No First Use" (NFU) NWS. Any country with an NFU policy must ensure that it has an assured second-strike capability. Missile silos, airfields and aircraft are easily detected by satellites and are hence easy targets. A nuclear submarine is very, very difficult to detect. Even if detected, it is extremely difficult to target, as it is constantly on the move at speeds of twenty knots or more.

Territorialisation of the Seas. Maritime powers have always wanted (as they still do) as much freedom of the seas, as possible; whereas non-maritime powers want as much ownership of the seas, as possible. With the UNCLOS, both have got much of what they wanted. Almost 40% of the ocean areas have become the Exclusive Economic zones of countries. The full claims for the world's EEZ have yet to be submitted by many countries and agreed to by the UN, and more important, by neighbouring states. Earlier we had neighbours and boundaries only on land. Now we have them at sea as well. The more the neighbours, the more are the problems. The larger the EEZ, the greater is the area of responsibility of the maritime Services.

Global Governance. Globalisation has made countries more inter-dependent and States will increasingly work together to ensure their economic development, as also to promote peace, stability and combat common threats. In future, therefore, one sees a form of "Global Governance" slowly but surely creeping to seaward to ensure that the "Freedom of the Seas", that the west holds so dear, is not misused by terrorists. The ISPS code, the Container Security Initiative and the Proliferation Security Initiative are manifestations of this trend. This will require the Indian Navy to patrol its area of interest, and work with other Navies, much more than it has done in the past.

Strategic Frontiers. What then is The Indian Navy's "area of interest"? Our land frontiers are well known. So also are our maritime boundaries with our immediate maritime neighbours. But our current area of interest lies far, far beyond our territorial sea and the EEZ. It extends all the way to the choke points that afford entry into the North Indian Ocean.

Extra-Regional Presence. Any nation with the capability can traverse the Oceans and arrive in force at the doorstep of another maritime state-no matter how distant it may be. Powerful Navies have indulged in "Gun Boat Diplomacy" in the past. While the phrase may be out of fashion these days, Navies continue to be used for the same purpose, by whatever name it may be called. It is well known that the strategic focus of the world has once again shifted to the North Indian Ocean, due to a combination of Terrorism and world energy reserves. The presence of extra-regional powers in the Indian Ocean is bound to last well into the foreseeable future. The Indian Navy consequently has to operate in the same waters as are being patrolled by the world's most technologically advanced nations.

Defence of Trade. Trade is the lifeblood of any economy–and so it is with India. Our economy is booming and this trade will continue to soar. Today 90% of the crude oil we use comes from across the oceans – be it imported or produced in our offshore oil fields. Our dependence on natural gas is increasing by the day. Over 95% of our trade by volume comes across the oceans. Any disruption of this trade lifeline, particularly any disruption in the flow of oil, will endanger the economic prosperity and security of the country. Defence of trade has always been a major mission of the Navy and this will continue to be so.

Maritime Diplomacy. The Navy works very closely with the External Affairs Ministry to further the interests of the country around the world. Towards this end it sends ships on overseas deployments to show the flag and build "Bridges of Friendship"– which was also the theme of the Navy's very successful International Fleet Review in 2001. Towards this end the Navy also trains a considerable number of foreign Naval personnel in its many training institutions. With many small nations on the Indian Ocean rim now getting huge EEZs there is a growing demand for assistance and suitable vessels to patrol these areas. It is in India's interest to meet these demands and supply equipment as and when requested. Since many of these countries cannot afford to buy such vessels we must be willing and ready to supply them at short notice, and free of cost. Budgetary provisions must be regularly made for such assistance.

Regional Naval Expansion. The Naval development plans of maritime states in the Asia-Pacific region clearly indicate that all are giving greater importance to maritime security than ever before– a trend that we must take note of.

The Threat. Very often I have been asked to identify the "Threat" that the Indian Navy is going to face. The immediate threat is well known, but I have always desisted from identifying others because "to name an enemy is to make one". But more important is the fact that in this respect the Navy has to think and plan differently than the other two services, which can clearly identify the threat across our borders. Because of the unregulated ocean space, ease of access and movement a threat can develop from the sea very quickly. So, unlike the other two Services, Navies are not built purely to counter known threats but to protect maritime interests. The larger a country's dependence on the oceans, and the larger its interests at sea, the larger its Navy has got to be.

FLEET MODERNISATION

Availability of Funds. The Navy is a capital intensive Service and it takes a long time to design, develop and build ships. The larger the ship, the longer is the time taken to design and build it. Taking a typical destroyer/frigate (The work horses of any Navy) it takes around 10 to twelve years from Government approval to commissioning, if the ship is to be designed and built in India. Assured funding over three plan periods (i.e. 15 years) is absolutely essential for any planned modernisation. Historically, the fate of Navies has been linked to the fate of their country's economy. Fortunately for us the Indian economy is doing very well and modernisation of the Navy (and indeed of the Armed Forces) can be easily funded over the next three plan periods in particular, and for the future in general. This statement is supported by published/stated figures for the Indian economy and the assumptions at sub-paras (d) and (e) below:-

- The GDP in 2004-05 was around Rs 2658750 Crores.
- The GDP has been growing at an average rate of 6.35% and very recently the PM announced that this year it will grow at 7% (for the first time the GDP growth in the first half of the fiscal year has been over 8%) and there is every possibility that it could touch 10% in the future.
- The percentage of GDP allocated for Defence during the latter 1980s varied from 3.08 to 4.24%. Since then this has gradually dropped, and from 1991 to 2005 the percentage has varied from 2.77 to 2.24. This was quite inadequate to fund the modernisation of the armed forces.
- We have been able to afford 3 to 4% of GDP for defence in the past and we can easily do so in the future. It must become stated Government policy that we will spend 3% to 4% of GDP for defence;

Besides making adequate money available for defence, it will also enable planned modernisation which has not really been possible in the past as, more often than not, the Budget has driven the "Plan" rather than the Plan driving the Budget. Assuming a modest 6.35% growth rate, the expected GDP at five yearly intervals is likely to be:

- 10-10 Rs 36,17,137 Crores
- 15-15 Rs 49,20,989 Crores
- 20-20 Rs 66,94,835 Crores
- 25-25 Rs 91,08,091 Crores
- 30-30 Rs 123,91,243 Crores

Share of the Defence Cake. How much each Service should get from the allocations for Defence has always been somewhat contentious. The Navy being the smallest of the three Services, has always received the least. As early as in 1988, General Sundarji had stated that by 2000 the Navy should get 20% of the Defence budget. He realized the value of a Navy in World affairs. Regrettably, this has not happened and it was only in 2002-03 that the Navy crossed the 15% mark and received the highest ever allocation of 17.6% in 2003-04. Since then it has hovered around the 17% mark and this should gradually be increased to 20% as India will certainly need a powerful Blue Water Navy as it takes up greater responsibility in world affairs. The peace process currently underway will ultimately give us a Peace Dividend that will allow us to reduce troops on the border. (Sub-continental Armies are perhaps the only ones that are amassed on the borders. The rest of the world takes boundaries for granted and respects them) For planning purposes, however, let us assume an allocation of 17%. Even with this, the expected allocations to the Navy as shown below (assuming only 3% of GDP is allocated for Defence) would be adequate to fund the projects/modernization being recommended :-

- XI Plan 2007-08 to 2011-12 Rs 92586 Crores
- XII Plan 2012-13 to 2016-17 Rs 125960 Crores
- XIII Plan 2017-18 to 2021-22 Rs 171366 Crores

Aircraft Carriers. For many years now the Indian Navy has been stating that it needs a minimum of three aircraft carriers to fulfil its missions. One is required to be operational on each coast and the third will normally be under maintenance. After much delay (it took over 15 years!), the Government finally approved the construction of the Air Defence Ship to replace the INS Vikrant, which was phased out in 1997. It took 8 years to get government approval to induct the Ex-Gorshkov (now christened Vikramaditya), which will replace Viraat in 2008/09. It is time now to place the order for the third carrier, which should really be a repeat of the ADS. Batch building of ships and standardization greatly reduce the life cycle costs of a ship. Moreover, for the third carrier we will not have to invest in a separate carrier air wing, as the intention and requirement is to have only two carriers operational at any one time. If approved now, we will have three carriers in the 2020s.

Strategic Forces. Now that India is a declared Nuclear Weapon state with a No First Use Policy it is absolutely essential that we put our second strike capability in Nuclear Submarines as soon as possible. There are many advantages in doing so and the actions of existing NW States are good indicators of the direction in which we should go. The Government should approve, start and fund such a programme at the earliest, as it is vital for the security of the country. The ultimate aim should be to have at least four such submarines so that at least one, if not two, are on patrol at all times.

Destroyers and Frigates. These ships are really the workhorses of the Navy, both in peace and war. Today, we have 11 destroyers and 11 frigates, which are far too few. In fact, after the 1962 war a study had recommended that the Navy should have 28 such warships – a target that the Navy has never been able to achieve. Forty years down the line much has changed and the responsibility of the Navy has increased manifold. In the next 20 years this figure must go upto at least 20 of each type. Five Leander Class frigates are already well past their prime and need immediate replacement. (One was earlier decommissioned without a replacement) Three project 17 Frigates under construction will replace the first three Leanders. The three Godavri class frigates will need to be replaced between 2010 and 2015 by which time they will be between 25 to 30 yrs old. Thus there is an immediate need to place orders for at least six more P17 frigates, just to maintain the current force levels of Frigates. Additional orders will need to be placed on MDL and GRSE to take the frigate numbers to twenty by 2025.

As far as destroyers are concerned, the first of the Kashin class destroyers will be 25 years old this year and the youngest (Ranvijai) will be 17 years. They will all need to be replaced between 2010 and 2020. Three Project 15A destroyers are already on order and it would be cost effective to increase this order to five so that they replace the five Kashins.

It will thus be seen that Mazagon Docks, the shipyard building both the P17 Frigates and the P 15A Destroyers, must deliver 9 x P 17 frigates and 5 x P15A destroyers between now and 2020 i.e. almost one ship a year – assuming that orders are placed well in time and no delays are introduced. Going by their past performance they will not be able to meet this target and so the only option to maintain present force levels will be to exercise the import option and a repeat order for the Talwar class destroyers recently imported from Russia is a very attractive option. A minimum of four should be immediately ordered to maintain force levels. Additional orders for the Talwar class and/or the Delhi Class must be placed a little later to take the destroyer fleet upto 20 by 2025.

Submarines: Submarines are a vital part of the Naval Fleet and ideal for dissuasion and sea denial operations, particularly against a vastly superior Navy. Their operational value in the Indian Ocean is much greater than in the other oceans as the hydrological conditions in our waters afford the submarine many advantages.

2020: DEFENDING INDIA

The Flashpoint. NATO's Allied Force saw induction of more than 400 planes into the Balkan skies. Phase-I witnessed cruise missiles, F-117 Nighthawks, B-2 bombers, F-15/16 Eagles, F-16 Falcons and B-52 bombers which rolled in from as the diverse directions and places as Adriatic Sea, Missouri, Italy and England. With that Kosovo moved to a new level of misery. The largest air attacks since WWII commenced on a country which does not threaten the global equilibrium nor its neighbours. And none know the precise exit strategy nor the endgame. However, this much is clear that the resultant giagantic refugee problem will heavily eat into the NATO manpower and resources for a long time to come.

Of late, unfortunately, the American foreign policy has been driven by ultimatums. Whenever, a disagreement occurs, the lone super power needs to deliver on such threats. But the air attacks without ground troops support cannot always win. So Osama bin Laden remains where he was. Saddam continues to visit his mistresses. And now NATO's credibility is up for grabs. The Balkans is likely to be the graveyard of air-attacks-alone theory.

For history argues that a determined infantry cannot be evicted by massive air attacks. The Kosovo spillover will not only impact on the health of the EU, but also put a question mark on the American global dominance.

However, Americans are likely to continue with such ill-advised actions on a variety of flashpoints worldwide in a desperate attempt to disallow emerging new power equations. This will further tie down in knots the NATO credibility. Let's try to visualise how India can re-organise internally to meet the new challenges arising out of the deteriorating international scenario.

The Indian Faultline. This faultline can be traced back to the Mauryan empire's unwise decision of renouncing war. Like corporate graphs, the military power graph of a nation either gradually creeps upwards or if not in use, the law of gravity pulls it downwards! Thus unwittingly, in subsequent centuries the neglect of the military component resulted in unprecedented foreign invasions. Incomprehension of the dynamics of military power by the subsequent rulers and the attempts to absorb, appease and amalgamate the invading armies put the foreign rulers at the seat of power in Delhi with ease. This is akin to allowing an adversary in a soccer match to dominate your half of the field. Obviously goals will be scored.

The other aspect of the Indian Faultline rests on the fact that majority of the Indian rulers employed the military power ruthlessly internally to pacify the outlying provinces (instead of attempting economic development) while refusing to correctly posture it to meet the threats from invasion. This short sighted approach continued on India's attaining independence. Many elders (product of a similar mindset) tend to defend the actions of Indian political leadership of 1947 on singular ground of inexperience. One tends to disagree because all it needed was to review the historical evidence of foreign subjugation and the leadership would automatically have deduced the reasons. And initiated corrective measures. This small exercise really did not require a very high calibre in leadership either.

On one hand, the international stability appears to be in a tail spin. Because the lone super power is determined to rise and shine at every flashpoint despite the time tested principle of never jump into somebody else's civil war. On the other hand, India is finally waking up to the fact that the world does not feed on morals! India needs to re-look and re-fashion its internal factors to meet the prevailing new external lawlessness.

The Have-Nots. Indians over the centuries have done to the Untouchables, what the Americans did to the Blacks. Suppression. The Blacks even today cannot easily rise in the American society because of one simple fear that they will return the favour in ample measures.

Fortunately for India, the Untouchables retain their levels of tolerance like the rest of the Indians. Therefore, rapid education and economic development of the backward/rural areas needs to be implemented on a war footing. Time lost in this respect will be directly proportionate to heightened levels of social disharmony which India can ill-afford as an emerging power.

Unity-in-Diversity. The Indian tragedy is that this slogan since 1947 has only harped on the aspect concerning *diversity,* encouraging divisive tendencies from Kashmir to Kanyakumari! For aspirations towards building a modem nation-state, the buzz word has to be integration and not disintegration. Give spin to integration by merging the MoD with Service Headquarters and right down the line to the Theatre Command. More efficiency at a much lesser cost with availability of a larger fire power.

A unique functional role model of unity in diversity for India is its military. Be it the Sikhs, Rajputs, Jats or the Madras Regiments, the cultural diversity is adequately maintained at the lower end of the spectrum. Uniformity through training is achieved at the higher end of the spectrum.

The social scientist and the economist must sit together with the military analyst to understand, innovate and devise methods to integrate the society accordingly. The military role model respects and encourages secularism and yet manages to effectively knit the diversity in a rare unity. Overall national uniformity in approach is vital for the national health and cannot be disputed. Nor should it be erroneously mistaken as militerization of the Indian mind. Internal harmony will also reduce consumption of military power within. Such surplus of military component then readily will be available to face the external threats. To develop national uniformity in approach, the following elementary steps are recommended.

- Post-independence military actions, battles and wars must be taught to students from the ninth standard onwards. This literature is not only secular but can galvanize the young through acts of courage, compassion and bravery exemplified by the Indian soldier, sailor and the airman. It will also be of immense help to create a larger vision of a diverse India in the young mind. Further, to hone the skills of civilian instructors in the teaching of post independence history in military science departments in colleges, officers from the three services should be put on deputation for two years under study leave provisions.
- On scrutiny, the only all India services are the Army, Navy and the Air Force. Indian Administrative Service or Indian Police Service merely adorn an all India nomenclature. For example an IAS officer from Bihar cadre normally ends up spending his professional tenure between Bihar and Delhi. This needs to be modified like the military. Officers of the civil services like IAS, IPS, etc. should be posted through out the country to increase their vision and interaction with diverse regions and communities. This will provide a fillip to integration.
- A major boost to uniformity in approach can be achieved by lateral induction of the military in civil services. Officers of the Armed Forces imbibe in them the best man and material management techniques that the country can offer. If they are laterally inducted into central and state administrative and police structures with their seniority intact, they will perform miracles in providing a responsive and a responsible administration. Similarly jawans can be absorbed in the state and central police forces. Training costs come down, efficiency goes up, shortages of manpower ends, and the military remains young. Besides, this simple measure bestows honour and recognition of the soldier's contribution to the nation. Above all this will act as a force-multiplier in national integration.

Internal Reforms. Analysing the Indian genius and skills, one factor stands out. It works the best in a free atmosphere. Scores of Indian fast food joints are now ahead of those owned by multinationals. Infact, for the first time, the latter are forced to cut down their retail prices and cater to the Indian palate. Modern banking facilities at a lesser cost provided by HDFC Ltd. Bank is ahead of the foreign banks. Zee TV revenues score over a foreign channel. Therefore, accelerated pace of internal reforms to free and unleash the Indian enterprenuial energy in the next five years is a must-must. Simultaneously lowering the over-whelming government structures by 35% in the next five years is mandatory for India to gain momentum. The system is not only clogged but eats up revenue in far excess of what it can collect. And hardly delivers. However, the social net for the next twenty years needs to remain intact till the have-nots are brought into the main stream through education. Here, I emphasize on the spread of education in the rural areas because this not only creates new skills and competence but helps check the explosion in population. In actualities, India can afford to export vast amount of brains and yet have an internal surplus! The government needs to exploit this factor.

Defending India. To defend India, we have everything going for us except a vision and a will to ruthlessly implement it. Indians must remember that despite building up of sufficient alliances in our region and out-of-the-region, we must not become complacent and neglect the growth of military power in future. Education of the masses, encouraging the free enterprise, developing the economy of the outlying provinces through an efficient administrative machinery on a war footing (and thus freeing the military power from enormous internal consumption), disallowing demographic changes in the border areas from outside in particular, and giving thrust to national integration while retaining diversity at the lower end of the spectrum are the areas that need to be conceptually worked upon. Simply, put to defend India, the India First generation must take over from the fading elders of India Last generation.

12 The Defence Scene and the Budget

India today is faced with an extensive defence and security parameter, 14,103 kilometres of land borders, including 7,000 kilometres of border with countries with which major territorial disputes still persist (Pakistan and China), a coastline of 7,600 kilometres and 2.5 million square kilometres of Exclusive Economic Zone (EEZ) to protect. Besides this, there are over 500 islands plus offshore hydrocarbon installations.

The land defence perimeter spans some of world's most difficult terrain, the Himalayas in the North, thick mountain jungles in the East and North-East and the rain swamps of the West. China continues to occupy 37,555 square kilometres of Indian territory and 5,180 square kilometres in Ladakh have illegally been transferred by Pakistan to China from Pakistani occupation of so-called Azad Kashmir which is some 78,000 square kilometres of territory. Pakistan's sponsorship of terrorism and insurgency in Kashmir and the North-East is of increasing concern.

China is a nuclear power. The Chinese armed forces, the world's third largest, are being continuously modernized. An expanding infrastructure in Tibet created over the years, sizeable ground and air forces together with a capability of rapid reinforcement enable China to be able to launch major offensive operations. Extension of rail, road and other infrastructural projects such as pipelines and air facilities are proceeding at a fast pace. The airfields in Tibet are being improved to take heavy military transport and civilian aircraft. The runway at Gongkor airport has been extended to 4,000 metres. China has held many exercises to reinforce her Army in Tibet.

In March 1989, the 149 Airborne Division was moved from its base in Sichuan to Lhasa in 36 hours. There have been other such exercises at regular intervals. Significant too is the move of the control line military headquarters from South-West China in the Lhasa area.

China is reported to have over 500 nuclear bombs/warheads. China is continuing with underground nuclear tests at Lop Nor. Out of the 500-plus nuclear devices that China has, about 200 are free-fall bombs capable of being dropped by a variety of Chinese aircraft. The bulk of the remainder are designed to be fitted into the large numbers of land-based missiles. China is also developing a range of missiles, for its surface naval vessels and its submarines as well as neutron bomb and laser weaponry.

Pakistan has waged three wars against India. Pakistan is currently sponsoring insurgency in Kashmir. It is fuelling terrorism and insurgency in the North-East. It is in the process of modernizing its armed forces. China is assisting it in building defence, industrial infrastructure, machinery and weapon technology. Chinese technicians are currently engaged in retrofitting and upgrading obsolescent aircraft and tanks.

Pakistan has the geo-military advantage of operating on interior lines. This gives it the capability of mounting a major offensive against India in a matter of days. It also gives her the capability of switching forces from one sector to another with great rapidity. India due to its geographical position and its exterior lines requires much more time to concentrate forces and to switch from sector to sector.

China has actively assisted Pakistan in developing nuclear weapons and missiles. It is reported to have made available underground testing facilities at Lop Nor. Pakistan is said to have produced some 15 nuclear warheads and has enough weapon-grade uranium to fabricate between 10 and 20 more war heads. Pakistan, with Chinese assistance, has developed the HATF 2 and 3 short-range ballistic missiles.

China has supplied Pakistan with M-11 missiles capable of being fitted with nuclear warheads and is assisting Pakistan in such a technology. Pakistan has linked its nuclear programmes to its claims on Kashmir. Pakistan's nuclear and missile development programmes should be viewed in this context.

Pakistan has a disproportionately large navy considering her coastline of some 700 kilometres.

It is developing the port of Gwadar near the Iranian border into a naval base with supporting airfield complexes-naval and air force approaches to the Gulf through the Straits of Hormuz through which a large proportion of our oil supplies pass. Pakistan is expanding her surface, underwater and air arms. Her recent order of four sophisticated French submarines is indicative of her designs in the event of hostilities to target our commercial shipping.

The possibility of Pakistan using nuclear weapons to achieve her declared aims cannot be ruled out. Pakistan, by issuing conflicting statements about its nuclear weapons, is creating a fog of nuclear deterrence.

The other factor in this geo-military equation is China. It is difficult to anticipate or legislate for Chinese intentions and actions. China still holds the territory it has seized in Ladakh enlarging its claims from that it originally mooted in 1962 by expanding claim lines. It still maintains that its border in the North-East is as per the survey of India map of 191 7, i.e., the Inner Line in Arunachal Pradesh.

Indian defence planners, both civil and military envision that any future conflict with Pakistan will be of short duration. Due to the present balance of forces any future conflict may be of longer duration. The pattern of a future war will also be different as industrial and infrastructural complexes are likely to be targeted.

China, despite recent protestations of friendship, looks on India as a rival in its path of political, economic and military hegemony in Asia. India must have the wherewithal to defend its border including Bhutan where we have a commitment to defend.

In 1974 we exploded a nuclear device a Pokharan. The decision to carry out this test was pragmatic.

Unfortunately the follow-up has been ambiguous. Had we gone in for a weaponization programme we would today have had the nuclear status of China, though in terms of nuclear arsenal a fraction of its capability.

Nuclear deterrence had kept the peace in Europe during the Cold War. The capacity to deter depends not only on the warhead but also on the delivery means. India should embark on a programme of fabrication of nuclear bombs/warheads. This should not present any great problem as we have sizeable stocks of weapon-grade uranium and the engineering ability to manufacture these.

To create a credible deterrent India requires to give priority to its missile development programme. It should aim to create both a first-and second strike capability. The Prithvi now being deployed can be fitted with a nuclear warhead. However, its short range of 150 to 250 kilometres gives it a limited coverage of targets in Pakistan.

China has the ability to strike Indian targets from the Tibetan plateau. The Agni with its planned range of 2,500 kilometres is not capable of reaching the Chinese heartland.

In order to create a credible deterrence against China it is imperative that work to increase the range of the Agni to 5,000 kilometres is undertaken on priority. The development of solid-state fuel missiles for use with our submarines and surface ships should be undertaken.

THREAT SCENARIOS

Indian force levels must be adequate to meet the following contingencies.

- Full-scale war with Pakistan. This combined with a holding action against the Chinese in Tibet and containment of insurgencies;
- Full-scale invasion by China with a holding action against Pakistan and containment of insurgencies;
- Low-intensity operations against large-scale infiltration in Kashmir;
- Naval operations in the Indian Ocean, Bay of Bengal and Arabian Sea.
- Policing of adjacent areas on request, e.g., Sri Lanka, Maldives, etc.

The Indian strategy should aim at force levels to counter these threats. The most likely threat scenario in the short term can be stated thus: Pakistan with subsidiary threat from China. In the long term the main threat is from China.

The major combat components of the armed forces of India and Pakistan are given in Table 1. In the case of China, Chinese capabilities of waging an offensive from the Tibetan plateau are relevant.

Though Chinese armed forces total more than 3 million China's capability to deploy troops on the' Tibetan Plateau is restricted by terrain infrastructural problems and logistics. An assessment of capabilities is as follows:

Ladakh	1 army plus 3-4 divisions
Sikkim	1 army plus 3-4 divisions
Arunachal Pradesh	3 armies 9 divisions

(A Chinese Army consists of a basic 3 divisions)

The total assessed capability is that of 17 Infantry Divisions. China's Navy has a blue-water capability. Presently her ability of operating in the Indian Ocean and Bay of Bengal is restricted to her submarine arm which has more than 100 submarines, a proportion of them having nuclear propulsion.

She has got Burma to agree to a railway connection to an Indian Ocean base for the Chinese Navy. Such a base will have a decided effect on the potential naval threat in the Bay of Bengal.

Table 1

	India	Pakistan
Army		
Armour divisions	3	2
Infantry divisions	22	19
Independent armoured brigades	5	9
Corps independent artillery brigades	3	9
Mountain divisions	10	-
Independent infantry brigades	7	9
Army aviation squadrons	14	15
Air defence brigades/groups	6	8
Para brigades	1	-
Navy		
Principle surface combat vessels (including 2 Indian Aircraft Carriers)	24	14
Submarines	15	6
Patrol and coastal	40	18
Inshore/Offshore	21	7
Air Force		
Combat aircraft *conisisting of :*	707	393
Fighter ground attack squadrons	23	7
Fighter air defence	17	9
Recconenance squadrons	1	2
Naval air combat aircraft	64	4
Helicopter (armed)	75	10

Defence Expenditure

India's defence expenditure has been sinking in real terms. Inflation, currently around 11 per cent, is expected to rise. India's defence expenditure as a proportion of GDP declined from 4.04 per cent in 1986-87 to 2.53 per cent as against Pakistan's 6.88 per cent and China's official figure of 6 per cent (actual reported to be significantly higher).

As a proportion of total government expenditure, Pakistan spends 26.52 per cent, China 23.8 percent and India 14.94 percent. India's defence expenditure share of governmental expenditure has come down from 17.27 per cent in 1987-88 to 14.94 per cent in 1993-94 and 13 per cent in 1994-95.

Defence allocations in 1994-95 were Rs 230 billion. This has been increased to Rs 250 billion in 1995-96.

The breakdown percentage in 1995-96 was : Army 53.96%, Navy 13.29%, Air Force 25.69%, Defence production 1.76%, R&D 5.28%

Lack of funds has resulted in mothballing tanks, ships and aircraft. This reduces immediate combat readiness. Pensions for defence personnel have been taken out of the defence budget and are met, from the consolidated fund of India.

Defence Production

There are 39 ordnance factories. These meet the armed forces' requirements and to some extent the paramilitary forces'. The production by the eight public sector undertakings particularly Bharat Earth Movers and Bharat Electronics has gone up.

Indian ordnance factories are producing a vast range of products, battletanks, infantry combat vehicles, self-propelled guns, field guns, anti-aircraft guns, mortars, small arms and ammunition, rockets and projectiles, bombs, grenades, mines, depth charges and other items. They also supply the railways, coal industry, paramilitary and police. Production of the 5.56 rifle has begun. India also exports various defence items.

In 1987, procurements from ordnance factories were shifted from the defence production head to defence allocation. This has had the impact of reducing the Army's allocations correspondingly.

Though R&D funding registered a growth in the last ten years from 2.05 per cent to 4.39 per cent in the last budget, the money allotted is inadequate. In 1987, the transferring of R&D to defence as a consequence had an effect on the total defence allocations. Funding for R&D despite the increase of 105.13 crore in 1995-96 is far less than what is required. Since R&D for defence also has a bearing on other allied research agencies it would be preferable that R&D is funded under a separate head and its funding suitably enhanced to meet defence research needs. The priorities are for the :

AIR FORCE-LCA, helicopter (ALH) and Agni

ARMY-main battle tank, missiles, radar and artillery

NAVY-weapons systems, missiles and sonar equipment

Not only has Pakistan's defence expenditure increased significantly, the Pakistani Military Capital Stocks have also increased, both qualitatively and quantitatively. During the last few years Pakistan has fabricated nuclear warheads (estimated at 15), and built up fissile stocks to fabricate a similar number. Pakistan has added to her arsenal during the last five years 600 main battle tanks, 775 armoured personnel carriers (M-113-A2), 185 combat aircraft/ Mirage and the Chinese F-7P). The navy bought 3 frigates from the UK. 3 modern submarines at US $600 million are on order from France. 18 missiles HATF 1/11 have already been deployed. An unspecified number of Chinese M-11 missiles have been inducted. Those have a capability of carrying nuclear warheads. Pakistan's defence budget for 1994 accounted for 34.53 of government expenditure at a total of Rs 237,795.2 billion.

Pakistan has received loans from Saudi Arabia and US for arms acquisition. Pakistan is reported to have siphoned off some 60 per cent of the weapons and equipment intended for the Afghan Mujahideen for equipping terrorists operating in Jammu and Kashmir.

Accurate figures for China's defence expenditure are difficult to assess. Estimates place it at US $31.18 billion. The Chinese armed forces are being modernized and more professional forces are being created in place of the cumbersome structure obtaining. China has developed a blue-water navy and is actively spreading its influence in Burma with a view to obtaining naval and air facilities in the Bay of Bengal.

In our case with an inflation rate currently around 11 per cent and soaring international prices for military hardware there are insufficient funds available for modernization. Approximately 60 per cent of the budgetary allocations are appropriated for the revenue account, pay and allowances, etc. The proportion available for the capital expenditure for combat and combat related stores including fuel and oil is hardly sufficient to maintain existing force levels. No major weapon system has been inducted since the Bofors deal.

The defence budget has increased by some 10 per cent. With inflation now at 11 per cent this would mean in real terms a decrease in defence allocations. It will be insufficient to maintain the status quo particularly as the proportion allotted to the revenue account will increase as a result of the upcoming recommendations of the pay commission.

The armed forces' expenditure in aid of civil power is increasing due to insurgency conditions in Jammu and Kashmir and the North-East. So far these costs have not been recovered from the Home Ministry allocations. Recovery of these dues will increase availability of funds for the armed forces.

The raising of the Rashtriya Rifles has not come up to the initial expectations. It was intended that these 36 battalions (enough infantry for 4 divisions) to be increased to 40 battalions would be financed by the Home Ministry. This has not been the case and the financing has to be borne out of the Army allocations. In the circumstances the Army could have raised regular infantry battalions which would have given the flexibility of using them both for counter-insurgency and if so required for induction into regular divisions or brigades.

For the record this was the system earlier where regular infantry battalions were raised on a reduced counter-insurgency establishment. These modified infantry battalions were used in the 1971 war with minimal reorganization. This system had the advantage of using the existing regimental layout and avoids the hybrid composition of the RR with all its attendant problems of milking regular units, postings, promotions and morale. It has aggravated the shortage of officers which is now in the region of 12,500. This is seriously affecting the operational efficiency of the Army.

The Army is manpower-intensive. The Army's ability to generate firepower and mobility are not commensurate with its manpower structure. Manpower has to be trimmed and firepower increased. The armed forces require new weapon systems and force multipliers. Obsolescent equipment requires upgradation.

Provisioning of maintenance spares and ammunition, petrol and oil are essential. Planning presently is for a short war. A future conflict is likely to be protracted. Due to the vulnerability of our sealanes it is essential that stocks and reserves should be held for a conflict of longer duration than those of 1965 and 1971.

The armed forces for their part should pay more attention to interior economy. Savings can be effected in manpower and consumption of petrol and oil. Establishments should be reviewed to cut out nonessentials. It will be noticed that the Pakistan Army has comparatively much fewer headquarters. A number of headquarters can be eliminated. The staff at Army Headquarters and lower state formations can be reduced. The present ratio of teeth to tail is too low. The establishment of units should be reviewed in this light. The armed forces must work out priorities of 'musts', 'shoulds' and 'coulds' as there will never be sufficient funds to meet all projections.

13 India's Defence Industry in the 21st Century

INTRODUCTION

Trends in the Global Defence Industry

The global defence industry has undergone profound changes in recent years. Changes in demand for military weapons and equipment, the allocation of resources for national security, national and international security priorities especially by major states, among others, have affected the defence industry in many ways. While the Cold War era witnessed a massive military build-up by many countries, thus fuelling demand for this lucrative sector, the immediate post-Cold War period witnessed just an opposite scenario. Demand for military equipment went down during the late 1980s and early 1990s. Budgetary allocations for security sectors fell.

Military downsizing occurred. In just a period of half-a-decade, roughly from 1987 to the early 1990s, the defence industry witnessed a different scenario and shrank considerably. It had to shift priorities to adjust to the new environment. In brief, since the end of the Cold War, the defence industry has faced numerous challenges from all quarters. Most of the decline in the volume of arms production took place during the early and mid-1990s. During this time, significant down-sizing, rationalisation and diversification (primarily into dual-use and civilian production) were witnessed in the defence-industrial sector.

Mergers and acquisitions during the 1990s resulted in the creation of a few giant companies like Boeing, Lockheed Martin, British Aerospace, Northrop Grumman, EADS, and others. This also resulted in many smaller companies either having to merge with big ones or having to shift their priorities toward civilian production, thus leaving the defence sector. Defence industries of major countries like the United States and of Western Europe were affected most during this period although countries like Russia, Israel, South Africa, Brazil, India, and others were also affected. Arms reductions during the 1990s were extensive and fetched a sizeable 'peace dividend'.

It was desirable that such a decade of disarmament should have been extended. However, as evidence suggests, indicators of disarmament and conversion now show stagnation; in many cases even a reverse trend toward a strengthening of military postures are witnessed. A decade of cuts in military expenditure ended in 1998/99 when it went up again. The upward trend in military expenditure is likely to continue in future. The 11 September 2001 terrorist attacks in the United States are likely to result in a major shift in defence-industrial developments because of their impact on security requirements at national and international levels. But this is not to suggest that the upward trend in military expenditure was a product of such an unfortunate event.

This trend had already started in the late 1990s, primarily because of increased military spending by countries like the United States and regions like the Middle East and South and East Asia. In this changed scenario, the defence industry seems to gear up to meet new challenges. As procurement budgets have started to swell again and are likely to stay that way, new opportunities are expected for the defence industry. In fighting terrorism, additional defence programmes initiated by countries like the United States will most likely change the structure of the defence industry. While it is expected that giant weapons producers, especially in the United States, are likely to benefit most from the on-going 'War on Terror', national defence industries elsewhere are also likely to reorient themselves to meet future challenges. In brief, the global defence industry, after a period of significant downsizing and rationalisation, is likely to enter into a phase of renewed attention. Demand for smart weapons, increased emphasis on military technology including investment in R&D, growing demand for aerospace and cutting-edge technology products, are all likely to boost defence-industrial activities in many parts of the world.

India's Defence Industry

Trends in global defence industry have impinged India in many ways. India's defence industry has witnessed significant changes since the end of the Cold War. In the 1990s, changes in both institutional and policy spheres became more prominent. The most far reaching change that has occurred in recent years in India's defence-industrial sector is related to its opening up to the market. Long protected as a closed sector, India's defence industry has now opened up for private participation. As if this was not enough, it is also showing enough willingness to become an exporter and dares to venture into the competitive global arms market. How far it will succeed in its objectives is examined elsewhere, but changes are certainly a product of and response to the contemporary changes in the global industrial defence scenario. At the same time, it is also showing willingness to diversify its range of products, which not only include modern weapons systems but also technologies for wide and popular civilian uses. The Indian defence-industrial sector targets the national, and even global, civilian market to sell its products, especially in the fields of civilian space, medical, and electronics. Thus conversion through diversification has been witnessed in many areas of defence production in India.

India's defence industry has come a long way from being at the lowest end of the production spectrum, catering to the maintenance and repair and overhaul of imported weapons, to a stage where it can boast of designing and developing a range of state-of-the-art weapons systems. Half a decade of defence-industrial experience in India shows that while it started from scratch, it has been able not only to learn and absorb various stages of production intricacies but also produce complex systems that are primarily an indigenous activities. Another important factor is that the Indian defence industry has produced various weapons systems under licenses acquired from various foreign sources.

Although the first Prime Minister of India, Jawaharlal Nehru, believed in 'self sufficiency' in arms production, which became a policy mantra for subsequent years, it had to be supplemented by what is roughly called 'self-reliance in defence'. Self-reliance does not preclude accessing external sources for technology and systems, or external help in any stage of the production cycle. It is the degree of dependency on external sources that is tested in the case of India's quest for self-reliance.

India opted to choose an incremental path, in which it was necessary to continue to meet urgent requirements through imports while striving hard on achieving indigenous capabilities in defence production. Both policies continued till the late 1980s and many of the components of both still continue till today. The 1990s witnessed a series of far-reaching initiatives in the field of national security, of which defence industry was a critical component.

The creation of six Special Task Forces to reform major aspects of national defence coordination and management, under the Chairmanship of the then Defence Minister in 1994 may effectively be considered as the first major step after a long time to initiate and implement much-desired reforms in the defence-industrial sector. This was followed by a series of intensive interactions between various organs of the armed forces, government departments and institutions like the Confederation of Indian Industries (CII).

The 'Army-Industry Partnership', a partnership between CII and the Indian Army to get acquainted with each other's needs and to facilitate channels of communication between the armed forces and the private industry, was a result of this process and, in turn, led to other cooperative initiatives. Events like India's nuclear tests in mid-1998 and the Kargil conflict in mid-1999 provided grounds for an intense debate on various aspects of

India's national security. Also, as a by-product of the current disinvestment programme, which is primarily aimed toward lessening or wiping out government control and responsibilities in state-owned public enterprises in India, the debate on a reform of the defence industry got a major boost as demands for a privatisation of and private participation in this hitherto closed sector grew more in tune with the changing times.

In January 2001, the Government of India initiated a series of major initiatives that, among others, included Foreign Direct Investment (FDI) up to about 26 percent and full private participation in certain sectors in the defence industry. This policy indeed marks a critical departure from the past. Followed by this, the Group of Ministers (GoM) Report on 'Reforming the National Security System' was made public in early 2001. This laid stress on reforms in all-encompassing aspects of national security, of which changes sought in higher defence management emphasised the need to create specific institutions like the Defence Acquisitions Board to adapt and facilitate changing needs of the defence industry.

While these far-reaching institutional and policy-oriented changes have been underway for quite some time especially since the early 1990s, the demand for private participation has assumed significance in recent years. In such a scenario, analyses of India's defence-industrial sector and policies have become critically important to understand the complex web of linkages that determine national policies in the defence-industrial sector. This, in turn, needs a closer look into the past performance of the defence industry, lessons learnt and a peep into the likely future course.

Research Objectives

The objectives are primarily four-fold. First, we will examine critical aspects of defence-industrial policies adopted by India in the past and link those to performance. It will examine the factors that have influenced India's defence production and their co-relationship with policies and decision-making in this sector. Second, we will examine the main trends during the 1990s, during which major policy changes occurred. It will critically examine the impact of such policy changes. Third, we will examine the contemporary scenario. Fourth and last, it will look into future problems and prospects. The last two are essential in understanding the intricacies involved in India's defence-industrial strategies and are expected to give some clues related to the future course of action in this sector.

Some of the major queries that will be examined here are: Why a quest for self-reliance in the past? Has the policy of self-reliance paid off? If not, what are the options for the future? Why the changes in defence-industrial policies during the 1990s? Are the objectives achievable? What are likely options for the future? Does it have scope for more diversion, thus leading to conversion through the increase in civilian production, in future? We will invariably try to find answers to these queries, although not necessarily in the same order.

Methods and Sources

We will follow a general descriptive-analytical approach. The scope is limited somewhat to policy analyses due to constraints in the availability of information. This is because India's defence industry has long been a 'closed' sector and thus been under exclusive government control. It is only in recent times that it has opened up, thus leading to an availability of information in a low to medium scale. We will also follow a historical method whereby it will emphasise linkages at policy-and decision-making levels to performance, and this is important in understanding the nature of development that this sector has undergone for the past half-a-century. Available data on specifics will be evaluated. Emphasis will be on an evaluation and interpretation of data from primary (especially government) sources. In brief, the overall approach will be descriptive and analytical.

Literature on the subject is scarce. At international level, the study of India's defence industry has attracted very little attention. The same is true at national level. Barring a few books, written by scholars like K. Subrahmanyam, Air Marshal Samir Sen, Major General Pratap Narain, Chris Smith, WPS Sidhu, and others, substantial work is not evident on this subject. Occasional research papers by G. Balachandran, Rahul Roy-Choudhury, Ajay Singh and others have also focused on limited themes. Secondary and tertiary sources are scarce. Primary sources, however, constitute the most important component of this study. Annual Reports (published by the Ministry of Defence, Government of India), Annual Reports of major Defence Public Sector Units (published by respective organisations), periodic reports published by the Comptroller and Auditor General of India, Parliament Secretariat and similar other reports constitute primary sources for this endeavour. Select interviews with senior government officers, analysts and industry-watchers have been taken into account.

INDIA'S DEFENCE INDUSTRY: A HISTORICAL OVERVIEW

Looking into the Post-Independence Era

The pre-independence (pre-1947) defence-industrial infrastructure in India was limited. It generally catered to the lowest spectrum of defence production—repair and overhaul of imported weapons systems. The then ruling British followed a policy of retaining strategic capabilities for themselves while allowing the native Indians to assist in the tactical dimensions, confined to minor works in most endeavours. An example of this policy is evident from the fact that while the Royal Air Force retained the strategic elements like the bomber force and used their own formations, the Indian Air Force (IAF) was left with only tactical elements—supporting them with secondary and tertiary roles that mainly included repair and similar minor works. The Walchand Aircraft Factory (WAF) in Bangalore was wholly engaged in repair and maintenance of aircraft at that time. From March 1942 till the end of World War II, it was employed for the servicing of American aircraft and was managed, for part of this period, by the US Air Force.

Mazagaon Docks (Mumbai) and Garden Reach Shipyards (Calcutta) similarly existed prior to India's independence to repair warships. However, apart from such single air or ship industrial units, India's defence-industrial capacity during times of pre-independence mainly consisted of what is known as Ordnance Factories (OFs). These factories had been set up primarily to supplement land-based weapons and equipment produced in

Britain. Before 1947, there were 16 OFs, all located on Indian territory.

The gun and shell factory at Cossipore (near Kolkata), established in 1801, an ammunition factory at Kirkee of 1889, a rifle factory at Ishapore of 1901, a gun carriage factory at Jabalpur of 1904, and others were built mainly to produce for the British forces. During World War II, possible threats to the sea lanes of communication in the Indian Ocean and requirements of the allied forces in the region, made it necessary to double the number of factories during this time. The filling factory at Khamara and the light machine gun factory at Hyderabad were amongst such new factories. In brief, pre-partition Indian defence-industrial capacities were confined only to a supplementary role and were placed at the lowest end of the production spectrum.

Post-independence, the Indian leadership wanted self-sufficiency in every sphere of activity. This objective was obvious because India was never allowed to develop industrial competencies. The same objective was no different in the field of defence production. Right from the first Prime Minister Jawaharlal Nehru, every successive Indian leader sought self-sufficiency in defence production.

The need to establish a comprehensive defence-industrial infrastructure thus constituted a primary objective of the political leadership. Right from the beginning, India's industrial policies emphasised 'core' industries to be taken care of by the central government and others by the states. Defence industries, considered as critical national assets, obviously came under the exclusive control of the central government. The first Industrial Policy Resolution of 1948, consequently revised under the Second Five-Year Plan in 1956, made it clear that core industries, including munitions, aircraft, shipbuilding, iron and steel, heavy machine tools, heavy electrical plants, atomic energy and similar others were to be placed under exclusive central government control. During this period, many industrial units related to these fields were established under the strict supervision of the central government, known as 'basic' (Schedule A) industries. The Defence Science Organisation was also established during this period to take up the challenge of undertaking R&D activities. As demands for defence R&D grew, this organisation paved the way for the creation of the Defence Research and Development Organisation (DRDO) in 1958, which to-date remains the most important contributor to India's defence R&D activities. It has got nearly 50 laboratories, spread all across the country, and other scientific establishments and institutions like the Council of Scientific and Industrial Research (CSIR).

At independence, India's defence-industrial production was mainly coming from the existing 16 OFs. These factories were engaged in the production of low technology items like small arms and ammunition, mines and other explosives. Their cumulative value of production was estimated at roughly US $7-8 million during the time of India's independence. Despite the first India-Pakistan War (1947/48) and the need to boost defence-industrial production, no new factory was built during the first decade (1950s). It was during the late 1950s that the need to construct more factories was contemplated. It is also during this time that peace time civilian production in defence industries was emphasised, especially by the then Defence Minister, V. K. Krishna Menon. The policy of production for civilian markets was primarily aimed at maintaining operational capacities during slack periods of demand as well as keeping the level of productivity high by the manufacturing units. By the end of the 1950s, the number of defence-industrial units almost remained the same. The production from these ordnance factories was still geared to low-technology items.

Apart from OFs, and various defence science and technology establishments, the Indian government also created a number of production establishments to take care of various productions in the field of defence. These, like others, were under the exclusive control of the government although they were created as corporations, commonly known as 'Defence Public Sector Units' (DPSUs). There are eight DPSUs in the country, devoted to the production of different military systems and components. They are: Hindustan Aeronautics Limited (HAL), Bharat Electronics Limited (BEL), Bharat Earth Movers Limited (BEML), Mazagaon Dockyard Limited (MDL), Garden Reach Shipbuilders and Engineers Limited, Goa Shipyard, Bharat Dynamics Limited (BDL) and Mishra Dhatu Nigam Limited (MDNL). Both, DPSUs and OFs, are administered by the Department of Defence Production under the Ministry of Defence. Both sets of industries have their own research and development units although the overall R&D activities are met by the DRDO. Bharat Electronics Limited (BEL) was the first DPSU, established in 1954, to manufacture electronic equipment primarily for the defence sector. Over the years, more than half of BEL's overall production has turned into products for the civilian market. And it is not the only production entity that has changed that way.

In the post-independence period, till the war with China in 1962, India's defence-industrial base was too weak to take the responsibility of all defence needs. The self-sufficiency model had been adopted since the beginning but as years passed and demands for security grew, India found it difficult to create an industrial base as it was hit primarily by two important factors – lack of sufficient funding and access to modern defence technologies. The Indian leadership was aware of these two problems but they also had a number of other issues to handle. The country was just independent, had already fought a war with Pakistan, did not even have a rudimentary industrial base, and faced numerous nation-building and socioeconomic problems, independence, found it pragmatic to follow a policy of controlling critical industries, including defence, though this is widely debated now. Although both defence and non-defence critical industries were under exclusive state control, the former—due to their strategic importance—became a 'closed' sector.

The leadership also desired and pursued what is commonly known as comprehensive industrialisation. This meant that more and more big industries emerged to cater to needs that were vast, like steel, coal, mining, etc. Thus, big state-owned companies like the Steel Authority of India Limited (SAIL) was established. This was also evident in the defence sector where large industrial units were created to cater to the demands of the vast armed forces. As mentioned, the two problems of lack of investment and access to technologies became acute as the defence industries expanded, making many units perform below par. Also, investment pattern in this sector was not uniform. Critical establishments like the

Hindustan Aeronautics Limited (HAL) and DRDO received more funds than others, such as OFs. The ever-growing demands of the armed forces and the problems in the defence sector in meeting those led many to criticise existing policies followed by the then ruling party. The government, in turn, was hard pressed for funds that were essential and was aware of long-term returns for investment in the defence sector. In brief, policies to maximise production in order to attain self-sufficiency in the defence sector although they were considered far-sighted, did not match expectations, thus leading to further constraints.

From Self-Sufficiency to Self-Reliance

The self-sufficiency in defence production was in fact realised from the beginning, and was complemented by the concept of self-reliance after a few years of persistence and failure. Self-reliance, as far as India was concerned, meant—apart from its own production base for support—a degree of dependence on reliable foreign sources for access to technologies, supply of components and complete systems. This, in turn, was debatable as foreign partners to achieve such long-term self-reliance were not forthcoming during the first few years as the West was considered to be unreliable both for military and political reasons. India tested self-reliance by meeting urgent and immediate demands through imports from abroad while simultaneously striving for indigenous capabilities in defence production. The west European weapons systems, primarily British, French and Swedish, were considered first choice in the Indian arsenal during the first few years; however, after the 1962 war with China, many western countries along with the United States were reluctant to co-operate with India which made a major adverse impact on India's defence production activities. The post-War scenario witnessed a slow entry of the Soviet Union as a major supplier, the position is still retained by its successor Russia.

The post-1962 scenario was marked by utter confusion in the decision-making circles, which in turn impinged the defence industry. India was humiliated in the war with China and thus started looking into its existent defence-industrial capabilities and found to its horror that all was not well. For example, the Indian Air Force (IAF) needed a high-altitude supersonic interceptor against the threat of the B-57 bomber of Pakistan (supplied by the United States) and the Tu-16 bomber of the Chinese Air Force (supplied by the USSR). The requirement especially assumed a serious dimension after the war with China, when India looked outward and found out that only three fighter aircraft worth-considering were available in the market. India neither wanted to buy the British Lightning nor the Soviet MiG-21, and preferred the American F-104. This system was already supplied by the United States to Pakistan and despite repeated efforts India could not obtain it. India's effort to upgrade the existing HF-24 to supersonic capability was not considered by the Americans, either. It was at this time that the USSR came to India's rescue when they not only decided to supply the MiG-21 and other weapons but also gave a go-ahead for license production. India's quest for self-reliance got a major boost through this license production arrangement. This was indeed a turning point in India's self-reliance activities. The Soviets proved to be a trusted friend whose military supplies constitute more than 70 percent of India's total weapons acquisitions now. This friendship immensely benefited India's defence industry as it improved many notable weapons systems and components from this experience. In brief, India's self-reliance model in defence production was given a life lease by the Soviets.

After 1962, India sought to make up for the lacuna as well as boost defence production to match requirements. New ordnance factories were planned and established during the next three decades. The number of OFs thus grew to thirty-five by the mid-1980s. And, by the mid-1990s, it had reached thirty-nine. The fortieth ordnance factory (at Nalanda, in the state of Bihar), started in 1999/2000. These OFs were established in different parts of the country: Ten of them cater to materials and components, ten for weapons, vehicles and equipment, ten for ammunition and explosives and five for other ordnance items. By the early 1990s, they were producing more than 1500 items of arms, ammunition, equipment and components. By the early 1990s, the OFs collectively reached place 45 on the list of the largest arms producing companies in the world, and were placed at 29 in 2000.

The OFs, with a cumulative work force of 1,75,000, have been engaged in various types of land-based weapons. During the period under examination, the bulk of the production, nonetheless, still constituted of large quantities of relatively low-to medium-technology items. These, among others, included small arms, anti-tank and anti-aircraft guns, mortars, associated ammunition, rocket projectiles, bombs, grenades, mines, transport vehicles, leather items, parachutes and ordnance clothing for the armed forces. The establishment of the Heavy Vehicle Factory at Avadi (in the state of Tamil Nadu) in the early 1960s was crucial for the production of tanks and combat vehicles. This is where the first series of tanks, called 'Vijayanta' were manufactured under license from the British firm Vickers. This was followed by the manufacture of the ex-Soviet T-72 'Ajeya' MBTs. Although this project was taken up during the 1970s, it finally rolled out in 1988. In some projects, however, the level of indigenization has been pretty high, for example, up to about 80 percent in the case of 'Sarath' infantry combat vehicles. The overall performance of the OFs during that period was modest, although a lot could have been done to improve the performance of many factories. Hindustan Aeronautics Limited performed modestly during this period. Created in 1964 through an amalgamation of two aircraft companies, Hindustan Aircraft Limited and Aeronautics India Limited, HAL has become the only major aerospace company. With a total work force of nearly 45,000, it stands as the 57th largest defence company in the world.

During the beginning, it was primarily catering to maintenance and overhaul but over a period of time has slowly developed itself to undertake assembly, license manufacture and indigenous design and development. During the 1960s and well beyond, it was engaged in various license manufacture projects, amongst others the MiG-21 series aircraft, HF-24 Marut transonic fighters, 'Kiran' HJT – 16 jet trainer.. Apart from this, it also undertook to license manufacture 'Cheetah' (Aerospatiale SA 315 B) and 'Chetak' (Aerospatiale SA 316 B) helicopters. Bharat Electronics, set up in 1954 to manufacture electronic equipment, was perhaps the only DPSU which showed positive production results during the same period. Other DPSUs such as BEML, BDL, MDL were engaged in production, which may again be termed as modest. Bharat

Dynamics Limited, established in 1970, is the other DPSU, which was engaged in the production of missiles and associated products. Except during the 1990s, it had engaged in the past in license manufacture of some of the low range missile series. To sum up: While the Indian defence industry was expected to raise its production level during the half a century (1960s to mid-1980s), both its objectives of self-reliance through indigenous activity and more active collaborative activity, have brought very limited results. Some analysts even term this phase as an 'era of license-manufacture', nothing more. While plant utilisation capacities remained at the lower end, with around 40 to 50 percent, the quality, range and mode of production was modest and generally confined to low and medium technologies.

Gaps Galore

From the early 1960s till the early and mid-1980s, license production and direct purchase and acquisitions remained the predominant form of supply for the Indian defence forces. Analysts like Ajay Singh argue that there was a gap of nearly three decades in India's effort toward indigenous production. This gap was especially evident in the fields of design and development, which constitutes the upper spectrum of self-reliance. A fighter aircraft between Marut and the Light Combat Aircraft (LCA), a basic trainer aircraft between HT-2 and HPT-32, an intermediate trainer between Kiran and an yet-to-be fully developed Advanced Jet Trainer (AJT) are some of the examples that typify both the technology and production gaps. Weapons for the army had been manufactured under license with no significant design activities undertaken till the 1980s when a tank and a small arms project commenced. The first was a Main Battle Tank (MBT, named Arjun) while the last is known as the Indian Small Arms Systems (INSAS). The Situation was a little better for the Indian Navy, where at least some ship platforms were designed indigenously. The period thus witnessed a time gap in the design and development while emphases were more on license production and acquisitions that led to two problems – below par quality performance of the defence industry, although the quantum of production was on expected lines and lack of or little funding for critical and strategic sectors of the defence industry including R&D. Analysts also argue that given the situation even half the allocation for acquisitions would have been sufficient to ensure delivery on time, if not at the required level of technology.

TRENDS IN THE 1980S AND 1990S

Defence Production during the 1980s and 1990s

The of model of self-reliance, adopted by the defence industry during the 1960s and continued since then, became more prominent during the mid-1980s. After a critical gap in access to defence technology for more than two decades, the defence industry started looking for enhancement of its performance level. This period was also witnessing profound changes in the international security environment. Global defence expenditures rose to an all time high in 1987 and then fell sharply during the late 1980s and early 1990s.

Major production initiatives were curtailed and funding slashed. The Cold War came to an end but South Asia faced a security threat of a different kind. The superpower involvement in Afghanistan left a huge quantum of surplus small arms, which were redirected toward armed violence in Kashmir and Northern Sri Lanka and the volume of general lawlessness and crimes grew manifold. This was also the time when Pakistan was developing its clandestine nuclear programme which reached a critical threshold in 1987. The decision to accelerate India's nuclear programme gained momentum as of the early 1980s when leadership received positive information on the fact that Pakistan was working on a nuclear programme. Although the option had been kept open since the late 1960s, Indian leadership had gone slow after the 1974 Pokhran nuclear test, classified by India as a PNE (Peaceful Nuclear Explosion).

As is mentioned before, defence production was quite modest during the previous decades and it was desired that it should pick up momentum. Hence, one may notice a kind of upswing in India's defence production activities during the early 1980s, which continued thereafter. This was due both to internal and external factors, as cited above, but was more driven by a sense of urgency that was long lacking. It is also interesting to note that while during the 1960s and 1970s the overall expenditure toward defence lay well below the 3 percent mark of the GDP, it started expanding beyond this mark for some years in the 1980s, only again to fall well below this mark in subsequent years. Major acquisitions from abroad coupled with major initiatives in indigenous defence production, including R&D, activities mark this period. The OFs during this period were engaged primarily in manufacturing a series of licensed production items and were also striving for indigenous design and development.

MBTs, ICVs, and small arms were some of the products which were produced with interest. In the MBT series, 'Ajeys', a licensed manufactured version of the T-72, was considered as a major step forward which emboldened the OFs further to produce 'Arjun', an MBT conceived during the 1970s and designed and developed in the 1980s and 1990s, which came out for serial production during the mid-1990s. Arjun is dubbed as a fine indigenous product by India although a minor portion of its components were imported which have subsequently been modified. Similarly, Sarath ICV was developed with full indigenous activities and is doing well for the armed forces. The latest generation INSAS, the 105mm light field gun, mortars, carbines, light machine guns, and related ammunition were produced in several of OFs. Of note is the latest generation of 5.56mm INSAS assault rifle, which is said to be an equivalent of an AK-assault rifle. Production of all these systems were going on with average to expected turnover during the 1990s. In the field of aerospace, a series of new projects were begun and licensed production continued during this period.

After the MiG 21 aircraft, Marut transonic fighter, HAL started looking for new products. Since the early 1980s, among others, it has taken up the license manufacture of Jaguar deep penetration strike aircraft (from France). The first aircraft of this type was delivered to the Air Force in 1987/88. HAL had already handed over the contemporary version of the Mig (named MiG-27M), which was license manufactured for the Indian Air Force. During the mid-1980s, HAL produced the first Dornier Do-228 transport aircraft and, had indigenously designed the modified version of the Kiran trainer by 1989/90,. In fact, production of Kiran MKII (license manufacture) and Dipak basic trainer aircraft had commenced in 1983/84. During the 1990s, it engaged in manufacturing the R-25 and R-29 B aero-engine for fighter helicopters. It is modernising the Air Force fleet of Jaguar and is also engaged in the overhaul of airframe and accessories of the Mirage-2000 series of fighter aircraft. Among its most recent pride, is the indigenously designed prototype of the Advanced Light Helicopter and the involvement in the initial stages for the Indian AWACS project and, along with the Aeronautical Development Agency (ADA, based in Bangalore), its responsibility for the design and development of the Light Combat Aircraft (LCA). The LCA has been in the news for quite some time because of long delays in flight testing. Tests of the engine for the prototype (GE-404, supplied by the General Electric Corporation of the United States), however, were successful. Apart from undertaking these programmes, which are primarily for military uses, it has contributed significantly to the civilian sector as well, as is explained later. It is worth noting that HAL has contributed at various stages to India's space programme. Light alloy structures, specially designed tanks, and many other components of India's PSLV programme were manufactured by HAL. It is during the early 1980s that India undertook a major initiative in the production of missiles.

In 1983, an Integrated Guided Missile Development Programme (IGMDP) was initiated under the Defence Research Development Organisation (DRDO). This programme was crucial to India's national security as for the first time it made a decision to produce its own brand of missiles. Although missile technology was and its applications were long in existence in many parts of the world, it took India some time because during the 1970s it was going for indigenous development only. For this purpose, a new DPSU, named Bharat Dynamics Limited (BDL), was created. Since its establishment in 1970, it has been engaged in production activities, both through license manufacture and, since the 1980s and 1990s, through indigenous development. In the latter, it is closely linked with the DRDO, which is responsible for R&D activities in missile technology.

BDL entered into an agreement with the French company, Aerospatiale for license manufacture of the SSI anti-tank guided missile. Production of this series was continued during the whole of the 1970s and early 1980s. It is to be noted that the content of indigenously produced parts in this missile was more than 70 percent while only the warhead contained more than 80 percent. This was hailed as a major success. The next series of anti-tank guided missile replaced SSII in 1985 when serial production of 'Milan' started. The first indigenously developed 'Nag' ATGM to replace Milan has been well underway for quite some time and has already been introduced with the armed forces. Two more versions of short range surface-to-air missiles, Trishul and Akash, after necessary tests and extensive user trials, have been inducted.

In surface-to-surface missile series, 'Prithvi' has already been inducted. It is claimed that more than 90 percent of these missiles are indigenously developed with very little components bought from abroad. BDL's most famous production is related to three versions of ballistic missiles, named 'Agni'. The 'Agni' is wholly indigenous in terms of its design and its re-entry and propulsion systems. It has three versions so far—Agni I, Agni II, and Agni III. Details of this series of ballistic missiles are explained in the subsequent section.

Three DPSUs are engaged in defence production for naval forces. Mazagaon Dockyard Limited (MDL) is the largest and one of the oldest in the Indian defence industry. Along with Garden Reach Shipbuilders and Engineers, it has been engaged in both repair, maintenance of warships as well as production. Both DPSUs have constructed a series of specialised vessels such as frigates, destroyers and submarines. In the late 1970s, after the successful construction of a series of Leander class frigates through license manufacture, the MDL undertook a follow on class of 3,600 tonne frigate, called 'Godavari'. This class of frigate was produced mainly during the 1980s. Also during the same period, it produced two larger 6,500 tonne-'Delhi' class destroyers as well as two 1,500 tonne-Shalki class HDW – 209 Type submarines 35. Indigenously built submarine 'Shankul' was commissioned into the Indian Navy in 1994.

In addition, both the DPSUs have built several patrol and coastal combatants for the Indian Navy and the Coast Guard. Production patterns during the 1980s and 1990s show that India has been able to initiate a number of projects for indigenous development in the defence sector. This has been partly possible due to increased allocation of funds for these projects as well as for R&D. Both the former and the latter have been given importance since the early 1980s. However, during the last two decades, funding was also cut or stopped many times, leading to a delay or abandonment of projects. This is common knowledge. For example, the project for LCA has been especially controversial as main reasons for its delay have been attributed to both funding and lack of access to technology. It is also expected that an increase in defence R&D (which is currently increasing and is expected to increase further) will boost indigenous production activities. However, the proportion of allocations for R&D still remains well under 10 percent.

Major R&D and Other Initiatives

As mentioned earlier, it was during the mid-and late 1980s, that the Indian defence industry got renewed attention. During this period, several projects were undertaken and carried out in the defence sector, many of which have been continued until today and are expected to continue in future. Many new projects have been added and are expected to be initiated in the near future. DRDO has been especialiy geared up to initiate and further R&D activities to boost and complement the defence industry in this regard. The DRDO, born out of the Defence Science Organisation during the 1950s, has contributed immensely to defence R&D in the country. With a network of nearly 50 laboratories/ establishments spread across the country, it has been considered as the main pillar of India's research activities.

Its achievements have been far and wide, most importantly including the IGMDP, MBT, LCA and other programmes. Under the IGMDP, it has been engaged in several series of missile programmes as explained earlier. Its latest endeavour includes the 'Agni' series of missiles with several tests conducted in recent years. The 2,500 km 'Agni II has been operationalised and is ready for induction in the armed forces. In addition to this, recent successful test of medium range Agni I (700-750 km range), single-stage and solid propelled, designed to fill the gap between Agni II and Prithvi, has been hailed as a major achievement.

It is also reported that the Agni I has been specially designed with Pakistan in mind. It is likely to be operational by the end of 2003 which will depend on the results of more tests this year. The Agni-III ballistic missile, with a strike range of 3,500 to 4,000 km, the technology not being too different from the earlier versions of Agni, is being developed and is likely to be tested by the end of this year. The solid-fuelled Agni-III will be both rail and road mobile to confer operational flexibility in deployment. It will be an entirely new vehicle, along with an inertial navigation system, to accord capabilities to deliver a one-tonne warhead. According to some analysts, a fourth version of the ballistic missile, named Agni-IV, in the range of beyond 5,000 km, is also underway. This would provide India with ICBM capability. If this was not enough, there are also reports that an ICBM programme, code named 'Surya' has also been started since the mid-1990s. This missile will probably be nuclear tipped and is likely to have a range of 8,000 to 12,000 km. It will be based on components developed from the Agni series and the Polar Satellite Launch Vehicle (PSLV) programme, the latter successfully initiated and undertaken by the Indian Space Research Organisation (ISRO). However, high ranking defence ministry officials and others responsible for such a kind of programme deny this. They argue that India does not need an ICBM programme as its security needs can be met effectively by IRBMs. Agni can act as a classic deterrent against any potential adversary, they say. According to a well-respected scientist, India is trying to develop a ballistic missile defence system like a hypersonic class of missiles and long-range detection and tracking radar with the objective of countering incoming missiles and other forms of offensive weapons. Hence, India has its eyes on developing defensive weapons systems development of weapons systems rest with DRDO, which in turn takes technical and other inputs from other scientific institutions like ISRO, the Indian Institute of Technology (IIT) and others, the production rests with the respective DPSUs and OFs. Missile production has been entrusted to BDL.

Apart from strategic weapons such as ballistic missiles, several tactical battle-field weapons systems have been developed and produced by India. The Prithvi, Trishul, and Nag fall under the latter category. Serial production of Prithvi missiles has been started by the BDL and delivered to the armed forces. Trishul and Nag have been periodically tested and serial production of these two missiles are expected shortly.

Another much publicised weapon system developed jointly by India and Russia, called Brahmos, a supersonic cruise missile, was tested recently. The first trial of Brahmos took place in 2001 and the second in 2002. The recent test of this missile took place from a naval vessel. High speed, stealth properties, advanced jamming protection and highly explosive warheads are some of the features of this missile which has a range of 290 km and a payload of up to 300 kg. This missile can be launched from multiple platforms – ship, land, submarine and air. The missile is expected, after a successful series of trials, to go into serial production by the end of 2003. Various versions will be developed, its air-to-ground version is configured to be fitted in the Su-30 MKI multi role fighter aircraft. All versions of this missile are also slated for sale on the international market.

Most recent developments in the fields of aerospace and other areas, in which India's defence industry is intricately involved, are many. They include the project on the Unmanned Aerial Vehicle (named 'Nishant'), which has cleared all tests. The Pilot-less Target Aircraft 'Lakshya', after a series of successful trials, is inducted into the IAF and Navy. The LCA programme, which started during the 1980s and had faced a lot of troubles, both financial and mainly technological, has been accelerated again since the late 1990s. Despite these difficulties, already forty-eight test trials have been conducted and the second prototype is already on its way to have flight trials. According to the Secretary, DRDO, Dr. V. K. Atre, five more prototypes are intended to be built and the aircraft is planned to be inducted into the IAF after initial operational clearance. The Air Force is expected to have four operational squadrons of LCA between 2010 and 2015. The task of such a huge order is taken up by the HAL, which is quite hopeful of meeting the expectation. Kaveri aero-engine for the LCA, an indigenous project to replace the GE-404 for the LCA, is currently undergoing high altitude tests in Russia. A success of Kaveri, the first endeavour to produce an advanced aero-engine in India, is certainly going to boost the confidence of both the scientific and defence-industrial establishments manifold. This will also signal, along with LCA, a new era in the field of aerospace in India. As a spin-off project, its marine version is also contemplated.

India is also developing a twin-engine Medium-range Combat Aircraft (MCA). This was disclosed at the 54th Annual General Meeting of the Aeronautical Society of India (in Kolkata) by no other than the President of India, Dr. A P J Abdul Kalam, who is also considered as the father of missile and nuclear technology. He said that the MCA programme was in the design phase. He also said that India was working on the design of a hyper plane, a re-usable and cost-effective hypersonic space vehicle. While reusable missile configuration and technology has not yet emerged in the world, Indian technologists have started working on a reusable hypersonic cruise missile system, an integrated design of multiple technologies derived from UAV, aircraft and missile systems 47.

A new Intermediate Jet Trainer Aircraft (HJT–36), perceived as an interim arrangement to replace MIG trainers as well as to finally replace the indigenous Advanced Jet Trainers, was planned to be ready for production from 2003. Design and development of a Test Bed for Pegasus engines for the Navy, successful flight trials of Pilot-less Targeted Aircraft Engines (PTAE), up-gradation of Jaguar, modification of air to air re-fuelling of Mirage, up-gradation and modernisation of MIGs are some of the other programmes which have been undertaken by both the scientific establishments and defence industry. Successful trials of short range Battlefield Surveillance Radars (BESR), and the three dimensional Medium Range Radars (CAR) have demonstrated DRDO's breakthrough in radar technology. In the field of Navy equipment, one important development is the Advanced Technology Vessel project for indigenous submarines, which is expected to take some time, at least till early in the next decade. According to newspaper reports, major work on this project is still pending and its status has caused some concern. According to the Defence Minister, indigenous construction of an aircraft carrier will be soon begin at Cochin Shipyard, which may take a decade to be completed. Given the nature and extent of activities in the field of defence science and technology, it is obvious that the industry seems quite upbeat to do the follow-up job of serial production of a number of ambitious programmes.

From Licence to Co-Production

The 'self-sufficiency' model adopted during the first years, with massive industrialisation in all core sectors of the economy including defence, was replaced by what is known as the 'self-reliance' model, which roughly commenced during the late 1950s and early 1960s. The self-reliance model, with primary emphasis on indigenous production and development and secondary dependence on imports from reliable foreign sources, continues to guide policy. As explained earlier, the half–a-century of technology gap and a performance below all expectations in the defence industry, from the early 1960s to the mid-1980s, led to a renewed emphasis on indigenous production activities. The period since the late 1980s and early 1990s thus witnesses a change in nature of defence-industrial production activities. The earlier era, among others, witnessed an increase in license production, which reduced indigenous production to a considerable extent. The present times, however, have witnessed more emphasis on indigenous production, a major change in this regard being the increasing number of co-production activities coming from various sources.

Although license production has been a stable form of production, it has not made India self-reliant in terms of upper-ends of defence production, especially in the field of design and development. With indigenous activities having its own weaknesses, especially financially and lack of or difficult access to foreign military technologies, other alternatives to fill the technology gap have been contemplated for some time. This is where the idea of joint design and development as well as co-production come in. Among other factors, trends in global defence industry have influenced this decision in many countries. On its quest for self-reliance in the 1990s and beyond, India has tried to follow this trend.

Several new projects in the Indian defence-industrial sector are planned to be jointly designed and developed, and India is keen on taking up this opportunity to the fullest possible extent. HAL has led the way in this. After the successful integration of several electronic components in the Su-30MKI by Indian scientists and technicians in recent times, the Russians are very interested in a partnership, initially in license production of the aircraft by HAL but incrementally substituted by joint production in future, which is unprecedented in this kind of fourth generation aircraft project. A new simulator which will make it possible to train pilots for the Su-30MKI is on the cards for India. HAL is going to produce this aircraft soon. Russia, in addition to this, has also proposed to become a partner in the ambitious fifth-generation combat aircraft project, of which details are not available. It has offered to design, develop and produce this project with India, thus sharing incurring costs.

Brahmos, as explained earlier, is a joint venture between India and Russia, which was expected to be ready for serial production. This cruise missile project started in 1998 and is said to be one of the major steps by India toward international collaboration. India's recent decision to initiate an Advanced Jet Trainer (AJT) project is also going to lead to the involvement of international collaboration partners.

The US aviation giant Lockheed Martin, which is interested in the AJT deal, is keen to offer technology transfer for this project. It has claimed that its model of an advanced trainer, the T-50 Golden Eagle, is the world's newest and only supersonic trainer. It has also shown an interest in close collaboration with defence companies in India, especially with HAL. Similarly, to get a share in the project, in which initially British Aerospace had been the front runner with its Hawk trainer aircraft, several British aerospace and defence companies are interested in joint ventures with their Indian counterparts.

This is the first time that, except for Russia, more and more front line arms producing countries are showing interest not in exports but, more importantly, in joint ventures and other forms of industrial participation. The Indian defence industry, especially since the last couple of years, has been experiencing noticeable changes. It is gearing up to take this opportunity which was previously quite limited. Industry watchers believe that the Indian defence industry is going to benefit from such swift changes in production policies in many ways.

Trends in Acquisitions

India's arms acquisitions, especially during the last decade, have been substantial. Two primary factors are attributed to this. First, the technology gap, which is either due to the long-lasting indigenous design and development activities during the 1960s to the 1980s and insufficient resources for R&D and production or the perception that arms acquisitions were only a short-term remedy (with an invitation for long-term difficulties, often ignored by decision-makers). Second, greater demands of security needs, where state-of-the-art weapons are necessary for national defence. A third factor, which is often cited by many analysts, is that of an inconsistency in arms purchases from abroad. While there have been arms imports throughout the time, the least active period was witnessed during the 1960s to the 1980s, in which an over emphasis on license production led to a situation in the defence-industrial sector where it was unable to provide requisite weapons at the right time, thus forcing the government to opt for immediate short term action in terms of imports.

The gap in the national arsenal became visible soon after the Gulf War, when India felt that it was way behind others in terms of overall defence preparedness. The most worrying aspect of India's defence preparedness was exposed when the Kargil conflict started in mid-1999. To its horror, it found out that it was ill prepared in terms of defence equipment as shortages of arms and ammunition were noticed. In brief, security needs were not matched by existing possession of weaponry and there was a need to fill the gap.

India has imported several weapons systems from many countries. The main source of weapons for India's military is Russia, which accounts for nearly 70 percent of the total purchases. West European giants like France, the United Kingdom and Germany have also supplied several systems. Italy, the Netherlands and Poland are some of the other European countries which have also supplied some weapons. New emerging suppliers include, among others, Israel and South Africa. The latter is considered to be a long-term reliable source of weaponry. The United States has recently also become an important supplier, despite the fact that there used to be times in which both countries had not got on well in the field of arms transfers. India imported a Mirage-2000 fighter aircraft from France. Recent reports also suggest that India is going to buy six 'Scorpene' submarines at an estimated cost of US $1.8 billion. There are also negotiations with the French on the purchase of 130 Mirage-2000H fighters amounting to an estimated cost of US $7 billion. Although such large-scale purchases often lead to procedural delays in India, it is quite hopeful of finalising the deals soon.

The Scorpene deal will also involve India in a different manner with the Mazagaon Dockyard Limited being responsible for the future transfer of technology for the building of the submarine in India. The French defence electronics company, Thales, has already signed an agreement with MDL in this regard. A contract (yet to be signed) regarding the purchase of Type-209 submarines from Germany is also in the pipeline. Also, a contract with Germany for SUT class Anti-submarine torpedoes for Type 209 ('Sishukumar' class) was supposed to be signed the status of which is not known yet. Italy has supplied 10 Seaguard TMX fire control radar and A244 ASW torpedos during the 2001/02 period for the Brahmaputra class frigates, produced by India.

Countries like the Netherlands, Poland, and Slovakia have supplied surveillance radar, armoured recovery vehicles and other systems. South Africa, considered a new partner in the military industrial cooperation, has supplied armoured personnel carriers (APC) in 2000. It is also involved in a new Ordnance Factory in India (40th OF at Nalanda). Israel, considered a potential future supplier and partner especially in the fields of defence electronics and aerospace, has supplied a number of items in the last half-a-decade. These include, among others, Heron and Searcher class UAVs, EL/M variants of aircraft, combat battlefield and fir control radar. A deal to supply Barak class SAM is in the pipeline while there is also a rumour that anti-missile defence systems will be supplied for which negotiations are going on. Its proposed sale of airborne early warning systems (AWACS) to India has recently caused discomfort to many countries, primarily the United States which is opposing the sale as it involves some US technology. Russia, the most trusted friend in the field of military and industrial cooperation, has been the main source of defence equipment. In the last decade or so, it has supplied Helix class AEW helicopters, MiG–29K aircraft, Su-30MKI (purchase worth more than US $5 billion in total) fighter aircraft, AA-11/12 class air to air missiles, naval and land versions of MRLs like BM-9A52/BM-23, T-90 MBTs, a wide variety of radar systems, SS-N-25 class anti-ship missiles, Krivak class frigates and others. The cumulative deal in the last five years (19972002) is estimated at US $6 billion. If this is not enough, Indo-Russian defence-industrial partnership has been gaining much momentum in recent times. India has recently been on the verge of finalising a deal to acquire the 45,000 tonne Kiev class aircraft carrier 'Admiral Gorshkov', Tu-22M3 (on lease) long-range strategic bombers, Akula class submarine and is expecting delivery of three Krivak class stealth frigates by March 2003.

In addition to these, both countries have signed an 'Inter-Governmental Commission for Military Technical Cooperation' recently to boost both military and industrial partnership. As the Indian defence industry is undertaking a series of joint ventures with Russia, both countries have also recently signed a protocol on arms exports under which exports of such systems are to be decided on a case-to-case basis.

One can witness a noticeable change in India's import of sophisticated weapons. During the 1990s, negotiations for arms purchases in many cases have involved discussion on joint industrial partnership. This is a clear diversion on the part of India as earlier it was based on outright purchase of complete weapons systems or license manufacture. In recent times, however, many formal and informal deals have included the willingness on both supplier and recipient's part to forge military technical and industrial ties. Informal understandings with major suppliers is paving the way for joint partnerships, which is benefiting Indian defence industry.

Civilian Production: Diversification as Key

It is often assumed that India's hitherto closed defence industry does not have much scope for civilian production. Similarly, conversion or diversion of military industry into civilian production has long been perceived as a non-starter in countries like India due to the obvious closed nature of its defence industry. During the Cold War period, the little conversion which was attempted in the West encountered a lot of problems. These ranged from technical issues of diverting military factories to civilian production to frequent changes in the political and security environments for military production during the 1960s and 1970s. Still, it was assumed that surplus arms production capacity could be quickly and successfully converted to suit civilian needs, once disarmament was decided upon.

The second phase of conversion, initiated by major arms producing countries in the West, started during and after the end of Cold War. Existing surplus defence-industrial capacities were tried to be converted through various means, including diversification, for civilian purposes. However, the process of conversion, considered a means to contribute to disarmament and peace, has faced many hindrances despite decisions to reduce military spending.

Still, conversion through diversification has been a major feature in India's defence industry which has not been discussed so far. In fact, many believe that India does not possess a sizeable industrial base to contemplate conversion – meaning that its facilities are still insufficient for conversion or diversion, which normally takes place in surplus capacities. But, on the other hand it is emphasised that enhancement of civilian production in the defence industry will benefit both the civilian and military sectors. Civilian production in the Indian defence industry had been encouraged since the late 1950s.

The primary goal of this attempt was to attain a greater degree of production efficiency and to maintain operational capacities during slack periods of demand. Mr V.K. Krishna Menon initiated this programme during his time (1958-62), which saw civilian products like coffee percolators, consumer electrical items, and engineering and construction equipment being produced by defence units. The war with China in the early 1960s, however, curtailed this activities as more emphasis was put on the establishment of a number of defence-industrial units. It is during this time that the aircraft producing company, HAL, was established, along with a number of OFs and DPSUs. It suffices to mention here that an initiative to begin civilian production in the defence industry was evident during the time when conversion was initiated in the West. Also, this initiative led to a similar process as was initiated in China where Lin Biao and other military political leaders initiated what is known as 'civil production during peace time and military production during wartime'.

Although the OFs had diversified into civilian production as early as in the 1950s, it received a major boost during the 1980s and 1990s. The diversification programme included a time-bound plan of action with strategies for each factory, and the appointment of professional consultants to identify products and potential markets.

This would enable the OFs to utilise their spare capacities. The former Minister of Defence, Sharad Pawar, had authorised the OFs to employ as much as 40 percent of their rated capacities for the production of goods for the civilian sector. Diversified products included a range of consumer goods for which quality certificates were awarded to five of the OFs. By the mid-1990s, the sale of civilian goods by the OFs had exceeded 10 million rupees. HAL, manufacturer of aerospace products for the defence sector, has also been involved in several products for the civilian market. These include high technology products for space and other programmes. It was involved in several products for the PSLV programme undertaken by ISRO. Since the late 1980s, it has started supplying spare parts for civilian aircraft. In 1993, it joined an Asian consortium to co-produce medium and small passenger aircraft. It also has a tie co-operates with Boeing to take care of the maintenance of Boeing 737 passenger planes in India. The percentage ratio of civilian production to the military in the defence industry, including the OFs and the DPSUs.

The Indian defence industry is optimistic about its civilian production. In a recent seminar on 'Current Trends in Embedded Technology and Applications', top defence scientists, including P. Rajkumar, Director of the Aeronautical Development Agency which has undertaken the LCA programme, are of the opinion that India's indigenous military systems are harnessing cutting edge technologies such as embedded systems, which, when allowed to trickle through into the civilian arena, could ignite huge markets.

Custom-built embedded units applied extensively to LCA and other aerospace systems have been in demand in the civilian sector, especially in information technology. National Aerospace Laboratory, a key unit of the HAL, has recently rolled out its first prototype of a 14-seater light transport aircraft, named 'Saras'. This aircraft is expected to enter into commercial production within the next two years. The market size of this category of aircraft is considerable. It is expected that production of this aircraft is going to benefit aircraft industry in India. DPSUs like Bharat Electronics have been engaged in civilian production in a big way.

In fact, BEL's production for the military sector is less than 50 percent. In the case of Bharat Earth Movers, it is less than 7 percent. Civilian production of two other DPSUs, Mazagaon Dockyard and Mishra Dhatu Nigam, lies at more than 50 percent. More than 350 items are produced by BEL for the civilian sector which are primarily meant for the communication market. Since 1992/93, it has also entered the cordless phone and cellular phone market.

Among others, it is now concentrating on the production of X-ray tubes for the world market. Other DPSUs are similarly producing a range of products for both domestic as well as international markets. The Indian defence industry has a huge potential for the civilian market. It is now entering into a phase of concentrated production. This means that industrial units are geared up to produce more and more dual-use items and at the same time concentrate on core areas of both military and civilian technologies. Spin-off and spin-on are both expected to constitute a major part in this strategy.

The opening up of the defence sector for private participation has not only created opportunities for the defence industry to venture more into the civilian market, the spin-on effect is also expected from the private civilian industries. The private industry in India is confident of contributing to this in future.

INDIA'S DEFENCE INDUSTRY IN THE 21ST CENTURY

Major Policy Initiatives

India's defence industry entered a new phase of self-reliance on the eve of the 21st century. Since the mid-1990s, several initiatives have been undertaken by the government to effect changes in the defence industry. Soon after the liberalisation of the economy was announced in 1990/91, the defence industry started realising the importance of civil-military interaction in the industrial sector. The private industries in India, which were thus far debarred from entering into defence production and whose role in the defence sector was limited to supplying spare parts and other minor contributions, started demanding a share in defence production.

In 1994, the then Defence Minister founded six Task Forces on major areas of defence modernisation, of which reforms in defence industry was an important part. This was carried out by the government in consultation with institutions like the Confederation of Indian Industries (CII). The CII, on its part was instrumental in bringing out a series of proposals in the broad field of private participation in the defence sector and armed forces–industry cooperation. Soon after this, the government initiated a programme called 'Army-Industry Partnership', under the auspices of CII which highlighted the importance of cooperative arrangements between the armed forces, defence industry and the government. After India's nuclear tests, various sanctions were imposed on India, of which sanctions related to the import of military and dual-use goods and technologies were considered the most important.

Sanctions were imposed on more than 150 items, which affected the progress of many defence products. However, the impact of sanctions on military technology was taken up as a another phase of challenge for the defence scientists as they had faced similar sanctions after the test in 1974. At that time they had faced more difficulties as the defence industry was not in a position to withstand such severe cuts which had resulted in delays in many major programmes. This time around, the defence industry had made significant progress to be able to withstand sanctions. After the Kargil conflict in mid-1999, the government started looking into security gaps and founded a committee under Mr K. Subrahmanyam. He brought out a major report on this conflict, which is known as the 'Kargil Committee Report'. This report, among other recommendations, highlighted the importance of reforms in higher defence management and reforms in institutional processes in the security sector.

The Government also founded a Group of Ministers' committee to look into major aspects of the overall security management of the country. The committee submitted its report to the government, which is known as GoM Report on 'Reforming the National Security System. This report highlighted the importance of self-reliance in India's defence industry and recommended several steps to introduce institutional changes into the system. Coupled with changes at institutional and organisational levels, India's defence industry entered an entirely new era after the Government announced a major change in policy by outlining codes of conduct for and inviting private participation in the defence industry. This is seen as by far the most important policy shift in the defence-industrial sector in the last fifty years. By doing so, the Government, through an official notification No. 5(37)/2001-FCI, allowed private sector participation up to 100 percent and permitted foreign direct investment (FDI) up to 26 percent. This decision has been hailed by both the private industry and the government-owned defence industry. Institutions like CII and FICCI, which represent interests and views of the private sector, have been instrumental in influencing such a marked change in policies. According to Mr Sushanto Sen, the Director General of CII, such a policy change is certainly going to benefit both the defence industry and the private sector.

In tune with the stated objectives of India's defence industry to achieve a higher degree of self-reliance and a desire to make its flagship units globally competitive, thus entering into competitive defence markets, the Government has also introduced some institutional changes that are expected to smoothen operations both at structural and organisational levels. Earlier, procurement procedures were considered cumbersome, and there were overlaps in organisational responsibilities of respective organs responsible for procurement. Under the new system, the Services Headquarters were integrated into the Ministry of Defence to provide closer interaction. The procurement structure is now a three-tier structure with the recent establishment of the Defence Acquisition Council (DAC) at the apex. Its primary role will be to accord in-principle-approval of long-term perspective plans (15-20 years), acceptance of necessity for the capital acquisition plan (5 years), identify 'Make', 'Buy' and 'Make and Buy' projects and monitor progress of the three Boards under it – the Defence Procurement Board, Defence Production Board and the Defence R&D Board. The Defence Procurement Board under the Defence Secretary will have the primary role of capital procurements and coordination. The Defence Production Board will be headed by the Secretary Defence Production and Supplies and will oversee all activities related to indigenous manufacture, progress in 'make' projects and will provide support to DAC. The Defence R&D Board will be headed by the Secretary Defence R&D and will oversee progress, monitor and report on all R&D proposals in consultation with the user service and production board. Other measures at institutional level include direct linkages between the armed forces and the Ministry of Defence through integrated headquarters, which include respective perspective planning branches. In sum, organisational and institutional changes brought about recently seem to complement policy changes.

Problems and Prospects: An Assessment

India's quest for self-reliance has produced mixed results. Some of the lessons that India has learnt in the past fifty years are worth noting here. First, a combination of factors have led to the indigenous design and development component of self-reliance slowing down to almost zero for over a quarter of a century after 1962. This has led not only to a huge technology gap but also contributed to severe difficulties in technology assimilation in the industrial sector. However, since the mid-1980s, activities toward achieving a greater degree of self-reliance have taken up momentum. The technology gap also widened the scope for acquisition of production technology rather than design technology from foreign sources. This in turn has created a license production regime at the cost of indigenous production. During the 1990s, the activities to encourage joint ventures and co-production in the defence-industrial sector is largely seen as a step to reduce license regime and boost indigenous industrial capabilities. How far this will achieve desired results are yet to be seen as such activities are only of recent origin and they need lead time to prove themselves.

For example, the market for Brahmos missiles is estimated to be large, but it depends on how much is it likely to penetrate the cruise missile market at a global level. Success of this kind will not only validate India's defence-industrial capabilities to meet domestic demands but also increase its confidence in many ways.

Second, private participation in the defence-industrial sector has started after a long delay. This is attributable to several factors, ranging from the socialist and protective nature of the defence sector to fears of what is called 'security diffusion'.

The latter especially relates to a fear of below-expectation performance by the private sector as it is hardly specialised to meet strict high military standards, hence compromising security standards. This kind of fear has been criticised by many who argue that private participation is essential in the defence sector which is primarily technology driven and capital intensive.

The recent opening up of the defence sector for private participation has generated a lot of interest in the country. Institutions like CII caution that while such initiatives are always welcome, the government should come out with a clear 'road-map' for the private sector participants in defence so as to enable them to prepare themselves for the new reality.

Fears regarding the ability of the private sector to match expectations of the country in the highly demanding and technology-dominated industrial sector are countered by industrialists like Atul Kirloskar (Chairman of Committee on National Defence, CII), who claim to have absolute faith in their abilities. Many also claim that given a chance, the secondary role of the private sector can be turned into a primary one in a short period of time. Some of the leading industrialists even claim that they have or intend to possess capabilities to produce complete weapons systems.

Several companies like Mahindras and Mahindras (M&M), the Tata Group, Kirloskar Brothers, Larsen and Toubro (L&T), and many others have already jumped into the fray to obtain orders from the defence industry. Since 2002, the Government has received more than ten applications from the private sector to manufacture weapons systems. It has recently awarded five licenses to L&T and M&M to produce military vehicles and some weapons systems.

Third, the government has emphasised measures to enhance the defence industry to cope with future challenges. Such measures are carried out by both OFs and DPSUs, apart from respective branches of the Government and the armed forces. Digitalisation, strict quality control, performance-related benefits, professional management systems, allowing the private sector to carry out R&D activities in the government-owned laboratories, are some of the measures which have come up in recent years and are likely to impinge the defence-industrial landscape.

A simplification of production and procurement rules promise better buyer-seller relations. There were some protests coming from employees' unions of OFs and DPSUs against privatisation. The Government has assured these unions that employees' interests will be borne in mind but that it will give priority to performance.

In one instance, the Defence Minister is reported to have appealed to the workers in one DPSU to not to worry about possible relocations due to privatisation and assured them to take effective steps to safeguard their interests. It seems that rationalisation of the defence industry is on the cards which might bring some unrest in the form of reduction of employment in the defence-industrial sector.

There are even rumours that some of the units, especially from the ordnance sector might be closed down. The private sector participants are, however, optimistic. They argue that their factories can effectively be converted into profit making civilian units. In several rounds of interviews with senior officers and industry analysts by the author, it seems that some of the industrial units may come under close scrutiny. Conversion to civilian production in their cases is not ruled out. In brief, significant rationalisation, diversification and closer private participation are coming and are likely to influence India's defence industry in many ways.

Conclusion

India's defence-industrial strategy is directed primarily toward achieving self-reliance. Presently, there is a clear imbalance in requirements by the armed forces. While roughly 70 percent of requirements are met through arms imports, the domestic sources supply the rest.

The current strategy is geared to reverse this trend with the primary aim of supplying three-fourth of the requirements through domestic sources.

India's decision to allow private participation in the defence-industrial sector is seen as a dual aim, namely to achieve much-needed capital and production enhancement and, secondly, to open up to the external market through their presence. There is also an effort to adopt suitable strategies to make select sectors like aerospace and electronics globally competitive.

DPSUs like HAL and BEL are now much in demand and are trying to become viable global giants, not to be included in SIPRI's List of Top 100 Defence Companies for their sheer size only but for their performance. And, the overall strategy is to make the defence-industrial sector act as a locomotive for economic development. In this regard, an emphasis on dual-use technologies and production is contemplated which could benefit both the defence and civilian sector.

The current strategy also looks into various options toward minimising the state investments in the defence sector while encouraging private and foreign portfolio investment in existing Indian defence companies. Such a tall order for the defence-industrial sector is often regarded as unrealistic by many in India but that is another matter. If recent changes in various policies related to the defence industry are supposed to have any meaning, then, despite all problems, there is something to be optimistic about in the Indian defence industry.

INDIA'S DEFENCE POLICY CHALLENGES IN THE 21ST CENTURY

The first macro problem that must be resolved, if India is to rise as a great power, is achieving higher rates of economic growth. The reason for that is simple. A competent military costs money and modern defence capabilities, which are sophisticated and effective, are priced in numbers that boggle the imagination. For a country like India, which has to deal not simply with questions of defence but also questions of development simultaneously, high economic growth becomes the only solution especially in those situations when India cannot choose between the objectives of defence and development. When one begins to think of the revolution in military affairs — the kind of capabilities today that characterize the military forces of the great powers — it is simply impossible for India to acquire such capabilities without sustaining economic growth of at least 7 to 9 per cent per annum consistently.

China is a good example. A country that has experienced close to double-digit growth for more than twenty years since 1978, still finds it hard to develop the kinds of sophisticated military capabilities it seeks to acquire across the board.

Therefore, one must be prepared for the fact that even if the Indian economy were to grow between 7 and 9 per cent consistently for the next twenty years, the best India would be able to do in the area of cutting edge defence technology is to acquire niche capabilities. But those niche capabilities may be enough for the specific strategic circumstances that it faces. The second macro problem that India needs to engage and satisfy is the development of an appropriate national vision and appropriate institutions designed to manage the acquisition of great power capabilities.

What substantive goals, defined in terms of national interest, does India really seek to service? The answer to this question cannot be defined in terms of platitudes like a "just world order." That is a useful phrase for a political campaign. It is a terrible criterion for defence planning and force structuring. The other aspect of this question of defining India's goals and creating the appropriate institutions pertains to the issue of whether India will be able to achieve the right balance between state control and societal autonomy. It is very important to realize that successful states in the modern era have been those that have maintained this balance in the most creative way possible.

The third macro challenge that I would highlight for your consideration is whether India is capable of exploiting the existing structure of the international system to its advantage. In this context, I think India should get rid of the notion of a multipolar world order as a practical outcome in the relevant future. Pursuing chimerical goals like multipolarity does not make for good policy. The international system, for all practical purposes, is going to remain a unipolar system for at least the next half century. By all indicators, if you define power in terms of comprehensive national strength, it is unlikely that the United States will face serious peer competitors for at least another fifty years.

Consequently, the challenge for India becomes, can it develop a viable strategic partnership with the United States that serves both mutual interests and India's own unilateral interests? Can India develop a relationship with the United States that helps it enhance and magnify its own power?

This is not to suggest that the United States is the only power in the international system. Clearly not — there are many others. This is also not to suggest that India's goals ought to consist solely of developing a relationship with the United States, or that India somehow is constrained solely to develop a relationship with the United States and no other. Not true. India has the flexibility to maneuver within the interstices of the international system. But at the end of the day, there is one eight hundred pound gorilla that has to be engaged. And that is the United States. That gorilla is not going to go away. That gorilla has already put its nose for the first time in modern history, into the physical environment of the subcontinent. And it is in India's national interest, and important for its capacity to generate and magnify its power, to develop a productive and a collaborative relationship with the United States that enhances the interests of the two countries.

First, India has to deal with the challenge of neutering internal security threats without undermining its capacity for effective external defence. This is harder to do than is sometimes imagined.

It is unfortunate that the principal security threat that India is going to have to deal with on a day-to-day basis is the threat to internal security. There is no running away from this problem. Historically, India dealt with this challenge by essentially throwing manpower at the threat instead of technology. And the reason it did this was simply because it enjoyed a surfeit of manpower and a deficit of technology.

There were two consequences to this strategy. One was that its approach to preserving internal defence was probably not as effective as it could be, because technology could provide that valuable supplement which was not available to India. The second consequence was that preserving internal security became extremely expensive and has now come at the cost of being able to acquire the new technologies required to raise a modern military force. It is a myth that India's manpower is cheap. Maintaining the size and kind of forces that India does, if maintained over the secular period, will undercut its ability to acquire the kind of RMA capabilities that wins modern wars. And this is going to require India to make very painful choices — painful choices about reducing its manpower strength and changing the inter-service budgetary balances, choices that it cannot make today because of the gravity, importance, and burdens of its internal security commitments.

The next micro issue is the need to preserve effective external defence, now in a nuclear shadowed environment. This brings us face to face with the vexed question of whether India has the capacity to successfully prosecute a limited war. Most commentary so far has focused on the issue of limited war as an example of Indian recklessness. People have chastised that limited war in fact represents a solution to India's external security problems. My take on the issue is somewhat different. I believe that limited war should be viewed not as a product of the proclivities of the state, but rather as a predicament resulting from a specific set of structural circumstances.

The transparent presence of nuclear weapons in the subcontinent for the first time makes unlimited wars untenable as a matter of state policy. This is not simply India's choice — it actually represents a dilemma of the nuclear age. And it is a challenge that faces India both with respect to Pakistan and with respect to China. In both cases, unlimited war is not feasible. There is also no guarantee that war is obsolete. And therefore the challenge of limited war confronts India squarely, both with respect to its northern and its western borders.

What does limited war mean for Indian defence policy? It means that India is now confronted with the task of being required to hit hard and effectively enough to punish an adversary, but not hit so hard or so effectively as to cause inadvertent escalation. This in turn leads to questions like "how do you avoid escalation?" Most commentaries have focused on this aspect of the problem. But there is another aspect to the problem, which has largely escaped attention. Because it is going to demand of India a new style of war fighting that New Delhi traditionally has been uncomfortable with and which historically it has been relatively incapable of. It is a style of war fighting that puts a premium on achieving very speedy decision on the battlefield and then terminating offensive action either before the international community intervenes or before the conflict degenerates into unavoidable attrition. Getting the Indian military to successfully prosecute a fast paced war that generates quick decisions is something that we have not seen in fifty years of India's independence. It is also the kind of war that traditionally the United States was not very good at. We preferred wars that allowed us plenty of time to mobilize, plenty of time to deploy, and then plenty of time to be able to grind down the adversary at our convenience. If India is to be able to prosecute the opposite kind of war, as the United States is now proficient at — fast, decisive, and yet limited — it is going to require an investment in new technologies and new operating skills apart from new doctrines and new concepts of operation.

Third, if India is to become a great power of the sort that it seeks to become, it also has to become a net provider of regional security, both in the sub-continental and in the extra sub-continental arenas. This is easier said than done; yet at one level it is the quintessential part of the definition of a great power. After all, what is the meaning of having great power capabilities if at the end of the day you cannot extend net security to others? And yet any Indian attempt to provide the kind of regional security that I am talking of, even in the sub-continental arena, is fraught with hazards because it risks deepening intra-regional rivalries and it risks deepening the suspicions India's weaker neighbours have of its capabilities and its intentions.

Finally, will India develop the organizational structures that are required to maintain and operate these capabilities if it seeks to provide the kind of regional security that is to be expected of a great power?

The fourth micro problem pertains to whether India can acquire an effective nuclear deterrent without breaking the bank. My view is that nuclear weapons are important for India's security in some limited sense, but it is also essential to remember that they are actually relatively obsolescent technologies. Nuclear weapons are now over fifty years old and they are generally unusable as instruments of international politics.

14 India-US Defence Pact-II: Commitments may Fetter Judgment

Indeed, the text of the accord itself says that in the context of the US-India Defence relationship having "advanced in a short time to unprecedented levels of cooperation unimaginable in 1995", and changes in the international security environment posing challenges to both countries "in ways unforeseen ten years ago", the new "framework", while building on past successes is designed to seize new opportunities by way of supporting the broader US-India strategic partnership as an "element" of it.

In tune with its unprecedented nature, it will be in force for an exceptionally long period of 10 years. The blunt truth is that this is an agreement between two unequal partners, one having all the trumps and the other in danger of being irresistibly forced to follow suit at moments of crisis.

Also, be it noted that India has got very little from the US for undertaking these obligations which are bound to be a strain on its resources and freedom of action. The US has been tight-lipped on India's bid for permanent membership of the UN Security Council, supply of dual use nuclear and space technologies and pressuring Pakistan to close down sanctuaries for terrorists operating against India. Well might the US Defence Secretary, Mr Donald Rumsfeld, rejoice: "The military-to-military relationship between our two countries is excellent.

It has been developed over a period of four-and-a-half years in ways that today are multi-faceted. We have advanced continuously in the relationship in terms of meetings and exercises and various aspects of it. And I feel very good about it and very positive about it."

"Shared Interests"

There are several features that distinguish the new 'framework' from the Agreed Minutes of 1995. For the first time in a formal agreement, called by whatever name, on Defence cooperation, it sets out the "shared interests" of the US and India in specific terms as including: Maintaining security and stability; defeating terrorism and violent religious extremism; preventing the spread of weapons of mass destruction and associated materials, data, and technologies; and protecting the free flow of commerce via land, air and sea lanes.

In the light of these wide-ranging goals, the two Governments bind themselves and their Defence establishments to a comprehensive charter of 13 (unlucky number!) different types of obligations many of which may constrain India to become a "client State" of the US.

Take, as examples, the obligations to collaborate "in multinational operations when it is in their common interest" and expand collaboration in missile defence. Conceivably, the Defence Policy Group set up pursuant to the Agreed Minutes of 1995 will decide what is in the common interest of both countries, but what happens when they cannot agree?

Further, there is no mention that such operations will be under United Nations' auspices. Which means that India has pre-committed itself to participating in them even if its troops were to be brought under the US military command.

As regards missile Defence, talks are going on for the induction of Patriot Advance Capability-3 missile Defence system into India.

Collaboration in missile Defence can easily result in India being drawn into the global missile defence shield being forged by the US as part of its own hegemonistic strategy.

Would India want this to happen? Or, take the commitment to "assist in building worldwide capacity to conduct successful peacekeeping operations, with a focus on enabling other countries to field trained, capable forces for these operations".

Peace-keeping cannot take place *in vacuo* or without regard to who are the aggressors and the aggressed. There will be situations in which it would be prudent for India not to get involved. But the obligation imposed by the charter is unqualified and may prove a source of contention.

Too Many Cooks

On top of it all, India seems to have boxed itself in the interlocking mechanisms envisaged under the "framework" and they can also become embarrassing millstones round India's neck in the future fettering free exercise of its judgment.

In addition to the existing Defence Policy Group and its various sub-groups that came into being after the signing of the Agreed Minutes, the pact "in recognition of the growing breadth and depth of the US-India strategic defence relationship" establishes a Defence Procurement and Production Group (DPPG) and a Joint Working Group for mid-year review of work.

The DPPG will oversee Defence trade, as well as prospects for co-production and technology collaboration, broadening the scope of its predecessor subgroup the Security Cooperation Group.

The Defence Joint Working Group will be subordinate to the Defence Policy Group and will meet at least once per year to perform a mid-year review of work overseen by the Defence Policy Group and its sub-groups (the Defence Procurement and Production Group, the Joint Technical Group, the Military Cooperation Group, and the Senior Technology Security Group), and to prepare issues for the annual meeting of the Defence Policy Group.

With so many cooks in the kitchen stirring the broth (and the hornets' nests as well!), it is problematic whether India's Defence establishment will have the time to look after its primary duty of safeguarding India's own Defence! In short, the whole purport of the "framework" and the charter of commitments seem to be to enhance "inter-operability" of which one of the concomitants would be integration of the structures of the two armed forces. Is India game for such a merger of identities?

(There are many foreign policy implications of the framework impinging on India's relations with China and South-Asian countries, which have not been touched)

Charter of commitments under the 'framework'

- Conduct joint and combined exercises and exchanges;
- Collaborate in multinational operations when it is in their common interest;
- Strengthen the capabilities of our militaries to promote security and defeat terrorism;
- Expand interaction with other nations in ways that promote regional and global peace and stability;
- Enhance capabilities to combat the proliferation of weapons of mass destruction;
- Expand two-way defence trade, not viewing defence transactions, as ends in and of themselves, but as a means to strengthen security, reinforce strategic partnership, achieve greater interaction between armed forces, and build greater understanding between Defence establishments;
- In the context of Defence trade and a framework of technology security safeguards, increase opportunities for technology transfer, collaboration, co-production, and research and development;
- Expand collaboration relating to missile Defence;
- Strengthen the abilities of our militaries to respond quickly to disaster situations, including in combined operations;
- Assist in building worldwide capacity to conduct successful peacekeeping operations, with a focus on enabling other

countries to field trained, capable forces for these operations;

- Conduct exchanges on Defence strategy and Defence transformation;
- Increase exchanges of intelligence; and
- Continue strategic-level discussions by senior leadership from the US Department of Defence and India's Ministry of Defence, in which the two sides exchange perspectives on international security issues of common interest, with the aim of increasing mutual understanding, promoting shared objectives, and developing common approaches.

15 Indian Defence Industry: Domestic Production and Imports —the Future Balance

INTRODUCTION

Ever since it gained independence from the United Kingdom in 1947 India has aspired to economic self-sufficiency in economic power and to be accorded the international status commensurate with its size and history. Increasingly, it has viewed the possession of a capable military supported by a home grown and state controlled defence industry and more recently a research and development capability as central to this strategy. India now has one of the largest and most significant defence production capabilities in the developing world.

It has nevertheless been spectacularly unsuccessful in growing its defence R&D capability. Indeed, having claimed in the mid-1990s, that it would significantly reduce its dependence on foreign suppliers for high-technology defence equipment by the middle of this decade, the country has therefore had to turn once again to the outside world to help it meet its defence needs. Many within the Indian military establishment and the government have also started to re-assess the viability of India's established approach to defence development. Thus far, attention has been largely focused on allowing private sector and foreign participation in defence production and R&D. Still, if the general experience of economic reform in India is anything to go by this will take time, and India will have to rely on imports in the interim.

Furthermore, the ability of India's defence industrial base to meet the country's high-end defence requirements in areas such as aerospace will probably remain limited, not least because the expense of designing and producing such systems is increasingly rapidly.

INDIA'S CURRENT DEFENCE PRODUCTION CAPABILITY

The foundations for India's defence industry are widely believed to have been laid in 1801 with the establishment of the Gun Carriage Agency in Calcutta by the East India Company. Although historically true, the birth of India's current defence industrial really came during the Second World War, when the decision was taken to establish a limited defence production capability in the country, to support the British war effort in Asia and the Middle East. Before then, the British had decided against establishing a significant defence equipment manufacturing capability in India, for fear of 'giving the natives access to modern military industry'.

Ordnance Factories and Public Sector Undertakings

At the end of the WW2 India's defence industrial capacity amounted to 16 ordnance factories, a clothing establishment, and an aircraft production plant; and the new government subsequently inherited this capability. No new factories were built in the first years after independence.

From 1958 onwards, however, the ordnance factories were steadily expanded. The war against China in 1962 (described by some as India's 'Pearl Harbour') prompted a further expansion in India's ordnance capability. By 1970, the number of ordnance factories had risen to 31 and by the 1980s the number had reached 35. Today the country has 39 ordnance factories. The Indian Ordnance Factories Organisation (OFO) is currently the largest departmentally run industrial undertaking in the country. In addition to its ordinance factors, India has eight defence focused public sector undertakings (PSUs). These are Bharat Electronics; Bharat Earth Movers; Mazagon Dockyards; Garden Reach Shipbuilders and Engineers; Goa Shipyard; Bharat Dynamics; Mishra Dhatu Nigam (Midhani); and Hindustan Aeronautics. The PSUs produce a range of defence equipment including helicopters, state of the art electronics, heavy trucks and tank transportation trailers, submarines, missile boats destroyers, frigates, corvettes, fast attack craft, guided missiles, and aeronautics. They also provide overhaul and maintenance facilities.

DEFENCE RESEARCH AND DEVELOPMENT

India also has a defence research and development capability: the Defence Research and Development Organisation (DRDO). The DRDO has its roots in the Technical Development Establishments (TDES) formed during the Second World War. These were amalgamated in 1959 to form the Defence Science Organisation (DSO). This, in turn, was amalgamated with the Defence Science Services in 1958, to form the DRDO. The organisation employs in the region of 25000 people (about 6000 of which are scientists and engineers and 10000 technicians). The DRDO draws on the work of 51 laboratories/establishments across the country, and (in theory at least) has close links with the eight PSUs. It also cooperates with 70 academic research institutions, 50 national science and technology centres, and some companies in the private sector. The organisation really came into its own in the 1980s, under the leadership of Dr. A.J.P Abdul Kalam, when a number of major programmes were launched. These were the: Integrated Guided Missile Development Project (1983); the Light Combat Aircraft (1983); the Advanced Light Helicopter; the Arjun Tank (first conceived in 1974); and a number of smaller projects, such as the Pinaka, a multiple barrel rocket launcher (MBRL).

Major Government Actors

India's defence planning system is centred on the Ministry of Defence (MOD), which uniquely, is manned only by civilians. In simple organisation terms, the Ministry of Defence (MOD) is the major coordinating body for defence production and R&D. It consists of three main departments: the Department of Defence; the Department of Defence Production and Supplies; and the

Department of Defence R&D. In addition to this, there is the MOD Finance Division, which exists at the same level. The Department of Defence (DOD) is headed by the Secretary of State for Defence. He coordinates the activities of the other MOD Departments and the three armed services.

The Department of Defence Production was established in 1962 after the war with China in order to create an indigenous defence production base, while the Department for Defence supplies was established in 1965, with a view to forging links between the civil industries and defence production units. The two departments were eventually merged into one 1984. The Department of Defence Research and Development, meanwhile, is headed by a secretary who is also Scientific Adviser to the Defence Minister.

Its main responsibilities are R&D planning and advising the Defence Minister on scientific aspects of military equipment. Several committees are also involved in the defence planning process: The Defence Minister's Committee (now replaced by the Defence Minster's weekly morning meeting); the MOD production and supply committee, which deals with matters relating to import substitution, domestic arms production, and the operation of the ordnance factories; and the Defence R&D Council, which formulates and reviews R&D defence programmes, and brings together the Defence Minister and the Directors General of the Council for Scientific and Industrial Research. The Chiefs of Staff Committee, which comprises of the three Chiefs of the Armed Forces, provides a channel for providing military advice to the Prime Minister. A defence-planning cell, which was established in 1965 with a view to improving liaison between the National Planning Commission and other relevant Ministries to ensure that overall defence planning is integrated with overall economic planning, is rumoured not to have functioned as intended.

APPROACH TO DEFENCE PROCUREMENT AND INDUSTRIALISATION

The approach that India has adopted in defence procurement and defence industrial development is similar to that followed other less developed countries (LDCs). Within this general model, however, the country's experience can be divided into three stages. The first was from independence in 1947 until the early to mid-1960s. The second went from the period following the Sino-India war (1962) and second Indo-Pakistan (1965) conflict until the mid-1980s. And the third went from the mid-1980s until the present day.

In the first period, India only possessed the ability to make things such as shells and other ammunition, small arms, guns and explosives; it also had a limited aircraft and ship maintenance capabilities based in Bangalore and Calcutta. Thus, it had to look abroad to foreign defence equipment suppliers, such as the United Kingdom and France to meet its needs. During the second stage, efforts were made to build up domestic production, mostly through assembly under license from the Soviet Union and the United Kingdom. (This programme was centred on the PSUs). During this period, the range of activities undertaken by defence sector was also deliberately widened to include previously peripheral items such as clothing. The third period started with large purchases from the Soviet Union by the former Prime Minster Rajiv Gandhi's government (1984-1989). During this period, India consistently spent over 3.3 per cent of Gross Domestic Product (GDP) on building up its armed forces. By the end of the decade, India had the fourth largest armed forces in the world, the fifth biggest airforce, and the sixth biggest navy. Likewise, India became the world's largest importer of conventional weapons, spending $US12.2 billion in the period, of which Russia was the largest supplier. By the end of the 1980s India was assessed as being able to assemble Complete Knock Down (CKD) and Semi-Knock Down (SKDs) purchased from foreign companies and production under license.

Furthermore, gradual improvements were also made in and greater attention paid to the country's defence research and development capability, as well as systems integration for the in-country assembly of weapons. Between the financial year 1991-1992 and the FY 1994-1995, for example, funding for military R&D increased by 36 per cent to UD$430/454 million. And in 1995 India announced its intention to double the share of the defence budget allocated to defence R&D to ten per cent of the total defence budget with a view to reducing the imported content of defence goods to 30 per cent by 2005. Broadly speaking the decision to allocate increased funds to defence R&D came at the expense of funding for more traditional procurement programmes.

The move towards defence indigenisation and the tensions associated with it in the 1990s did not occur in a vacuum; indeed it arguably happened earlier than India either predicted or was ready for. For example, the 1991 economic crisis that best the economy forced India to reduce defence spending as a percentage of GDP, from four per cent in the late 1980s to below three per cent in 1994, while the amount of funding allocated to procurement was slashed. The end of the Cold War and the collapse of the Soviet Union, meanwhile, led to the end of the supply of cheap and subsidised weaponry from Moscow. As the previously centralised Soviet arms industry was now spread across the new Republics, India also found it increasingly difficult to acquire spare parts for much of this equipment. Against this backdrop, indigenous R&D was apparently seen (*or at least presented as*) a way around the problem.

India's approach to defence industrial development from Independence onwards is also closely related to its approach to economic development generally. Crucially, a significant proportion of India's defence production and R&D base is entirely under state control. This is the result of the Industrial Policy Resolutions of 1948 and 1956. These placed the development of all key sectors of the economy, such as machine tools, railways, iron and steel and defence production, under state control. (Both the Mazagon Docks and the Garden Reach Shipbuilders were brought under public ownership in 1960).

The large-scale participation of private sector companies in defence production, in the meantime, is limited to providing components to the PSUs. Even though the manufacture of components, assemblies and sub-assemblies was opened up to the private sector in 1991, the Indian armed forces procure 250 per cent more from the public than the private sector. A survey of 500 top companies in Indian in the same year also reported that only 30 of them had (or are currently) involved in defence contracts.

CHALLENGES TO INDIA'S CURRENT DEFENCE PRODUCTION AND RESEARCH AND DEVELOPMENT CAPABILITY

India's experience of developing its defence industry and research and development capability over the past decade has been mixed.

Ordnance Factories and PSUs

Outwardly, both the ordnance factories and the PSUs can be considered successful enterprises. The country's ordnance factories are capable of providing the Indian military with a significant proportion of their ammunition and low level material needs. In the period 1992/93-1997/98, for example, India only imported 11 per cent of its total ammunition needs.

India is also planning to open a 40th Ordnance factory in the near future. Furthermore, speaking in the Indian Parliament, the *Lok Sabha,* on 4 July 2000, George Fernandes, the Indian Defence Minister, stated that the country's ordnance factories recorded a surplus of Rs 780 crores (a crore is ten million rupees) during the period 1999-2000. In addition to this, Fennandes stated that due to last year's Kargil conflict, output increased from 33 per cent to 900 per cent for ammunition items; 20 per cent to 108 per cent for clothing items; and 76 to 233 per cent for cables.

More generally, an overall increase in output value of 34.6 per cent in 1999-2000, as compared to the value of issue in 1998/99. The picture for the PSUs is similar. Output in the sector has been rising rapidly since the 1980s, and all the companies have started to move into profitability. According to the latest MOD, moreover, the value of production in 1998-1999 (Rs 7205.55 crore) registered growth of 15.57 per cent over that in 1997-1998 (Rs 6234.75 crore). In addition to this all the defence PSUs reportedly earned a profit in 1998-1999.

Set against that is the fact that these two elements of India's defence industrial base continue to receive large amounts of money from the government in the form of government loans. Between them they also employ in the region of 300000 people. The picture is further complicated by the fact that almost half the production of the PSUs goes to the civil sector; a small proportion of the

Ordnance factory production also goes this way. (Put another way if is arguable that, certainly in the case of the PSUs, it is the production of equipment for civil use rather than for military use that is actually making money).

Against this backdrop, questions have been raised about their efficiency and ability to meet production targets, as underscored by the fact that it has taken Garden Reach Shipbuilders 12 years to build the Indian Naval Ship (INS) Brhamaputra; three times longer than it would take Russia's cash strapped shipbuilders to do. Traditionally, the price of purchasing systems and platforms from the PSUs has also worked out more expensive than purchasing them from abroad. For example, back in 1956 it was estimated that the cost of independently producing under license the HS-78 plane would be in the region of US$320000; come the end of the 1970s it stood at $1.5 million per unit.

Indigenous R&D

The success of India's indigenous R&D efforts is even more questionable: despite considerable investment through the 1990s nearly all major programmes implemented in the 1980s are experiencing time and cost over-runs.

The IGMDP: Covering the Prithvi and Agni short and medium/ long range ballistic missiles, the Nag anti tank missile, and the Akash and Trishul surface to air missile, this programme has scored a number of notable and high profile successes. For example, the Prithvi has been tested regularly since 1988 and three versions of the missile (150km, 250km, and 350km ranges) are now believed to be in (or close to) production.

The Agni was first tested in 1994 and in a 1998 missile test the missile flew close to 2500km. According to some reports, moreover, the missile is now operational. The Aksah, Nag and Trishul, meanwhile, are expected to enter service soon. However, none of these missiles are entirely indigenous. Some reports suggest, for instance, that five to ten per cent of the technologies used in the Prithvi are imported from abroad.

The Arjun: India's experience of designing an indigenous tank has been less successful.

Take the example of the Arjun tank. Originally, expected to be in operation service by 1985 the tank has suffered from continued problems, such as problems with the engine overheating. Limited production of the tank has now started; however the Indian Army has cut back on the number of tanks that it is ordering. *The LCA* The story of the LCA is almost identical to that of the Arjun tank. The programme has experienced delays since its inception in 1983 for a variety of reasons. And the first flight-test, originally scheduled for 1996, is now not expected to take place until some time in 2002. The cost of the programme, in the meantime, has increased from Rs 560 crores. This increased to Rs 2188 crores in 1993, when approval was given to enter the Full Scale Engineering Development Phase-1.

Other Programmes: The picture is much the same for a number of other less high profile programmes, such as the Pinaka, MBRL. This was initiated in 1986 with a budget of Rs 25.6 crores. This was subsequently increased to 49 crores. The system underwent troop trials in October 1999, moreover, but is still waiting for acceptance by the Army before entering full production. A similar story emerges for products such as the Indian Small Arms System (ISAS). The only product deemed to have been a complete success is arguably the ALH.

The failure of many of India's R&D programmes and its reliance on the outside world for key technologies is confirmed by a number of by external assessments, such as the United States government Military Critical Technologies List (MCTL). For example, India's capability to manufacture, gas turbine engines, and human crew systems (aeronautic systems technology) is not even considered worthy of a mention in the MCTL. Likewise, its ability to manufacture the systems necessary to ensure that a combat vehicle is superior to the technology that it is confronting. India scores a little better in the area of Marine Systems Technology, where it is rated to have limited Sub-surface and Deep Submergence Vehicle Capability.

One area where India is deemed to have been successful is in the area of Means of Delivery Technology for nuclear and other non-conventional weapons, where it is rated as having a sufficient Theatre Ballistic Missile Capability (TBMC), some ICBM capability;

and a sufficient Cruise Missile capability. By way of a comparison, outside the core-areas of competency that it has developed, India's defence production and R&D capabilities do not compare that favourably with other developing countries such as China, which has managed to develop its defence industry across a broader spectrum.

Consequences and Responses

India's inability to meet its top end defence needs have been compounded by the approaching obsolescence of a number of platform and systems; a problem that has been made even worse by the fact that Indian has not made any major defence purchases for the past ten years. Crisis in Kargil has also impressed the need to introduce new equipment on the armed forces-according to the reports, for example, the Indian military assessed Pakistan's Ukranian T-80s as being 'almost a generation ahead of what we had'.

In response, as far as major systems and high-technology products are concerned, the government has reversed the pattern of the 1990s and shifted the balance of procurement funding away from its home grown programmes and back towards external procurement. This re-evaluation started in the late 1990s and has progressed since there. Thus in 1996-97 and 1997-98 the DRDO's share of the defence budget decreased in real terms for the first time in that decade. At the same time, India announced its decision to purchase 40 SU-30MK fighter/bombers from Russia in India's largest ever defence deal. Likewise, even though India announced that it would increase its defence budget by 28 per cent to $13.94 billion (2.5 per cent of GDP) in 2000-2001 this March, funding for domestic R&D was only raised by 5.2 per cent; the percentage of the defence budget allocated to defence R&D has also slipped to 4.4 per cent of the total budget. At the same time, while this year's defence budget has seen the amount of money for R&D fall in relative terms, the funds for the purchase of defence equipment from abroad have been steadily increased since 1998.

Reviving the Russian Link

Despite the challenge to their defence relationship that occurred following the end of the Cold War and the economic crisis in

India, Russia and India still managed to maintain close defence ties throughout the latter part of the 1990s. For example, the two countries signed a long-term defence cooperation programme in 1994; a number of agreements for the upgradation of Indian defence equipment were initialled; India also agreed to buy 40 SU-30MKs in 1997; and according to the Russian Vice Premier Liya Klebarov, defence sales to India account for between 20 and 25 per cent of the annual total export of Russian military goods, making it India's largest arms supplier. It comes as little surprise to find, therefore, that much of the money allocated for procurement will be spent in Russia.

Although many of the deals have been under negotiation for some time, the visit of the Russian president, Vladimir Putin, appears to have broken the logjam. Thus, India and Russia officially agreed to extend their defence cooperation programme until 2010. Furthermore, India announced its intention to buy Russian arms worth more than $2 billion. Intended purchases include, additional Su-30 long range fighter bombers, a number of which will be made under license in India, more than 300 T-90 Main Battle Tanks (MBTS), one third of which will also be made in India, the ageing Soviet-era aircraft carrier, the Admiral Gorshkov, which will be provided for free but would cost $500 million to refurbish; an, as yet, unspecified number of MiG-29s for the ship; and a number of Smersh MRBLs.

European and Other Suppliers

India has also looked to solidify its links with European suppliers. For example, although the details of the deal have yet to be finalised the British based company BAE SYTEMS is also believed to have secured the deal to provide India with the Hawk advanced jet trainer aircraft. (India has been negotiating this purchase for over a decade). France has also been particularly successful, recently concluding an agreement to sell India additional Mirage 2000 fighters.

Outside Europe, India has established a close defence procurement relationship with Israel, which is thought to have provided it, among other things, with equipment suitable for border surveillance. Furthermore, reliable sources have suggested that the Phalcon early warning plane (AEW) that Israel was building for China but recently agreed not to sell to Beijing after pressure from the United States will be delivered to India. South African arms exports have also managed to carve out a small niche for themselves in the country. A number of Eastern European nations are also looking to provide India with new equipment and to help it upgrade its existing inventory. Quite simply, these purchases will fill those gaps that have appeared in India's armed forces in recent years.

The Fourth Phase-All Change in Indian Defence

In hindsight it appears that India, along with other LDCs, has learnt the lesson that while it is one thing to produce equipment such as ammunition and manufacture other people's platforms under license, it is another all-together to be able to locally design and build high-technology weapons systems, particularly in an environment in which the R&D programmes of the developing countries are producing increasingly sophisticated and indeed expensive weapons systems. At this stage, however, nobody is talking about getting rid of defence production and R&D-India is still officially committed to purchasing 70 per cent of its defence needs from indigenous sources by 2010. Rather, a growing number of military officials and businessmen are now calling for a radical shake up in the way in which India approaches defence procurement and indigenisation, largely by allowing greater private sector and possibly foreign participation.

Promoting Privatisation

Of course, interest in promoting greater private sector participation in defence is not new: as stated earlier the law was changed in 1991 to allow the private sector to provide components as well as assembly and sub-assembly to the military. Likewise, in 1994 the country's former Prime Minister Narashima Rao gave a speech in which he noted that 'the domestic arms industry must be opened up to private investment and competition'.

However, in a sign of growing convergence between the government and the private sector on the need for change the Confederation of Indian Industry (CII) and the Ministry of Defence (MOD) agreed in 1998 to establish six task forces to look at the subject. They recommended 1) reviewing the existing partnership between the MOD, industry and the military; 2) evolving strategies for long-term partnerships between these group; 3) studying the existing capacity of the defence PSUs and ordnance factories; 4) exploring the possibility of joint ventures; 5) developing joint marketing arms for exports; and 6) leveraging India's strengths in information technology in the defence sector.

Both the government and the military appear to be embracing these suggestions. For example, in July 1998 the Defence Minister, George Fernandes, called for greater cooperation and interaction between the Ordnance factories, the PSUs, and the DRDO. Speaking at a September conference organised by the Confederation of Indian Industries (CII) and the Indian Airforce (IAF), meanwhile, the Chief of the Airforce, Air Marshal A.Y. Tipinis, called for much greater participation from private manufacturers in the production of aircraft and weapons support systems. At the same conference, Vijay Kapur, Chairman of the CII National Committee on Communications, stated that: 1) the private sector should be allowed to manufacture arms and armaments and that the government should review its industrial policy accordingly; 2) that foreign collaboration should be allowed; 3) that arms and armaments currently in the 'reserved' category should be moved to the licensed category; 4) that industry should come forward as a partner with the services and not as contractors; and 5) that the government should fund private sector R&D.

He concluded that if these steps were followed India would be able to soon meet its defence requirements indigenously. In an interesting development, at an earlier CII conference, George Fernandes, also welcomed the suggestion that the private sector be allowed to play a larger role in defence research and development (R&D) by calling on the private sector to compliment the role of the DRDO.

The main advantage of private sector participation in defence R&D and/or increased government funding for private companies engaged in defence R&D is that the government can tap into the private sector's recent success at IT R&D. Private sector involvement should also serve to reduce costs as these firms operate on free-market principles.

Drivers of Change

Interestingly, this willingness to consider a change of direction is not only the result of the failure of India's ambitious R&D programme, but also due to a number of domestic and international factors. *The End of the Cold War:* In addition to the defence production issues and problems with Russia, the end of the Cold War has had a number of often contradictory impacts for Indian defence planners. On the one hand, India, like China was shocked by the quick success that the Allies scored over the Iraqis during the Gulf War.

Particularly, the sight of a large army equipped with much Soviet equipment struggling to compete with European and North American technology was not lost on the Indians, convincing the country's senior military officials of the needs to introduce high-technology equipment. Likewise, India was disturbed by NATO intervention in Kosovo on the basis of support for human rights. America's desire to deploy a National Missile Defence (NMD) system has also been opposed in India. (Its opposition is partly related to the fear that advances in technology in this area will undermine the limited advances that India has made in its own nuclear and missile capabilities).

On the other hand, thanks to its emergence as a major IT power, India's decision to fly in the face of international convention and conduct nuclear tests in May 1998 has been largely forgotten by the international community and particularly the United States. The crumbling of the traditionally strong bonds between Pakistan and America in the wake of Pakistan's decision to test nuclear weapons shortly after India; the Kargil crisis have helped this process of rapprochement. In response, India has attempted to maintain and build on its existing relationship with Russia, particularly in the area of defence sales, while establishing new ties with the United States in both the economic and diplomatic spheres.

Global Defence Industry Restructuring: Since the end of the Cold War global defence spending has decreased by 28.6 per cent between 1990 and 1999. Over the same period there has been a rash of consolidation among major arms producing companies in the United States and Europe. The decreasing size of the major producers' home markets has encouraged them to look abroad to new markets, in which defence spending is still growing. The impact of this process on India has been two-fold. Firstly, as the process of globalisation continues there is growing scope for partnerships to be established between Indian defence producers looking for access to new technology, and foreign defence manufacturers keen to tap the sales potential in the Indian market and also its strengths in areas such as IT.

They may also wish to use the country as a platform from which to launch its products into other markets. Domestically, meanwhile, those civil servants and bureaucrats at the heart of the Indian government are unlikely to have missed the fact that process of privatisation and consolidation in defence was a reaction to declining defence budgets after the Cold War. And that these new companies are often leaner and more competitive than their predecessors; while strategic alliances and joint ventures are now the rule rather than the exception in the sector due to the rising costs of designing and producing the next generation of defence equipment.

The Election of the Bharatiya Janta Party (BJP). The BJP led coalition government is more committed to tackling defence issues than its predecessors. Examples abound: in May 1988, shortly after first coming to power, it presided over India's first nuclear tests since 1974; while March 2000 saw the government reverse the downward trend in defence spending established in the 1990s. From the start the BJP government has also made an effort to articulate what the country's defence and security policy was, in opposition to the previous government, which according to the BJP was merely to assure Indians and indeed the world that India actually had such a policy.

Economic Reform. India's economic reform programme has gained momentum since it was introduced in 1991. Crucially, it now has support from across the political spectrum. As the government slowly retreats from the 'commanding heights' of the economy, moreover, greater attention is starting to be focused on the benefits to be gained from allowing greater private participation in defence, which to a large degree explains the involvement of the CII. India's moves towards privatisation, however, have not been plain sailing. Despite moving away from its policy of 'Swadeshi' or self-reliance, there remain elements of the BJP who still oppose the process; the same is true of many of the country's citizens. Efforts to dismantle the so-called 'Permit Raj' through a process of 'dis-investment' have also progressed more slowly than many had hoped, due largely to bureaucratic opposition and inertia.

Information Technology: India is quickly becoming a major player in the field of information technology (IT). For example, there are currently 340000 software professionals employed in the country-in 1996 there were only 180000-while India's technology schools are producing 100000 software professionals a year. The country has also developed its own super-computing capability, the Paran, which it has exported to Russia. India's strength in IT having a major impact on India's economy: total exports of IT related products amounted to about $9 billion in 1999. This sector of the economy has also managed to attract significant amounts of foreign investment, much of it into the cities of Bangalore and Hyderebad. The emergence of India as a major IT power is interesting for a number of reasons.

For instance, although the principle of IT development was supported by the late Prime Minister Rajiv Gandhi in the 1980s, the sector has grown up outside the normal regulation and red tape associated with the Indian economy. Dominated as it is by private sector companies it has also proved to be rather more innovative and flexible than other industries. Additionally, information technology has been India's bridge with outside world: its technicians and programmers are at the forefront of the IT revolution in the United States and are being courted by Japan, Germany and the United States. Attracted by the loosening of government control over the economy, moreover, many of these people are now returning to India, thereby breathing new energy into the economy.

ASSESSMENT OF MOVES TOWARDS PRIVATISATION

As a result of the above, increase private sector participation in defence production is increasingly being pursued: according to the latest reports more than 300 companies have already registered their interest in participating in the defence sector. Thus far, the following areas appear to have borne the greatest fruit.

IT and Communications. According to the MTCL India's capabilities in areas such as super-computing and software development are very strong indeed. With this in mind, it is understandable that a number of senior military figures have recently made clear their desire to upgrade the Armed Force's communication and IT capabilities through private sector involvement.

Speaking during an August 2000 CII seminar, for instance, General V.P Malik observed that: "the private sector, which had not previously participated in defence production, had expanded in size and reach and now has the capability to produce non-lethal items such as communications and IT related' products He also stated that: 'the army would be requiring radios of all types, ATM switches, optical fibre cable, satellite systems, power sources of all types and micro and macro cellular systems' and that the Army was looking at buying these technologies off the shelf from private companies.

Service Contracts and Outsourcing: There is a growing interest in outsourcing to the private sector within the military The IAF, for example, is exploring the possibility of privatising its base-repair depots, accounts, and areas of administrative work. According to the Chief of the Air Staff, Air Chief Marshall A.Y. Tipinis, there is also scope to involve the private sector in the maintenance and operation of fighter aircraft, air-launched guided missiles and ground to air missiles as well as support equipment such as radars, communications networks, and specialist vehicles. Outsourcing is also an option for the PSUs; indeed they are increasingly shedding the production of low technology items to the private sector.

For example, both Bharat Electronics and Garden Reach Shipbuilders have developed a network of small-scale industries and ancillary units around them. Likewise, the ordnance factories have been sourcing various raw materials and small parts from a range of indigenous industries. Some effort has also been made to involve the private sector in the production of middle level technologies: for example, at one stage Kirloskars was involved in the development of an indigenous engine for the Arjun tank.

Foreign Participation. There is mounting evidence to suggest that the country's eight PSU's will be allowed to enter into 'strategic alliances' and partnerships with foreign defence manufacturers. George Fernandes, stated that 'India provides an excellent opportunity for the developed and developing world to source cost-effective goods and services from our defence production industry' He also talked of the 'opportunities that India offers for joint-ventures, technology transfers, and co-production facilities for export to other markets'.

Currently the amount of foreign investment in the Indian defence sector is small. But a number of foreign manufacturers have already taken him up on the offer. During the visit of the Russian President Vladimir Putin to India, the two sides signed a new military and technical cooperation agreement to establish joint ventures for the production of a variety of armaments and military hardware and establishing joint sales and marketing structures for the products.

The Russian government is also thought to be considering investing a share of proceeds of its recent sales to India for creating after-care and upgrading facilities in the country. Looking to the future it is possible that Russian companies will invite their Indian (and Chinese) counterparts to participate in the development of next generation weapons systems. Russia is not the only country assessing this option. Somewhere in the region of 20 partnership agreements covering a range of cooperative arrangements, including co-production of aircraft equipment, joint development of communications equipment, and cooperation in software and electronic design, are believed to have been signed between British companies and the eight PSUs. Similar discussion have also been held with France, Poland and others. Every effort is also being made to ensure that these partnerships are not limited to the public sector.

Research and Development: There is some reason to believe that private companies will be encouraged to participate in defence R&D. Participation in this area received a significant boost following the May 1998 nuclear tests, when the imposition of sanctions on India prompted the Defence Research and Development Agency (DRDO) to open up eight labs in non-strategic areas to private participation. In addition to this, the DRDO now claims to have 'various levels of partnership' with 250 industries.

Defence Exports: In a related development, the government is now actively assessing the possibility of increasing exports of defence related equipment. Traditionally, modern India has eschewed the option of selling arms abroad, and relatively speaking its defence exports are minimal, although a defence exports cell was established in 1973. In recent years, however, the country has held a number of defence export shows in cooperation with the CII, while Indian PSUs have participated in defence shows abroad. Currently, the main products exported are from the country's ordnance factories and include small arms ammunition, explosives, rockets, spares for rifles and guns, clothing items, parachutes, aeronautical stores, communications equipment, and components and subsystems. India's main export markets are Asia and Africa although some equipment has gone to Europe. Old export markets are also being expanded and new ones being sought out: following a visit to Vietnam in March 2000 by George Fernandes, for example, both countries, who signed a Protocol on Defence Cooperation in 1994, initialled a new agreement to enhance defence cooperation in areas of training. Algeria is also considering buying defence equipment from India, including spares for its MiG combat aircraft, and helicopters, vehicles, night vision devices and communications equipment. India's hope is probably that it will be able to use the revenue from sales to reduce its own unit purchase costs as well as provide an extra flow of money into defence R&D.

Future Prospects

Despite these positive signs, at this stage there are still a number of factors inhibiting increased private sector (and possibly even foreign) involvement in defence production.

The main stumbling block is that in order to increase private sector involvement the Indian government would have to scrap the 1948 and 1956 Industrial Policy Resolutions. This is unlikely at this stage because many of the country's bureaucrats and politicians fear that such a decision will lead to mass lay-offs and possibly social turbulence. (Incidentally, these same individuals are also against the privatisation of India's other PSUs). As is traditionally the case, pressure against change is also likely to come from both the management and the workforce from within the sector. In short, the momentum and support for the economic reform programme in India has yet to gather the momentum necessary to allow fully fledged private participation and competition in defence production. Private participation in the sensitive areas of defence R&D is likely to be limited due to concerns about security.

Substantial foreign participation in the form of joint ventures particularly with Western companies, meanwhile, is likely to be limited by concerns about security and the reliability of Western suppliers in meeting their obligations. (By way of an example, the fact that a number of Indian Navy SeaKing helicopters have been stranded in Britain because they contain American parts, which the country is restricted from selling to India as part of the sanctions imposed following the May 1998 nuclear tests, is believed to one of the reasons why the deal to sell the BAE SYSTEMS Hawk has been further delayed) Organisational problems within the MOD are also likely to hinder any advantages to be gained by through the greater involvement of the private sector. The isolation of defence production from defence R&D, for example, is seen by many in India as inhibiting sensible planning and management of India's defence programmes.

CONCLUSION

Despite all the problems and challenges of the past decade India is unlikely to abandon the dream of establishing its own defence industry. Paradoxically, however, it is becoming increasingly apparent to all concerned that the only way that the country will be able to fulfil (even partly) its ambition of designing and manufacturing its own top-end defence equipment will be to dismantle the system of public ownership on which it is based. As the process of globalisation and consolidation in the defence industry continues to gather pace and the price of designing, developing and producing modern defence equipment increases rapidly, India's aspirations would also be greatly helped if it could rapidly involve foreign companies in the process of defence production.

Five to Ten Year Forecast

In the near term (5-10 years) the evidence collected in the paper suggests that this is unlikely to happen. Rather, the development of a hybrid model in which the core of PSUs and the DRDO will be maintained, while private sector participation will be sought in non-sensitive/peripheral areas such as IT and communications will probably dominate. This process will be complemented by an increased effort both to seek partnerships with largely Russian put possibly some European defence companies.

However, if past efforts to establish joint ventures with Indian companies in both the civil and defence sector are anything to go by the scope of these will be limited. India's attempts to increase its defence exports profile partly as a way to fund its indigenous R&D programme will also be limited to the sale of low and middle level technologies to cash-strapped and politically isolated regimes, such as Algeria and Vietnam. The perceived need to modernise its armed forces quickly, which has taken root in the wake of the Kargil crisis and the impending obsolescence of many of its existing platform, however, means that India will continue to look abroad to full-fill the majority of its top-end defence needs. This will be reflected in the division of resources within the defence budget, which is also likely to continue to grow over this period.

Ten to Twenty Year Forecast

Potentially, India's long term prospects (10-20) years are better. There is a good chance, for example, that by 2010 the Indian government will have made real advances down the path of economic reform and that the climate for private sector participation and perhaps even the privatisation of the PSUs will be more favourable. Crucial to India's success, however, will be its ability to bring together its civil and military R&D capabilities, not only in non-military/dual use areas, but across a broad spectrum. India could also use its strength in IT to strengthen its partnerships with foreign defence manufacturers and secure maintenance, upgrading and possibly production facilities in return. Parallel to this, and bearing in mind the fact that future defence platforms, such as the JSF, are unlikely to be single country ventures, there are also added advantages to be gained from India linking itself into those foreign companies associated closely with this process; indeed it may even be able to contribute in certain key areas. If this happens, although it is unlikely that India will be able to produce 70 per cent of its requirements domestically, it will certainly be able to source more from domestic producers, and more crucially will benefit from its access to technology, and participation in R&D programmes. (It is possible that India will be able to reduce its total reliance on imports to 50 per cent, although it is still unlikely to be able to produce whole systems indigenously).

Final Assessment

Naturally, this rather rosy outlook depends on India's willingness to accept not only the advantages of privatisation, but more importantly the direction in which defence industries today are going.

Arguably, the room for companies focused solely on their home markets and expecting to provide their militaries with state of the art defence equipment, not only in the developed world but also in the West, is shrinking rapidly, due to the rising cost and sophistication of the systems involved.

Put another way, participation in regional or global defence programmes will become the norm. India, with its growing strength in the new economy, has the chance this time not to miss the boat, although there is always a danger that misplaced nationalism and an unclear understanding of developments will prevent it from making the most of the opportunity.

DEFENCE INDUSTRY

The first set of major policy changes were promulgated by the Government to give a fillip to our stagnating and moribund defence industry. The fundamental underpinnings to the policy changes were two: firstly, bring in the private sector; and secondly, opening the door for foreign companies by permitting up to 26 percent investment, so that technology inflows are facilitated. It was perhaps rightly believed that these were the two principle measures that were required to catalyse our ailing military industrial capabilities.

While most observers welcomed the policy announcements, there was considerable scepticism over the Governments' resolve to implement them. Could a system that was wedded to the philosophy of state led industrialisation for almost fifty years, change course that easily? Unlikely! Then there was the problem of our establishments' recognised and reputed talent for conceptualising great ideas, but seldom demonstrating the capacity to execute them. However, after having out-of-habit taken recourse to castigating the Government, it would be prudent to also try and understand its compulsions and concerns. The first is that given the nature of the UPA Government, no reforms can be implemented without the Left's concurrence.

The Left's dogma is to stonewall any measure that appears to threaten the interests of the PSUs and the Ordnance Factory Board (OFB). Thus the Left would not be inclined to acquiesce to proposals that contemplate the relaxation of state control over most core industrial sectors. Similarly, the defence PSUs and the OFB, would also not be willing to dilute their monopoly of their defence market.

Then there is the problem of the huge investments and the capacities created in all our Government owned defence industrial under-takings. Logically, it cannot be any one's case, that these assets are permitted to decay instead of putting them to optimal use. With the private sectors' case for a level playing field, the fear that over time, the Government owned defence industrial establishments would be progressively edged out of business, is genuine.

The third concern, and not easy to counter, pertains to the argument of national security. Since the private sector is not under Government control, in times of a crisis it may not respond to national requirements in the same manner that a Government owned unit would do. It is a combination of the preceding concerns that explain the Government's hesitation in letting go the control that we have witnessed since the policy changes were promulgated in May 2001.

Having acknowledged the issues, it must be conceded that these are not new or unique to us. All nations have had to grapple with the same set of dilemmas, and since we are in the catch-up game, our problems ought to be easier to solve, for we have the experience of other countries to learn and benefit from.

So, while the Government at one level remained wedded to the policy of reforms, in its implementation, it dragged its feet. Consequently, the practice of doing business only with the Government owned industries did continue unchanged for three to four years, much to the frustration of the private sector. This ambivalence of the Government impacted negatively on the private sectors' attempts at collaboration with foreign companies. It should therefore be accepted that foreign partnership was, and is, vital for our industry to take off.

Indigenously we do not have the technology, nor the know-how, for state-of-the-art systems that the defence services aspire for. Since foreign defence companies were unclear of the Governments' intent, they were not prepared to enter into collaborative arrangements with the private sector. For quite a while they remained cautious, indulged in fence sitting-hedging their bets.

The air was finally cleared with the Government's announcement of the Defence Procurement Policy of 2006. The most significant features of this policy were its 'offset clauses' and the concept of RURs (Raksha Utpadan Ratnas). Of the two, it is the offset policy that has the potential to yield spectacular results in energising our defence industry.

The billions of dollars of business that this policy will bring to the Indian industry has generated unprecedented excitement among our domestic players. In excitement lies the challenge. They will have to be prepared to absorb complex technologies and engineering skills, and then manufacture components, assemble subsystems, and systems, at a cost that is competitive and sufficiently profitable.

Ever since the idea of the offset policy was mooted, all foreign multi-nationals have been lobbying intensely to sabotage it. Arguments-that the policy would push up prices, that the Indian industry is incapable of absorbing high technology 'direct offsets', that monitoring mechanisms cannot be effective etc-have been in the air for a while.

The Government is considering some relaxation in the policy. The areas mentioned were the adjustment of the cost of technology transfer against offsets, banking of offsets and the acceptance of indirect offsets. Though these issues may merit consideration, it would be somewhat premature to accept policy changes even before we have begun. The pressure on foreign vendors to fulfil their offset obligations must remain undiluted. Concurrently, we must concentrate on finding satisfactory solutions to the issues being raised. Having dwelt somewhat cursorily on policy issues, an objective assessment of our present industrial capability and its growth potential would now be in order. The Defence industry cannot be viewed in isolation. It has to be a manifestation of the nation's overall industrial and technological capabilities. Often we tend to ignore this fundamental.

The first place to begin this survey would be to look at the captains of our industry. There is a growing realisation that they have arrived. Globally, they are winning admiration and recognition. In the early nineties, when the first steps of liberalisation were initiated, they nurtured apprehensions about their survival.

Having successfully negotiated that phase of transition in our economy, they have at the beginning of the twenty first century emerged with renewed strategic sense that has a global sweep. Witness the takeovers and the expansion plans of quite a few of our companies. Just a decade ago, who could have imagined, that the Jaguar brand car would be owned by an Indian Company? They have in the recent past displayed vision, and matched that vision with the capacity to implement.

The next requirement is of the work force. It is abundantly available in all categories; managerial, technical and in terms of working hands-our biggest asset being the young age profile of our people. Some intervention can be expected from the government in its labour policies. But being a politically sensitive issue, the Industry will have to live with this problem, till a change becomes environmentally possible.

In terms of spheres in which we have advanced to global standards our range has remained somewhat limited to the automobile sector, pharmaceuticals and a few other disciplines. We have hardly any capabilities in electronics, communications, optics and in the field of aviation. Our industrial policies should focus on these voids. To become a meaningful player in the defence sector, these technologies are vital.

Our biggest strength is software services. Infosys, Wipro and TCS are globally among the best. In addition, there are a host of second tier companies, clocking rapid growth, while doing both domestic and international business. Unfortunately, this strength has not been effectively harnessed to give the requisite impetus to our defence industry. Particularly, because the new generation of weapon systems and related support systems, are all heavily dependent on extremely sophisticated software, the cost of which may be as high as 30-40 percent of the total value of the platform. Electronics we know takes up another 30-40 percent.

The Left and a few other groups have consistently opposed the opening up of the defence industry to the private sector. They have repeatedly been claiming that the public sector units can produce all that our armed forces need. A brief look at their track record will establish that such confidence in the state owned establishments is quite misplaced.

We have 39 Ordnance Factories, 8 Defence PSUs and 50 Defence Research Laboratories, ie. close to 100 establishments, all well equipped, extravagantly staffed, with some excellent scientists and managers, and yet no creditworthy achievements to show. And what equipment do they produce which is to the satisfaction of our Armed Forces?

It would be difficult to list any, other than the ALH from HAL, which has the potential to be a good product. The DRDO might want to take credit for the Agni (1 and 2) and the Prithvi. These are good systems but lose a fair amount of their sheen since they come twenty to thirty years after similar systems were inducted in China.

Our process of reforms in the management of the Government controlled defence research and production establishments, have regrettably floundered. Many studies have been done, yet-to all intent and purposes-the drift continues. Over the last three to four years the Government has been pushing for public private partnership. The idea being that such association would bring about the desired efficiencies in the public sector. But the problem is that such forced marriages do not really work. Driven by expediency, some private companies, may consider coming to an under-standing with PSUs for the short term, but such arrangements are not likely to be conducive to the real growth of the defence industry.

The policy of opening up of the defence industry to the private sector was successful in attracting quite a few industrial houses-large, medium and small, to enter the fray. Even prior to the formal opening of the defence sector, some had indirectly been in the business by manufacturing components, subsystems and systems-for integration by the defence PSUs.

Besides, our nuclear and space programmes had involved the private industry. Such companies have executed sophisticated design and engineering jobs that include special metals and alloys, and therefore have acquired the confidence to take on the development and manufacture of defence systems.

L&T, Tatas, Mahindras, Godrej Boyce, Bharat Forge and more recently Punj Lloyd, are some of the major industrial houses that have staked their claim for defence contracts. Following them, are a large number of second and third tier companies covering a wide range of technologies.

The basic handicap of all these companies at the time the policy change was announced in 2001 was their lack of domain knowledge. They did not know weapon systems, or what force multipliers were, or how the procurement procedures worked. They also did not know how the global arms market operated. They were equally unaware of the equipment profile of our armed forces and their future requirement.

Even though these companies inducted service officers whose advice was available, lack of personal knowledge of the business inhibited executives from pursuing projects that entailed taking investment decisions. Increased involvement in the defence sector; and interaction with the defence services, the procurement arm of the Ministry of Defence, and the big multinational defence companies, over the last five to six years; has impacted positively on the confidence levels of company executives.

The role of defence service officers in galvanising the industry merits special attention. Other than these officers, not many in India, have any idea of modern warfare, military organisations, weapon systems, munitions and the support systems. Such domain knowledge within the industry is imperative. All over the world companies engaged in the business of military hardware extensively employ service officers to develop products and promote business. Not only this, even governments in order to support domestic industries, lend serving officers and men to participate in trials or make presentations. We may recall some of the service-industry seminars held in Delhi in the recent past which had serving officers endorsing products.

Unfortunately, the environment that we have nurtured in India discourages our retired/retiring officers from being employed. If employed they cannot be optimally used because of the establishments' attitude towards them. Who benefits? Only the foreign companies and maybe our adversaries!

This must change. By encouraging the absorption of service officers by the defence industry, the nation will reap multiple benefits. Firstly, the users would have access to informed inputs on developments, which would contribute to better decisions on choice of systems and the formulation of specifications. Rather the industry would gain from the expertise of these officers in an area which they have much to learn about. Secondly, to some extent, the problem of rehabilitation of officers who retire at relatively younger ages would get addressed. It is important that the Government revisits this issue.

The central issue facing the defence industry is access to contemporary technology, its absorption and assimilation, and then the use of domestic research and development to graduate to next generation systems. South Africa, Israel, China, South Korea, Brazil, and even Singapore, have learnt to successfully navigate this cycle.

There is no reason why we cannot emulate their example. In our case, so far, technology transfers have taken place only to the OFB and the defence PSUs. Their experience should not become the only basis for drawing conclusions on this subject. The appetite for growth of the private sector, and its new found confidence, would undoubtedly yield different results.

A survey of the global defence market will reveal that we are currently the biggest importers of defence systems. The US and China do spend more but they mostly buy domestic. The figures of our projected purchases are being regularly quoted in thousands of crores. They do give us sufficient strength to extract terms that could be used to considerable advantage. Look at the pending procurements: some 200 helicopters, 126 advanced fighters, approximately 800-1000 artillery guns, and half a dozen submarines. Each of these would run into billions of dollars. The conclusion is obvious-buy sensibly.

With these purchases in the pipeline, if we did not get all the technologies we need, we will have only ourselves to blame. Procurement terms must state our purchase imperatives unambiguously. As a matter of fact we could consider modifying our procedures when acquiring big ticket items.

Take the case of advanced fighters. All contenders have proven comparable systems. The differences essentially stem from design philosophies and the source of subsystems and systems that have been selected for integration.

The gaps in features are so narrow that quite often the choice can be a matter of individual predilection. The same arguments can be applied to the helicopters we want or the submarines. Selection could therefore be based on the totality of the package a vendor offers and not just the L-1 criteria after qualifying. To what extent and in what manner is technology being offered? What are the long term buy back agreements?

What kind of investments is the vendor making in India? For such high value transactions we must extract much more than what we have done hither to. We need to therefore delve deeper into the manner in which we pursue major acquisitions. There could also be a case for some coordination with say the Civil

Aviation Ministry taking into account the carriers that Air India would be planning to induct. An important caveat at this point would be in order: under no circumstances should the views of the concerned service headquarter not be the ultimate deciding factor.

While charting the strategy for the development of our domestic defence industry we must identify technologies that require special attention; technologies where our capabilities merit quantum upgradation. It can be assumed that the DRDO, the services headquarters, and also the CII, would have undertaken studies on this subject. Our acquisition plans must look at integrating the road map that we should have drawn for technology inflows and digestion. Electronics, optics, communications and avionics, are generally the areas that we should be focusing on. We have for a few decades depended exclusively on Bharat Electronics for all our communication requirements as also all our electro-optical products.

Today Bharat Electronics may be a profit making company but has little to offer in terms of future technologies or next generation products. The same story applies to HAL, notwithstanding the successful development of the ALH, which should have been offered at least ten years earlier.

There is therefore a strong case to encourage private sector companies to enter these fields. The logic that since the Government has made investments in creating capabilities, all orders must be confined to these companies has proven over time to be counterproductive. A change in approach is long overdue. India urgently needs an HAL/BE in the private sector. The Government must encourage and support their emergence.

The subject of exports has also been grossly neglected. There may be a Joint Secretary in the Department of Defence Production responsible for promoting exports, but he can do little under the present dispensation. Pakistan's Ordnance Factories have consistently exported more than us. No defence industry can expect to sustain itself purely on the basis of sales in the domestic market.

Our private sector, unlike our Government owned establishments, have understood this. But they need much more support. The Government and the industry have to work together in a closely coordinated manner. Witness the way in which over the past few months the Heads of Governments of Germany, UK and France have brought with them the captains of their defence industries to India. The agenda requires no amplification. Here again we must push to get our act together

If India's defence industry is today on the threshold of transformation, considerable credit must be given to the role played by the CII. FICCI has also contributed, but only marginally. We may recall the first Army-Industry Partnership Seminar conducted in the mid nineties under the aegis of the CII. Many of us sceptics murmured-'what's the point?' But CII persevered. It continued with its efforts to nudge the industry and simultaneously influence our policy makers. It has also been actively persuading the big global players to look at teaming with the Indian industry. The results though slow, in the coming times would soon be there for us to witness. Having reached thus far, the CII must not take its foot off the pedal. Much more still needs to be done.

Before concluding, some of the suggestions made are listed below:

- Protection to the PSUs and the OFB from domestic players must be progressively withdrawn.
- A major overhaul of the functioning control, organisation and functioning of the OFB and the defence PSUs has been long overdue. Can we not figure out a way to move forward on this issue?
- Pressures to dilute the 'offset clause' of the DPP must be resisted. What we should be focusing on is the mechanisms for monitoring post contract implementation.
- Encourage the absorption of service officers in the defence industry. The rules of interaction with industry representatives must change. The MOD and the services headquarters should be more accessible to domestic industry. Currently doors for foreigners open up much more easily.
- Put in special efforts to promote and assist the growth of the private sector in the areas of aviation, communications,

electronics and sensors (optics). There should be a comprehensive action plan for the acquisition of key technologies. The Government and the industry should work in concert on this issue.

- Re-examine our procurement policies and strategies for major purchases. Given the nature of the global market we can perhaps extract much more from our big deals.
- The growth of our defence industry can only be sustained if its business model takes into account the imperative of exports for sustenance.
- The laudable role played by the CII merits recognition. Both the Government and the industry should continue to encourage the CII to step up its activities to accelerate reforms and change.

Our vision for India in the next two decades would be flawed if it did not envisage a sizeable, vibrant and sophisticated defence industry for us that is globally competitive and has the capacity to research and develop new state of the art cutting edge technologies.

Our industry has acquired a new found confidence. All it needs is direction and support form the Government. The launch of the Nano within four years of it being conceived has been inspiring. We hope the global awe it has attracted is repeated time and again. We want Nano clones now coming out of India's defence industry stable

With increasing outsourcing opportunities, the Indian aerospace and defence industry is emerging as a key participant in the Asia Pacific aerospace and defence market. Apart from India's perceived viability as an outsourcing hub for aerospace and defence products, the overwhelming involvement of the Government in areas of supply and demand cements its advantage in the industry.

The Government's pro-active soliciting of international cooperation has seen production moving to India, generating more opportunities for the country. Export competitiveness has been given priority, hence, there has been an increased thrust towards reduced import dependency.

The Indian economy is one the fastest growing in the world, reflecting the successful reform process initiated in 1991.

The Indian Government has gradually opened its key sectors to foreign participation and foreign investment in the Indian aerospace and defence industry which currently has a 26 percent cap. Meanwhile, since two-thirds of the Indian population depends on agricultural income, reforms in this area are widely considered necessary to aid economic growth.

Development of the agriculture sector, trade, as well as capital liberalisation, and improvement in investments, are some vital areas being focused upon by the current Government. The *Frost & Sullivan* Country Industry Forecast service for the Indian aerospace and defence industry uses a macroeconomic perspective to provide a focused analysis of the industry.

This service covers an array of issues pertaining to the industry including political stances, trade policies, industry regulations, as well as their overall impact. Besides enabling decision makers to assess the impact of non-market forces, this analysis also helps in identifying new opportunities in the industry. In addition,. it provides a strong base for preparing business contingency plans.

16 The Indian Experience in the Use of Military Helicopters

BATTLEFIELD MISSIONS OF MILITARY HELICOPTERS

Helicopters can transport troops and support them with both logistics and fire support. The modern military helicopter has become an integral part of warfare, being employed on several battlefield missions, as part of naval aviation and in air combat.

It is both an attack and transport platform. In its battlefield role, the helicopter is used for air assault and air mobility operations, on attack missions (anti-armour missions, for example) scouting and reconnaissance missions and anti-personnel area suppression. How a helicopter is used on the battlefield depends on the specific role it is given, the weapons provided and the operational doctrine of the user. The Persian Gulf war in 1991 demonstrated the kind of integration that the helicopter must achieve in the battlefield. Air mobile forces are today capable of all-weather, day and night operations in the FEBA, even deep in enemy territory.

The Indian Experience

The Indian experience of the use of helicopters for military purposes, started in the sixties when they were used as air mobility platforms in North-East India. The Indian Army used helicopters to induct and de-induct troops in counterinsurgency (CI) operations in Manipur and Mizoram. Simultaneously, plans were drawn up to employ helicopters for crossing water obstacles to capture important bridgeheads.

During the 1971 Indo-Pak war, GOC 4 Corps used helicopters to ferry troops across the Soorma river with the intention of cutting off the Pakistani 202 brigade withdrawing from Sylhet. In 1964, No. 105 helicopter unit of the IAF flew in Manipur in support of the Army in Cl operations.

Tusom Kaulem, Chasec, and Kungai were places to where Army troops were helilifted from Imphal. The No. 105 unit flying Mi-4 helicopters was also active in NEFA, Nagaland and Manipur during this period. In 1966, 5 Para was involved in CI operations in Mizoram.

The helicopter was used for air mobility operations, both for short notice operations and for long-range pre-planned Cl operations. These came to be called Special Heliborne Operations (SHBO). In 1967, the Home Minister of the MNF was captured near Dariung. Similarly, Sainghakha, the Defence Minister of the MNF was captured in another HBO. The same year Lieutenant General Sagat Singh as GOC 101 Comm Zone area launched an SHBO into Bangladesh to hit Mizo training camps located there. This mission was however unsuccessful.

During the 1971 war, plans were made to helilift a battalion of 4/5 GR to seize Sylhet in December 1971. The HBO to capture Sylhet was launched on 7 December. With only nine helicopters available, it was possible to lift only essential elements of the battalion. Over the next few days, the main strength of the battalion was transported.

It later transpired that the enemy had estimated the helilanding of troops to be of brigade strength. The capture of Sylhet bottled up a better part of the enemy there. On 9 December, the Meghna waterline was secured around Ashugung. Lieutenant General Sagat Singh now decided to make a dash towards Dhaka. Shortly after last light on 10 December, Mi-4s began their journey across the Meghna. In the next 36 hours, over 110 sorties were flown.

The Mi-4, which normally carried fourteen troops, now had twenty-three men on board. 311 Mtn Bde was amongst the first units across the river, landing at Narsingdi. 4 Guards with a detachment of artillery was flown to Narsingdi on 9 December. Two days later, 10 Bihar was lifted to the area. The battalion secured the road and rail links over the local Brahmaputra the same day. The next day 4 Guards were in control of Narsingdi. The area thus became a base for further operations against Dhaka by this date.

The next hop for the helicopters was to Daudkandi. From here brigade HQ and two battalions moved to Baidha Bazaar on 14/ 1 5 December, without supporting arms and artillery. The value of HBOs during the 1971 war was proved beyond doubt as they speeded up the pace of operations and surprised the enemy in many places.

It is important to note that the success of HBOs in the 1971 war was facilitated by the air superiority achieved by the Air Force. The peacekeeping operations in Sri Lanka also saw extensive use of the helicopter both in attack and assault roles. During the build-up in the Jaffna Peninsula in October 1987, the IAF carried out some 3,000 tactical transport and assault helicopter sorties in twenty days. Mi-8s of both Nos. 109 and 119 helicopter units operated throughout the Northern and Eastern provinces of Sri Lanka.

Helicopters were used for insertion of units for search, raid, domination of selected areas and subsequent extraction. Helicopters were used in the initial stages in the siege of Jaffna to land troops of the Sikh Light Infantry.

They were also used as observation posts to control large-scale ground operations in built-up areas. The Mi-8 helicopters did good work in Sri Lanka and provided support to the army, usually under fire. The battle for Jaffna saw the Mi-8s flying supply sorties, as no roads were open. The Mi-24 attack helicopters performed particularly well in the later stages of Operation Pawan, providing covering fire to troops and performing independent attacks on LTTE camps.

The helicopter has been used by the armed forces as elevated command posts and observation posts for the artillery regiment and have seen regular deployment in Siachen and other parts of India, where the terrain is inaccessible. The UN mission in Somalia saw the Chetak helicopters of the IAF being used as aerial convoy escorts on scouting missions and CASEVAC.

Despite extensive doctrinal studies and actual operational experience, it took fifteen years for the Army Aviation Corps to be set up. The main problem delaying the formation of this Corps was the battle for its control by the Air Force and Army. Despite the passage of time, the struggle continues for the control of aviation assets within the services.

In 1985, India decided to convert 54 Infantry Division into an air assault division. One of its brigades acquired training in amphibious operations, and another one was given air mobile training in January 1987. But the division could not acquire enough helicopter assets. Insufficient helicopter assets meant that the division could only be used in more air mobile operations from transport aircraft.

The helicopter as an air mobility platform has been used by regular infantry units, para commandos, and special forces. The Mi-8/17s are operated generally for commando roles, supply and personnel mobility, SAR and logistics support tasks. The Mi8s can also be armed and used in attack roles. The Chetak is mainly used for casualty evacuation (CASEVAC), communications and liaison duties. With the formation of the AAC in 1986, the Chetak and a certain number of Cheetah helicopters were transferred to the Army. The IAF still flies armed Chetaks in an anti-tank role, as well as for CASEVAC, while the Cheetah is used for FAC flights. At present the IAF has 11 Squadron with 50 Mi-8, 50 Mi17 and 10 Mi-26 Halo helicopters.

Air Assault Operations

The main areas where air assault operations can be carried out are, the plains of Punjab and the desert of Rajasthan. Limited HBOs can be carried out in J&K, for raids preceding a main attack. The employment of helicopters along the Line of Actual Control (LAC) will enhance the combat potential of forces. 'The IA could reduce its presence along the watershed to a mere tripwire, keeping adequate resources concentrated in depth and carrying out speedy heliborne deployment once the opposing Army commences its build-up.

The use of helicopters in the East against China are hampered by the mountainous and jungle terrain, but can be used to helitift mountain troops to salient heights in a specific topographic area. In the event of a border war with China, helicopters will be used in both attack and utility roles. In Arunachal Pradesh, the thick jungle and ever-changing weather makes fixed wing flying and attacking difficult. Thus attack helicopters will be essential.

Similarly, transport helicopters contour flying' will be supported by attack machines. The induction of troops into enemy territory in conjunction with conventional military operations will be essential in the future. These troops are to be earmarked for limited holding operations and must seek to achieve surprise. All such operations need a great amount of planning and coordination. The weather will determine the conduct of operations over varying terrain. To that extent, helicopters will have to be configured for that specific role. As part of the main ground attack, India should use helicopters to infiltrate special forces into enemy territory to carry out clandestine operations.

On the other hand, the Indian objectives could be to obtain a bridgehead, to carry out limited holding operations, or to secure and hold a particular area. Such operations will call for close cooperation between ground forces and helicopter units. In mountainous and jungle terrain, the helicopter is best suited for vertical envelopment and replenishment.

The operations in the Siachen Glacier largely depend on helicopters; 109 Helicopter unit of the IAF was active during the initial phases of Operation Meghdoot in 1984. In the jungles of the Northeast, HBOs were used to land-scouting teams, ambush parties and interdiction groups, both for conventional and unconventional operations.

The helicopter is also a crucial platform for maritime survey and combined operations. This is important given India's huge maritime environment and island territories. The Westland Sea King used by the navy may be used to helilift troops to meet any contingency, such as threats to our off-shore assets.

For long-range border patrolling and policing, helicopters are used for observation and surveillance, combined with the insertion of ORTs to interdict intruders which will help in reducing active manpower deployment on the border. In India it is necessary to provide police and paramilitary forces with the necessary helicopter lifts to enable them to reach various "hot-spots".

Conclusions

Proper integration of the helicopter in the Indian armed forces will necessitate two things. First, the doctrines evolved have to be made operational as a part of the training. Second, it must be realized that air assault and air mobility operations are inter-services operations and the future will witness the increasing importance of combined operations, in,an all-weather, day-and-night conflict environment.

Therefore, the setting up of a joint command HQ will not be out of place. Ideally, both services should have their own helicopter assets. But for air assault operations sufficient assets must be given to the air assault division. The IAF's present assets of Mi-8/17s and Mi-26 helicopters are just adequate for battalionsize operations. Alternatively, an "airmobile brigade" trained in 1987 could be given an integral fleet of Mi-17 helicopters.

It has been suggested that the air assault division for India be divided into three brigades, consisting of one parachute and two helicopter-borne battalions each. As seen earlier, India lacks the requisite asses, both serial and otherwise, to make the whole division air-assault capable.

Therefore, it makes sense to plan operations at the brigade level using the assets of India's parachute regiment for this purpose. Such organization combined with joint operational command is essential for air-assault operations.

In a resource-starved country like ours, the effort has been and must be to make the best use of available resources. Given this fact, India must look for a multi-utility/attack helicopter combined, as it may not be financially possible to acquire mission-dedicated helicopters. In this sense, the ALH being developed by HAL has to be capable of a dual role. The ALH will have a maximum take-off weight of 5,000 kg with two engines. And will have a crew of two and will carry 12-14 passengers or troops. Whether, it will be configured for a dual role remains to be seen.

It is a moot point whether India needs to consider a merger of attack and utility roles in one platform. But on the whole a merger of roles makes sense, being more cost-effective.

The main thrust at present should be for proper integration of the helicopter within the armed services. A doctrine has to emerge for its use as an assault platform, and its command and control problem must be sorted out. It goes without saying that its utility as an air-mobility and air-assault platform need not be over emphasized. This is something that needs special attention in the future acquisition.

17 Indian Foreign Policy

INTRODUCTION

The foundations of India's foreign policy were laid during the freedom movement when our leaders, even when fighting for independence, were engaged with the great causes of the time. The principles of India's foreign policy, that emerged then, have stood the test of time: a belief in friendly relations with all countries of the world, the resolution of conflicts by peaceful means, the sovereign equality of all states, independence of thought and action as manifested in the principles of non-alignment, and equity in the conduct of international relations.

DEFENCE POLICY

India believes in a policy that promotes peace and international cooperation. However, the country has a land frontier of 15,200 km, a coastline of 7,516.6 km and an exclusive economic zone of 2.2 million sq. km, island territories, vital offshore installations and airspace. The armed forces, therefore, have to be kept prepared and well equipped to repel any external threat. The country's armed forces are well trained, disciplined and free from politics. The accent in defence planning is on increasing indigenous capacity and a reliable mechanism of inter-services, inter-departmental and multi-level coordination and monitoring has been devised to help defence planning. The current strategic and technological scenarios as well as future projections are taken into consideration in preparing the defence plan. Periodic review addresses any unexpected development or threat to security.

Army

Even after the end of Cold War the global strategic environment continues to be uncertain and unstable. Some old conflicts may have ended, but the rise of religious fundamentalism and ethnic assertions have heightened tension in many parts of the world. In such a scenario, the Indian Army cannot afford to lower its guard. It needs to constantly upgrade its critical weapons and induct state-of-the-art systems to ward off threats from potential adversaries.

Navy

The Indian Navy has to guard not only a large coastline, but also offshore oil, sea bed reserves and sea-lanes that are used for 97 per cent of the Indian trade. Indigenisation being an important consideration even in expansion plans, some of the recent acquisitions by the Indian Navy like the destroyer "Bombay", frigate "Beas" submarine, "INS Shankul," were all made in India, one of the few countries to have the technology for submarine construction. The Indian Navy has also pioneered in Asia the idea of docking a submarine on pontoon, which will help in carrying out all dry dock routines. To further maritime diplomacy and cooperation, joint exercises were conducted with a number of countries. Naval ships also exchanged visits with a number of countries. The Indian Navy also has the proud distinction of participating in all the 13 Indian expeditions to Antarctica.

Air Force

Though the Indian Air Force is only 62 years old and, like the other services, suffers from resource constraints, it has made tremendous technological advancements in recent years, which have helped in indigenisation of a vast range of equipments and sophisticated technology. This has also enabled the IAF to upgrade and integrate state-of-the-art weapons and avionics in the existing fleet. The MiG 21 BIS is currently being upgraded with the help of Russian agencies. Progress has been made in developing Light Combat Aircraft, air defence radars, pilot less target aircraft and air-to-ground weapons. Overhaul facilities for the MiG 29 and Mirage-2000 are also being set up. The proposal to acquire advanced jet trainers has been approved.

The electronic warfare capability, crucial in modern-day wars, and precision-guided munitions capabilities of the IAF are also being upgraded and soon the entire IAF fleet will be equipped with global positioning system sets.

DEFENCE RESEARCH AND DEVELOPMENT

A network of 50 laboratories work under the Defence Research and Development Organization. The Department of Defence Research and Development is being developed to match and even surpass international standards in critical technologies. A national mission has been launched to achieve self-reliance in defence systems from the present 30 per cent to 70 per cent by 2005 A.D. Good progress has been made in the Integrated Guided Missile Development Program. User trials of the Prithvi surface-to-surface missile have been completed. Flight trials were undertaken to evaluate the beam-gathering system of the Trishul surface-to-air missile. Further tests were carried out on the medium-range surface-to-air missile Akash. The anti-tank missile Nag was tested in captive helicopter flights. The third launch of the Agni vehicle was completed and the project completed.

Indian Ocean

Over the past two decades, the Indian Ocean has become an arena of great power rivalry and confrontation. This has naturally led to greater tensions in the region. The littoral and hinterland States of the Indian Ocean have expressed their unified and determined opposition to outside military presence and called for its elimination in the United Nations Declaration on the Indian Ocean as a Zone of Peace. India hopes that the great powers and major maritime users will join the efforts of the littoral States of the Indian Ocean in achieving this objective.

18 India's Defence Minister: Improve Quality, or Else

At a international arms conference in New Delhi, Indian Defence Minister Pranab Mukherjee warned domestic arms makers to sharpen their skills or perish in the face of intense competition from foreign rivals in a globalizing world. AFP reports that the warning came amid reports of military complaints over the quality of hardware and spare parts supplied by India's own arms industry. The warning is valid to a point, and private sector procurement is finding a niche in India. Still, there may be less here than meets the eye. According to AFP, India opened defence production to the private sector in 2001, and permits direct foreign investment of up to 26% in joint projects.

State-owned defence firms annually procure goods worth 120 billion rupees ($280 million) from private businesses, while state-owned ordnance factories outsourced production work worth 190 billion rupees ($443 million) to private companies.

DID Op/Ed: India's software development community, which boasts more Level 5 CMMI firms than anywhere else in the world, shows that quality is not a foreign concept to Indian organizations per se.

As DID has noted in our coverage of India's annual Ministry of Defence report, however, large segments of India's arms industry are government-owned. Given the number of jobs (read: votes) dependent on these enterprises, the political reality is that closing these firms or even substantially reducing their workload would be extremely difficult. As such, threats of competition and closure are unlikely to mean very much to large sections of India's defence industry.

DID has also covered India's new foreign procurement rules, with their high levels of required local industrial offsets, and its procurement system difficulties that include development programs and other projects that miss their completion targets by over a decade.

Exhortations alone will not fix underlying systemic problems, and the incentive patterns that contribute to them. This is as true in India as it is everywhere else in the world.

NEW FOREIGN PROCUREMENT RULES IN INDIA

India has set new guidelines regarding military acquisitions from other countries. The most controversial clause of the new guidelines, which came into force on July 1, 2005, includes a key offset clause for any foreign vendor who wins a defence contract worth over $70 million. Under the offset clause, any qualifying defence contract with a foreign vendor will not become effective until after that vendor has concluded the offset contracts for the required 30% of the total cost.

This means that the foreign vendor will have to buy defence or other specified equipment from Indian industry. In addition, the government has also incorporated a new clause stating that the lowest bidder for a program may not necessarily be the winner of a contract, as considerations of strategy and politics may also be taken into account.

These clauses could particularly affect the planned purchase of 126 light multirole fighter planes. Due to existing arrangements, the requirements tilt the playing field somewhat toward the MiG-29, and raise the bar for U.S. aircraft like the recently-presented F/A-18E/F Super Hornet.

DRDO PRODUCTS

Light Combat Aircraft (LCA) Test-flown Successfully

The maiden flight of the first Light Combat Aircraft (LCA) Technology Demonstrator 1 (TD1) aircraft took place at 1018 hrs on 4 January, 2001. The flight was successful and met all the test parameters set for the flight. The flight lasted 18 minutes. This is a significant landmark in the LCA project and marks the entry of LCA into the Flight Test Programme. The aircraft was piloted by Wg Cdr Rajiv Kothiyal of the National Flight Test Centre, ADA, headed by Air Marshal P Rajkumar, PVSM, AVSM, VM.

LCA is an advanced technology, single seat, single engine, supersonic, light-weight, all-weather, multi-role, air superiority fighter designed for air-to-air, air-to-ground and air-to-sea combat roles. The purpose of flight test programme: was to validate a number of advanced technologies incorporated in LCA. These include: Unstable configuration, quadruplex fly-by-wire digital flight control system, integrated avionics with glass cockpit, advanced composite materials for primary structure and a novel utility systems management system.

The LCA programme was conceived in 1983. The project definition phase was completed in 1989 and the full scale engineering development (FSED) phase-I was sanctioned in 1993. The development effort for LCA is spearheaded by the Aeronautical Development Agency (ADA), an autonomous society under the Department of Defence Research & Development. ADA is responsible for project design, project monitoring and promoting the development of advanced technologies of relevance to the LCA. The principal partner of LCA is Hindustan Aeronautics Limited (HAL) and its divisions located in Bangalore, Hyderabad, Lucknow, Nasik, and Korwa.

The DRDO laboratories that have participated in the design and development of LCA are: Aeronautical Development Establishment (ADE), Bangalore; Defence Research & Development Laboratory (DRDL), Hyderabad; Combat Vehicles Research & Development Establishment (CVRDE), Avadi; Electronics & Radar Development Establishment (LRDE), Bangalore; Gas Turbine Research Establishment (GTRE), Bangalore; Centre for Artificial

Intelligence & Robotics (CAIR), Bangalore; Advanced Systems Integration & Evaluation Organisation (ASIEO), Bangalore; Defence Bio-engineering & Electro-medical Laboratory (DEBEL), Bangalore; Research Centre Imarat (RCI), Hyderabad; Aerial Delivery Research & Development Establishment (ADRDE), Armament R&D Establishment (ARDE), Pune; High Energy Materials Research Laboratory (HEMRL), Pune; Centre for Military Airworthiness & Certification (CEMILAC), Bangalore; and

Defence Metallurgical Research Laboratory (DMRL), Hyderabad. The other collaborating organisations are:

Public Sector Undertakings

Bharat Electronics Limited (BEL), Bangalore

Mishra Dhatu Nigam Limited (MIDHANI), Hyderabad

Bharat Heavy Electricals Limited (BHEL), Hyderabad

Indian Petro-Chemicals Limited (IPCL), Vadodara

Bharat Heavy Plates & Vessels (BHPV), Visakhapatnam

CSIR Laboratories and other Autonomous Organisations

National Aerospace Laboratory (NAL), Bangalore

Central Scientific & Industrial Organisation (CSIO), Chandigarh

Structural Engineering Research Centre (SERC), Chennai

Central Electro-Chemical Research Institute (CECRI), Karaikudi

Central Machine Tools Institute (CMTI), Bangalore

Government Toolroom & Training Centre (GTTC), Bangalore

Ordnance Factories

Ambajari, Ambarnath, Medak, and Avadi

Indian Air Force (IAF) Establishments

IAF Programme Management Team (PMT), Bangalore

Aircraft Systems & Testing Establishment (ASTE), Bangalore

Institute of Aerospace Medicine (IAM), Bangalore

Central Servicing Development Organisation (CSDO), Bangalore

Academic Institutions

Indian Institutes of Technology (IITs) at Mumbai, Kanpur, Kharagpur, Chennai, and Delhi

Indian Institute of Science (IISc), Bangalore

Jadavpur University, Kolkatta

PSG College of Technology, Coimbatore

Private Sector Entities

Machine Tools and Reconditioning Limited (MTAR), Hyderabad

Kobayashi Limited, Hyderabad

High Energy Batteries Limited, Hyderabad

Turbotech, Bangalore

Southern Electronics, Bangalore

Kumaran Industries, Bangalore

Shanthi Gears, Mysore

JS Lamps, Delhi

Walchand Industries, Walchandnagar

Sanghvi Aerospace, Ahmedabad

In addition, 300 small and medium scale firms participated in the project. The LCA programme, thus, is a national aeronautical endeavour encompassing all available talents in the country across a wide spectrum availing the services of institutions and industries, both public and private.

MAIN BATTLE TANK, ARJUN

Main Battle Tank (MBT) Arjun is a multi-laboratory programme of DRDO with CVRDE as the lead Laboratory. It is a state-of-the-art tank with superior fire power, high mobility, and excellent protection. Twelve Mk 1 prototypes of MBT Arjun have been manufactured and their performance tests have provided satisfactory results. Some of the breakthroughs achieved by CVRDE during the development of MBT Arjun are in Engine, Transmission, Hydropneumatic Suspension, Hull and Turret, and Gun Control System.

Fire Power

The superior armour defeating capability of the indigenously developed Fin Stabilized Armour Piercing Discarding Sabot (FSAPDS) ammunition and 120 mm calibre rifled gun give MBT ARJUN an edge over contemporary world tanks.

A computer-controlled integrated fire control system incorporating day-cum-night stabilized sighting system guarantees a very high first round hit probability and reduced reaction time to bring effective fire on targets. The stabilization system for the main armament, slaved to the sighting equipment in elevation and azimuth, with a high and accurate laying speed, allows fire on the move.

The superior fire power of MBT is based on:

- Accurate and fast target acquisition capability during day and night and in all types of weather.
- Shortest possible reaction time during combat engagements
- Ability to accurately engage targets on move
- Capability to destroy all possible enemy armour at maximum battle ranges
- Excellent first hit probability

Main Armament

The rifled 120 mm ARJUN gun together with the newly developed super velocity ammunition, can defeat any contemporary armour used in tanks. The electro-slag refined gun steel tube is autofrettaged to withstand higher gas pressures. A thermal jacket prevents irregular temperature distribution on to the tube due to the weather influences.

Secondary Armament

A co-axial 7.62 mm machine gun for anti-personnel and a 12.7 mm machine gun for anti-aircraft and ground targets are provided as secondary weapons.

Gunner's Main Sight

Gunner's Main Sight consists of a day-sight, thermal sight, a laser range finder and a stabilized head common to all the three channels. The common sighting head mirror is stabilized in elevation and azimuth. The day-sight provides dual magnification.

The thermal imager provides night vision facility to the gunner and the commander to observe and engage target in total darkness and in the presence of smoke, dust, haze and light camouflage. Integral with the main sight is the laser range finder by which targets can be ranged accurately.

Panoramic Sight for Commander

Commander's panoramic sight enables the commander to effect an all round surveillance in the battlefield without removing his eyes from the sight and without being disturbed by the turret motion. The field of view is stabilized with the help of a two axes rate gyro-mounted on the platform of the head mirror. The sight offers dual magnification.

Ammunition

Two types of ammunition, viz, FSAPDS and HESH have been developed for this armament. The highly lethal

FSAPDS ammunition which is the main battle ammunition of the tank has accounted itself admirably during the trails. In addition, the anti-helicopter round to combat the air threat to armour is also under development.

Mobility

Low ground pressure, high power-to-weight ratio and new design concepts in transmission suspension and running gear result in highly mobile and agile weapon platform.

The remarkable mobility of MBT which also adds to its protection is the result of:

- High performance engine
- Robust and effective transmission system particularly flexible hydropneumatic suspension.
- Optimized running gear with its high shock energy absorption.

Due to the high power-to-weight ratio and low specific ground pressure, MBT is fast, highly manoeuvrable and extremely mobile to cross the most difficult terrain with ease. High acceleration rapid braking capabilities with excellent steering characteristics make MBT agile in the battlefield. Adequate fuel storage capacity and relatively low fuel consumption allow for an optimal operational range. An important criterion for the mobility of any AFV is the effective performance of the driver. Excellent vision systems both for day and night provide most effective means of observation in all battlefield conditions. The need to keep the crew's fatigue including that of driver at the minimum level over long periods of continuous operation, have been taken care of.

Protection

All round protection from anti-tank ammunition is achieved by the newly developed KANCHAN armour to a degree much higher than available in present generation tanks. The high degree of immunity is achieved by.

- The computerised design and simulation
- A fabricated turret housing lightweight compact KANCHAN armour
- Careful dimensioning of wall through optimal slopes and angles
- A low silhouette

Crew Comfort

Ergonometry, using anthropometric data of Indian troops, has been kept in view while designing the fighting and driving compartments to fully exploit the outstanding features of the weapon system. Hydropneumatic suspension provides excellent ride comfort for crew eliminating fatigue even on the extended runs.

Specifications

Dimensions	
Overall length (with gun forward)	10.638 m
Overall height (with gun rear)	9.546 m
Overall height (with AD gun mount)	3.03 m (Turret roof: 2.32 m)
Overall width	3.864 m
Combat weight	58.5 tons

Technical Characteristics	
Max speed	70 km/hr
Max speed on cross country	40 km/hr
Ground pressure	0.84 kg/sq. cm.
Engine power	1400 HP at 2400 rpm
Engine characteristics	V 90° Turbo charged diesel, 10 cylinder water cooled
Power-to-weight ratio	24:1 HP/ton
Gear box	4 fwd +2 rev gears Epicyclic gear train, Torque converter, Mech lockup clutch & hydrodynamic retarder
Steering	Double radii, mechanical steering with neutral turn
Suspension	Hydrogas
Shallow fording	1.4 m
Vertical obstacle	0.914 m
Trench crossing	2.43 m
Gradient	35 deg
Gun	120 mm rifled
Rate of fire	6-8 rounds per minute
Ammunition	39 rounds (FSAPDS/HESH)
Co-axial machine gun	Mag 7.62 mm Tk 715 A
Anti aircraft machine gun	HCB 12.7 mm
Fire control system	Director type
Gun control system	Electro-hydraulic
Night vision	Thermal imaging
Ballistic computer	Digital
Crew	4 (*Cmdr,* Gnr, Ldr. Dvr)

MISSILES

Prithvi

- Completion of Development of Army version and induction in service (with one type of warhead).
- Dev. of 2 more type of warheads is nearing completion.
- Dev. of Air Force Version of Prithvi.

- User Training and documentation, ESP for Prithvi.

Trishul

- Proving of 3 beam guidance.
- Proving of Sea skimmer role.
- Development of Trishul combat vehicle (Dev and user version).
- Development of Airforce launch, Airforce Radar vehicle.
- Dev Trials of Naval version completed.
- Advanced stage in dev. trials of Army and Airforce system.

Akash

- Realisation of Ramjet Propulsion Technology.
- Realisation of phased Array Radar (Dev & user version) and other ground systems like BCC, BSR and 3D-CAR.
- Completion of TOT to BDL for Assembly & Integration.
- Successful flight against electronic target.

Nag

- Realisation of Nag Missile carrier (NAMICA).
- Realisation of Day Version Seeker.
- All weather seeker under advanced stage of development.
- Dev. flight from Tube Launcher and NAMICA.

Agni

- Successfully established Re-entry Technology with Carbon-Carbon Heat shield.
- Sagardhwani
- The understanding of ocean behaviour is essential for the design of underwater sensors. DRDO has therefore designed and constructed a multipurpose marine acoustic research ship, Sagardhwani. The ship is equipped with 10 modern laboratory facilities, sophisticated sensors and state-of-the-art handling gears. The data collection is a continuous process based on annual mission plans drawn. It generates a vast database and analysis reports in the form of atlases published regularly to provide vital inputs

to design organisations and the Navy for operational purposes.

- INS Sagardhwani, the floating laboratory, records ocean environmental data for analysis, from various locations at the sea for civil and military applications. It is equipped with facilities to carry out research through observation programmes in physical and chemical oceanography; marine meteorology, acoustics, and geology; and geo-acoustics. Data can also be stored in computers connected to individual equipment.

INS Sagardhwani is also equipped with navigational aids including satellite navigator, GPS, navigation computer, Decca navigator, survey echo sounders, Doppler speed log, navigational radar, gyro compass, and magnetic compass. Software deployed include SURPLAN for planning of cruise tracks, PROFILE for geo-scientific and oceanographic studies, and OLTAP for monitoring the navigation, quality and, graphical display of data along tracks during marine surveys.

KAVERI

Kaveri Engine is a technologically complex and vital system for the LCA as well as its future variants. It incorporates state-of-the-art technologies and provides the required thrust for indigenous competence in this critical area.

Kaveri Engine-The Power Plant for LCA

With three decades of rich experience in the field of aerogas turbine engines. DRDO has designed and developed the contemporary high performance bypass military engine christened as Kaveri. Four prototypes of Kaveri engine and two prototypes of Kabini engine (Kaveri core) have been assembled and are undergoing extensive ground testing. Kaveri engine is a two-spool bypass turbofan engine having three stages of transonic low pressure compressor driven by a single-stage low pressure turbine. The core engine consists of six-stage transonic compressor driven by single-stage cooled high pressure turbine. The engine is provided with a compact annular combustor with airblast atomisers. The aerothermodynamic and mechanical designs of engine components have been evolved using many in-house and commercially developed software for solid and fluid mechanics.

Kaveri three-stage transonic fan, designed for good stall margin and bird strike capability, handles an air mass flow of 78 kg/s and develops a pressure Combustion Chamber Liner ratio of 3.4. The six-stage variable capacity transonic compressor of Kaveri develops a pressure ratio of 6.4. The variable schedule of inlet guide vanes and two rows of stator is through FADEC control system to open the stator blades in a predetermined manner. High intensity low UD ratio annular combustor of Kaveri engine incorporates air blast injection of fuel for uniform outlet temperature profile and reduced carbon emission.

Kaveri high pressure turbine is provided with an efficient cooling design incorporating augmented convection-cum-film cooling for the vanes and combination cooling for the rotor blade to handle up to 1700 K turbine entry temperature. Kabini engine comprising high pressure compressor, combustor and high pressure turbine has undergone high altitude test at facilities abroad successfully demonstrating the flat rating concept of Kaveri engine assembly and in particular the combustor high altitude ignition and stability performances.

Kaveri-Special Characteristics

Air-mass flow	:	78 kg/s
By-pass ratio	:	0.16
Overall pressure ratio	:	21.5
Turbine entry temperature	:	1487-1700 K
Maximum dry thrust	:	52 kN (5302 kg)
Maximum dry SFC	:	0.78 kg/hr/kg
After burner maximum power thrust	:	81 kN (8260 kg)
After burner maximum power SFC	:	2.03 kg/hr/kg
Thrust-to-weight ratio	:	7.8
Application	:	Indian LCA

Kaveri engine has been specifically designed for Indian environment. The engine is a variable cycle-flat-rated engine in which the thrust drop due to high ambient, forward speed is well compensated by the increased turbine entry temperature at the spool Kabini altitude test speed. This concept has been already demonstrated with high temperature and pressure condition in DRDO's High Mach Facility. Kaveri engine is controlled by Kaveri full authority digital control unit {KADECU), which has been developed and successfully demonstrated at DRDO's test bed.

Fin Stabilized Armour Piercing Discarding Sabot (FSAPDS) ammunition is the most lethal kinetic energy ammunition, capable of destroying all known tank armour up to direct shooting range. The 125 mm FSAPDS (soft core) ammunition has been successfully designed and developed for enhancing the fire power of existing T-72 tank.

Design Aspects

The FSAPDS ammunition has been designed as a two-piece separate loading ammunition, capable of:

- Being fired from smooth bore T-72 tank gun
- Stowage in tank within the existing space
- Loading by auto-loader without affecting the rate of fire
- Ballistic performance to conform to the existing T-72 sight graticule pattern
- Defeating all NATO targets at a range of 2500 m

Principle of FSAPDS

FSAPDS is a sub-calibre projectile (penetrator) successfully designed to meet the ballistic requirement in the gun and at the target. The full calibre shot provides a large base area for the propellant gas to work against in accelerating the projectile to a high velocity.

The heavy sub-calibre penetrator provides high kinetic energy, concentrated over a small cross-sectional area. To get maximum penetration at the target, the length-to-diameter (L/D) ratio of the pene-trator needs to be increased to the maximum extent possible. Accordingly, this design caters for L/D ratio of about 15, which makes this penetrator capable of defeating all triple NATO targets at a range of 2500 m.

Penetration of the target depends on the behaviour of the material of both the armour and the projectile and it is governed by the kinetic energy of the projectile. The greater the kinetic energy of the projectile and smaller the area over which the energy is applied, the better will be the penetration.

The mechanism by which the penetration by this tungsten alloy penetrator at hypervelocity is effected, includes hydrodynamic deformation, mushrooming, macro-scopic plastic deformation, erosion, localised plastic deformation, brittle fracture, adiabatic sheer bending and melting/ thermomechanical interaction. Basically, this ammunition has achieved superior penetration power due to suitable mechanical properties of the tungsten-based alloy used for penetrator and its proper shape given to it for better stability to avoid ricochet at higher angle of impact at the target end

Description of Ammunition

The complete round consists of two cartridges, an FSAPDS shot with a supplementary charge attached to it, called the secondary charge (or the front cartridge) and a main powder charge called the primary charge (or the rear cartridge). The secondary charge consists of a shot which includes the tungsten alloy penetrator, three-segmented aluminium sabots, a tail fin for stability in flight, nylon bands, rubber seal, a tracer and a combustible cylinder with propellant charge.

The primary charge consists of a combustible cylinder with propellant charge, a steel cup which functions as the obturator and an electromechanical primer screwed on to the steel cup base.

Functioning of FSAPDS

The combination of HE, HEAT and FSAPDS ammunition, as per the requirement, can be stowed in the tank bins and loaded into the barrel by an automatic loading mechanism. When the round is loaded and fired from T-72 tank, the shot exits the muzzle and gases and aerodynamic forces acting on the sabot segments cause it to separate from the sub-projectile. The fin stabilised sub-projectile will continue to fly on its extremely flat trajectory to the target. Flight of the sub-projectile can be observed with the help of burning tracer.

Technology Involved

Manufacturing Technology

FSAPDS components are sensitive and sophisticated in nature and demand utmost care during their manufacturing and assembly. The dimensional and weight accuracies in various components are maintained to very close tolerance limits to achieve optimal overall performance of the ammunition.

Great care has been taken in selecting the operation layout for various components and other manufacturing facilities to minimise the rejection rate. Because of the intricate design and the need for close tolerance limits, major components are manufactured in combination with NC/CNC, high productive semiautomatic machines.

By introducing NC/CNC machines in flexible manufacturing system (FMS) mode, provision has also been made for machining operation of components for other calibre FSAPDS ammunition. Automatic online inspection of components has been introduced stagewise to ensure quality control and to increase productivity.

POWDER METALLURGY

The technology know-how developed on laboratory scale for the manufacture of high strength, high density tungsten alloy rods was converted into mass production methods and production established at HAPP. The heavy alloy rods are made from constituent powders through sintering process. The homogeneity and density along the entire length of the rod is maintained through inbuilt monitoring devices on the heating furnaces and online inspection at different stages.

Performance

Accuracy	<0.3 miles
Penetration	Can defeat all NATO targets at a range of 2500m and beyond
Range	Effective lethal range up to 3000m
Behaviour	Functions satisfactorily at extreme climatic conditions

Surface Coating

Two critical aluminium components are exposed to very high temperature zones during launch. To withstand the environment, hard anodizing at sub-zero temperature as a surface protective coating was established for this purpose for the first time in Ordnance Factories. This also enhances the shelf life of the ammunition against corrosion.

Ultrasonic Flaw Detection Techniques for High Density Materials

Since the tungsten alloy manufactured by sintering method has density more than 17 g/cc, the flaw detection becomes critical. No suitable ultrasonic equipment for detecting the flaw below 0.8 mm crack size was available in the country. It was imported as a tailor-made equipment and successfully commissioned at HAPP. This unique non-destructive testing method gives reliability on mass scale for getting the penetrators tested.

Establishment of Polymer Materials

The technology for two critical components made out of Nylon 6/6 and silicon rubber were established with stringent specifications. These are critical items for enhancing the performance of the ammunition.

Semi-Combustible Cartrige Case

This technology, developed on pilot scale, was successfully transfered to the trade for meeting the bulk requirement of the Army.

Testing and Evaluation

The testing and evaluation facilities used during design, development and production stages have been augmented by high speed cameras, tracking radars and other critical instruments to suit the bulk production requirements.

Technology Transfer

The transfer of technology of this ammunition has been completed in record time and production agencies have been geared up to produce more than 40000 rounds per annum with high reliability of the ammunition. This product, engineered to stringent production and quality assurance specifications, has enhanced Army's self-reliance and fighting capability. Moreover, the country could save precious foreign exchange to the tune of around Rs 200 crores per annum.

125 mm FSAPDS ammunition developed by DRDO has enhanced Army's self-reliance and could save the country foreign exchange of around Rs 20 million per annum.

An ophthalmic laser (*Nd-Yag*) photo disruptor known as *Drishti*-1064 has been developed under the aegis of SBMT. *Drishti* is used for capsulotomy and iridotomy. In the former, a cut is made in the membrane formed after cataract surgery to create a central opening thus restoring vision. Iridotomy is a procedure wherein the same laser is used to create a hole in the iris creating an alternate pathway for the outflow of aqueous humour thereby reducing the intra-ocular pressure in cases of glaucoma. The prototype of *Drishti*-1064 was evaluated by LV Prasad Eye Institute, Hyderabad, by carrying out more than 100 posterior capsulotomy and iridotomy procedures in a span of 15 months.

The technology has been transferred to Bharat Electronics Ltd., Pune and SBMT for productionisation. First production prototype, PT-1, is undergoing clinical trials at Guru Nanak Eye Centre, Delhi. Significant technological expertise in the area of lasers for use in Defence technology has resulted in this high-tech equipment for the common man. The cost of this equipment is reduced to one-third as compared to the imported one.

Bibliography

Alperovitz, Gar. The Decision to Use the Atomic Bomb. New York: Vintage Books, 1996.

Arend, A.: International Law and the Use of Military, London, Routledge, 1993.

Bellamy, C.: Knights in White Armour: The New Art of War and Peace, London, Random House, 1997.

Chandra, R.: Judicial System in India, Lucknow, Print House (India), 1992.

Damrosch, L.F.: Law and Force in the New International Order, Boulder, Westview Press, 1991.

Davies .A.: Telecommunications and Politics. The Secentralised Alternative, London, Pinter, 1994.

Heimanson, Rudolph: Dictionary of Indian Military, N.Y.: Oceana Publications, 1967.

Huntington, S.P.: The China Modernisation Military and the State, N.Y., Vintage Books, 1964.

Jones, W.H.: Government and Politics of India Military, London, Hutchinson, 1971.

Mary, W.: Asian Power and Politics: the Cultural Dimensions of Authority, Cambridge, Belknap Press, 1985.

Posen, B.R.: The Sources of Indian Military Doctrine, Ithaca, 1984, Cornell Univ. Press.

Rhodes, Richard, The Making of the Atomic Bomb, New York: Simon and Schuster, 1988.

Rosen, P.: Societies and Military Power: India and its Armies, Ithaca, Cornell University Press, 1996.

Simon, D. : Public Administration and Policy of Indian Military, New York, Knopf, 1950.

Simon, D. : Public Administration, New York, Knopf, 1950.

Index

A

Advanced Light Helicopter, 71, 87, 93, 237, 269.
Advanced Technology Vessel, 80, 97, 242.

D

Defence Industry, 78, 115, 116, 122, 127, 137, 242, 243, 244, 245, 247, 248, 268, 273, 276, 286, 288, 296, 297, 298, 299.
Defence Planning, 47, 48, 49, 50, 51, 52, 53, 54, 57, 58, 60, 61, 65, 66, 70, 73, 269, 270.
Defence Policy, 47, 48, 54, 60, 156, 157.
Defence Production, 48, 49, 114, 115, 116, 123, 269, 270, 272, 275, 278, 280, 283, 285, 286.
Defence Research, 48, 77, 121, 125, 128, 134, 138, 139, 140, 229, 237, 269, 284, 292, 312.
Defence Research and Development Organisation, 48, 121, 128, 134, 137, 138, 139, 140, 229, 269.
Defence Staff, 52, 60, 61, 71, 73, 118, 121.
Defense Projects, 80.
Democracy, 62, 144, 145, 156, 157.
Development Organisation, 48, 77, 121, 125, 128, 137, 138, 139, 140, 145, 229, 237, 269, 313.
Domestic Production, 267, 271.

F

Fighter Aircraft, 25, 35, 83, 97, 104, 129, 136, 166, 177, 232, 234, 237, 241, 246, 247, 283.

I

India Defence Industry, 114, 124.
Indian Aircraft Carrier, 90.
Indian Defence Forces, 1, 3, 13.
Indian Defense Projects, 80.
Indian Navy, 15, 17, 32, 33, 39, 65, 98, 111, 113, 115, 119, 235, 264, 280, 321, 322, 326.
Indian navy, 92, 116.
Intermediate Jet Trainer, 91, 242.

M

Military Intelligence in India, 17.

N

National Security, 23, 39, 43, 44, 47, 53, 54, 60, 68, 69, 128, 157, 235, 238, 239, 251, 305.

O

Organisation, 7, 12, 17, 18, 19, 21, 22, 65, 66, 70, 71, 75, 77, 117, 121, 125, 134, 229, 237, 239, 240, 268, 269, 297, 313.

P

Projects, 50, 53, 56, 60, 69, 80, 118, 122, 126, 139, 142, 143, 144, 145, 147, 175, 177, 192, 204, 212, 233, 310, 311.

W

Weapon System, 27, 91, 140, 187, 188, 189, 195, 219, 241, 317.

♦♦♦